DISAPPEAR HERE

Violence after Generation X

Naomi Mandel

THE OHIO STATE UNIVERSITY PRESS / COLUMBUS

Copyright © 2015 by The Ohio State University.

Library of Congress Cataloging-in-Publication Data
Mandel, Naomi, 1969– author.
  Disappear here : violence after Generation X / Naomi Mandel.
    pages cm
  Includes bibliographical references and index.
  ISBN 978-0-8142-1286-8 (cloth : alk. paper)
    1. Violence in literature. 2. Violence—United States—20th century. 3. Generation X—United States—20th century. I. Title.
  PN56.V53M36 2015
  809'.933552—dc23

                              2015010172

Cover design by Janna Thompson-Chordas
Text design by Juliet Williams
Type set in Adobe Sabon
Printed by Thomson-Shore, Inc.

Cover image: Young woman with knife behind foil. © Bernd Friedel/Westend61/Corbis.

♾ The paper used in this publication meets the minimum requirements of the American National Standard for Information Sciences—Permanence of Paper for Printed Library Materials. ANSI Z39.48-1992.

9 8 7 6 5 4 3 2 1

To Erik
with love
and
x x x

contents
. . . .

illustrations
· · · · · · · · · ·

acknowledgments

. . . .

I am deeply grateful to Malcolm Litchfield and Lindsay Martin for welcoming my manuscript to The Ohio State University Press, to Sandy Crooms for inviting me to submit this book to the Press, and to the manuscript's outside readers for their suggestions and support. Tara Cyphers was a patient and kind editor. I thank Martin Boyne for his quick and careful indexing and Kristin Ebert-Wagner for her magnificently persnickety copyediting.

This book has great and generous allies. Marco Abel's timely and thoughtful comments pushed me to make my argument stronger, and I am grateful to him for being the kind of scholar who likes to disagree. Alain-Philippe Durand created opportunities for me to share and shape this work. He encouraged its evolution at every stage, and I am grateful for his friendship. Ryan Trimm read drafts of these chapters and asked challenging questions and gave me his unflinching support in the face of myriad institutional hurdles. Carolyn Betensky and Travis D. Williams directed me to useful resources, gave me detailed and thoughtful feedback, and talked me down when necessary. John Hodgkins and John Schwetman assured me I was making sense. Though I have yet to meet them in person, E. Gabriella Coleman and Christine Henseler have been very generous with their time and encouragement. For their continued advocacy of this project and its author, I can never hope to repay my teachers Gabriele Schwab, Rey Chow, and Michael P. Clark (who, after looking at an early draft, said, "I'd read that book").

A Project Completion Grant from the University of Rhode Island's Council for Research funded my work with Matthew J. Balliro, a careful, thorough, and resourceful researcher, in the summer of 2014. Grants from the University of Rhode Island's Provost Faculty Development Fund and Beaupré Hope and Heritage fund enabled me to share early versions of this work with students, scholars, and colleagues at other institutions. I am grateful to Art Redding at York University in Toronto, Shuli Barzilai at The Hebrew University, Efraim Sicher at Bar Ilan University, Milette Shamir at Tel Aviv University, and Vered Lev Kennan and Shahar Bram at the University of Haifa for inviting me to speak. Grants from the University of Rhode Island's Center for Humanities defrayed some of my research expenses and costs of permissions.

Melissa Ramhold at Corbis Images provided prompt, cheery, and invaluable assistance in acquiring permission to include "Vulture Watching Starving Child" (© Kevin Carter / Sygma / Corbis), "City Workers in London Watch News of Terrorist Attacks in America" (© Reuters/Corbis), and "Young woman with knife behind foil" (© Bernd Friedel/Westend61/Corbis). Mar Williams graciously allowed me to reproduce his art. Andrée Rathemacher and Angel Ferria of the University of Rhode Island Library offered helpful guidance on fair use for the screen grabs included in this book. Sections of V for Vendetta are reprinted with permission of DC Comics. The following is reprinted with permission:

"Free of Hope"
Words and Music by Vic Chesnutt
Copyright © 1995 Ghetto Bells Music
All Rights Administered by BMG Rights Management (US) LLC
All Rights Reserved. Used by Permission.
Reprinted by Permission of Hal Leonard Corporation

"Down for the Real"
Words and Music by Derek Murphy, Lorenzo DeChalus, James Preston, Jay E. Nichols Sr., Jerome Dickens, and Ralph Rolle
Copyright © 1994 UNIVERSAL MUSIC CORP
All Rights Reserved. Used by Permission.
Reprinted by Permission of Hal Leonard Corporation

A version of chapter 5 was published in *Novel: A Forum on Fiction* in Summer 2012. I am grateful to the editors of that journal for kind permission to include it here.

At the University of Rhode Island, I have been fortunate in the support of Galen Johnson and Richard McIntyre, Directors of the Honors Program; Winifred Brownell, Dean of the College of Arts and Sciences; and Donald H. DeHayes, Provost and Vice President of Academic Affairs. Stephen Barber, Mary Cappello, Kathleen Davis, David Faflik, and Jean Walton are bracing and inspiring colleagues; Michelle Caraccia, Kara Lewis, and Dawn Cute (we miss you, Dawn!) are the kind and capable staff who sustain us. Most of *Disappear Here* was written while I was serving as Director of Graduate Studies for English, and I am deeply grateful to the students in the program whose enthusiasm for this difficult profession inspired me to work early in the morning and late at night. Jason Shrontz developed memorable tutorials in the music of the era; the students of ENG 379 and HPR 412 were patient as I wrestled with early versions of these ideas, and Andrew J. Ploeg and Mihaela P. Harper (look out for her work on anomie!) taught me more than I taught them.

I have the great good fortune to be cared for by Dr. Asaf Bitton, Dr. Lynae Brayboy, Dr. Karmela Chan, Dr. Jean Smith, Dr. Valerie Thomas, and Robin Whewell (RN, CDE) and I am grateful for the countless hours they give me. I am especially grateful to Dr. Barry Wall, without whose counsel and compassion I would surely disappear.

My sister, Jessica Mandel, sustained me with Slayer-strength hugs and directed me to *The Hunger Games*. John Dyer, Ohad Flinker, Aaron Stern, and Seth Yurdin were the litmus test for this topic: when their polite interest transformed to manic gleam, I knew I was on to something. Carole Sklar, Jacqueline Rokotnitz, and Diane Strommer opened their homes and allowed me to write, rest, and play surrounded by beauty. I am grateful to Joni and Nunu Rokotnitz for hours of good talk and good fun, and to Pablo Adi for all the fine meals and elegant conversation.

Miriam B. Mandel is my mother and my mentor. Her copyediting genius, editorial savvy, and professional wisdom helped this book into the world. I can only hope to emulate the clarity and rigor of her writing, and the alchemy of conviction and care with which she navigates life's challenges.

Jerome Mandel is my father and my muse. His own prose sings. He was the first reader for many of this book's chapters: seeing them through his eyes spurred me to make them better. If his quick humor and anarchic kindness glimmer in these pages, I will be proud.

Erik Sklar is my partner and my hero. He gives me tech support and life support. He always comes up with the name for the thing when I'm in the throes of aphasia. He never complains when I send him for fast food at dinnertime or drag him to conferences on his vacation. His love and courage sustained me every step of this journey. My fellow Xer, I dedicate this book to you.

The Middle Children of History

GENERATION X refers to people who were born in the 1960s and 1970s and came of age in the final decades of the twentieth century.[1] Uneasily placed after the postwar Baby Boomers and before contemporary Millennials, X is a cohort that eludes definition. Growing up, Xers witnessed the formation of the EU and NAFTA and the resilience of ethnic conflict worldwide. They registered the rise of postmodern culture and the entrenchment of corporate Empire. They were lured by upward mobility and stalked by financial crises. They donned Ray-Bans and checked out. As Tyler Durden, the anarchist hero of the cult film *Fight Club*, puts it: "We're the middle children of history, man. No purpose or place. We have no Great War. No Great Depression. Our Great War's a spiritual war . . . our Great Depression is our lives."

---

1. The range of birthyears offered for "Generation X" varies from the narrow 1965–1976 (Hornblower) to the inclusive 1960–1980 (Henseler, *Global*). Douglas Rushkoff sets 1964 as the starting birthyear; Philip Jenkins includes Americans born between 1963 and 1979; Neil Howe and Bill Strauss's *13thGEN: Abort, Retry, Ignore, Fail?*, widely cited in scholarship on Generation X, defines the "13th Generation" birthyear range as 1961–1981. I adopt Christine Henseler's 1960–1980 range for this study, in part to affirm the global perspective of her work, and in part to affirm Daniel Grassian's early point (with which Henseler agrees) that Generation X is best defined not by dates but by media events and cultural products (Grassian 14; see also Henseler, *Global* 27 n.4).

In *Fight Club,* Tyler organizes underground combat groups that draw on this underlying disaffection and resentment and transfigure it into violence. But the local fight clubs coalesce into a conglomerate, Project Mayhem, a highly structured terror organization. The twin towers that collapse in the film's final scenes are the culmination of this process, and attest to violence's eruption from the gap between image and experience, a lacuna that Xers chronically inhabit. "We've all been raised on television to believe that one day we'd all be millionaires, and movie gods, and rock stars. But we won't," Tyler tells his fight club members. "We're slowly learning that fact. And we're very, very pissed off."

Disappear Here asks what Generation X has to teach us about violence onscreen, online, and in a literary text. Like Tyler, I argue that their historical situation puts Xers in a unique position. Formed and fashioned by media events, schooled by consumer capitalism and its relentless dialectic of complicity and co-option, Generation X saw the epistemic certainty of violence—its quality as real or documentable—disappear, and found no reliable cause or *ism* to replace it. Consequently, Xers approach violence not from a sense of opposition to the culture from which they feel excluded, but by awareness of their complicity in it, a position that cancels out any moral or political conviction—hence the GenX catchword "whatever." But X is not merely a generational appellation. The letter marks the cultural experience that defines this group: varied, uncertain; stuck in an empty area, its value as yet to be determined; a shifting target, informed by the media, detached from or rejecting commitment. And X marks the spot from which a new approach to violence, the real, and "real violence" can be formulated today: *after* Generation X.

It is common for champions of Generation X to counter their reputation as disaffected and affirm, "We Care." Such an attitude, claiming solidarity with traditional activism, is nostalgic and inaccurate. It elides the implications of the X itself, its association with specificity and negation, multiplicity and menace. Xers were dismissed as slackers, hackers, and losers, and derided as volatile and apathetic. But even though they had no Great War or Depression to define them, Xers' lives were tinged with violence. They were haunted by AIDS and hunted by the demons of crack and meth. They played increasingly graphic video games. Many of them experienced the devastating, accretive violence of divorce and downward mobility. All lived the slow transformative violence of revolution. Xers witnessed the rise of the home computer,

FIGURE 1. *Fight Club* (1999). Screen grab. Edward Norton and Helena Bonham Carter, their silhouettes almost identical, face a pair of exploding skyscrapers. This image (which departs from the novel, in which just one skyscraper collapses) propelled a number of critics to read *Fight Club* as presaging the terror attacks of September 11, 2001. © Fincher/Fox.

the fall of the USSR, and the establishment of Empire—both capitalist and fundamentalist. As the planes struck the World Trade Center on September 11, 2001, Xers entered middle age.

But their reputation for chronic disaffection persists. A *Time* magazine profile rehearsed the stereotype: "Net surfing, nihilistic nipple piercers whining about McJobs; latchkey legacies, fearful of commitment. Passive and powerless, they were content, it seemed, to party on in a Wayne's Nether-world, one with more antiheroes—Kurt Cobain, Dennis Rodman, the Menendez brothers—than role models" (Hornblower). The music critic Touré recalls "the rise of a mysterious sexual plague and a powerful drug ruining society and harbingers of the end of American global dominance: All of that had the feel of the beginning of the end of days. [. . .] This was not something we could march to change. This was something from which we could do nothing but unplug" (64–65). Even today, "Generation X" is generally evoked—if at all—to signify an empty area, a value yet to be determined. "The label itself has been somewhat of an enigma, a question mark, a blank, an identity [. . .] twisted into a demographic that seems to contribute little, disregarded as dark matter lost in disillusioned space," writes Generation X scholar Christine Henseler ("What's in the Label?").

What would we learn by affirming X's persistent reputation as the alienated generation, the ones with nothing to believe in? What if we took seriously their anthem, "Nevermind"? *Disappear Here* argues that X's association with negation, ambivalence, and multiplicity lends it philosophical and critical heft, resurrecting the investment in the aporetic that lent ethical weight to the discourses of poststructuralism and deconstruction, and reclaiming the hermeneutics of suspicion that powered the important critical work of the previous century. Xers, the latecomers to that century, heirs to unparalleled technological advances and witness to technology's destructive capacity, initiated a move away from traditional approaches to violence, a move that is discernable in the fiction and film that Xers create. *Disappear Here* traces this move, and addresses its implications for judgment, critique, and action today, as Xers assume key positions in culture and society.

My first chapter, "Why X Now? Crossing Out and Marking the Spot," sets forth the stakes of this study and situates it within existing scholarship on Generation X. Important work has been done by John M. Ulrich, Christine Henseler, Daniel Grassian, and Martine Delvaux; together with Douglas Coupland's writing in the 1990s, Douglas Rushkoff's edited *GenX Reader,* and Neil Howe and Bill Strauss's seminal *13thGen: Abort, Retry, Ignore, Fail?,* this work sets the stage for my project of determining how Generation X thinks about violence, and how we—Boomers, Xers, Millennials—may think of violence *after* Generation X. I argue that Generation X's experience of violence is defined by paralysis, menace, and complicity; that Xers, raised on TV, accustomed to video games and to remote control over the image, and attuned to the prevalence of entrenched racism, invisible violence, and corruption, are uniquely poised to rewrite the relation of violence to the real. Novels by Bret Easton Ellis, Douglas Coupland, Colson Whitehead, and Jay McInerney help me define this X attitude.

Xers stress the formative impact of media on their development. In chapter 2, "Nevermind: An X Critique of Violence," I trace how, with the rise of home media, CNN, reality TV, and the censorship of images during the Gulf War, Generation X witnessed a revision of how the reality of "real violence" is traditionally signaled or signified. In the course of this revision, violence's epistemic validity, and its reliability as a way to demarcate reality and distinguish reality from fiction, vanished— with crucial implications for judgment, affect, and ethics. Turning to a history of violence in twentieth- and early-twenty-first-century philosophy (Walter Benjamin, Georges Bataille, Hannah Arendt, Michel Foucault, Elaine Scarry, Jacques Derrida, Giorgio Agamben), I articulate the specific questions that Generation X poses to representation and critique, drawing on theories of media, the image, state power, and pain, and articulating a concept of fidelity with which to think about the interrelation of image, violence, and truth *after* (that is, according to) Generation X.

"Fidelity" means faith: historically, possibly the most creative and destructive of human capacities. Fidelity to a god, a nation, a law, an ideal, or any *ism* can take the credit for most, if not all, major episodes of human violence. Though I note evocations of "fidelity" in the 1980s and 1990s in economics, postmodernism, and religion, my approach to this concept is best captured by the alternative rock band Eve 6's hit song "Inside Out": evacuated by lack, entranced by oblivion, X finds "nothing but faith in nothing." To extract the implications of this attitude I turn to Alain Badiou's work with "fidelity" in *Being and Event* and *Ethics: An Essay on the Understanding of Evil*. Returning to Generation X, I reposition their notoriously affectless worldview, defining an approach to violence as a moving target, using, in chapter 3, the novels of Bret Easton Ellis, who coined the phrase "Disappear Here" in 1985.

Chapter 3, "The Game That Moves," focuses on the novels Ellis published between 1985 and 2010, a crucial quarter century that spans the turn of the millennium. Ellis, a poster boy for Generation X and a touchstone for popular culture, produced fiction that has been taken for real by readers, activists, and critics. My discussion of six of his novels—*Less Than Zero, The Rules of Attraction, American Psycho, Glamorama, Lunar Park,* and *Imperial Bedrooms*—traces a process of subtraction: value, values, affect, and volition come into view and disappear. To document this process (that extends to the author himself) I set Ellis's work against the background of discourses on literary violence elaborated around them: the paradigm of complicity associated with Generation X; the literary mode of "blank fiction" described by James Annesley, Elizabeth Young, and Graham Caveney in the UK in the 1990s; and "the extreme," articulated more recently by Mario Perniola in the EU and by Alain-Philippe Durand and myself in our co-edited *Novels of the Contemporary Extreme,* which documents the phenomenon in fiction from North and South America, Europe, and the Middle East (I stress geography to underscore that Ellis's fiction articulates discourses of violence in global contexts. Ellis is widely translated and read). For all these scholars, critics, and theorists, Ellis's novels are foundational: they serve as a starting point from which to reflect on violence in literature, film, and digital culture.

Chapter 4 addresses the spectacular terror attacks on the United States on September 11, 2001, widely assumed to be a defining event for Generation X. These events were so inextricably tied to their televised quality that terrorism emerged largely as media spectacle, subject to manipulation, dulled by repetition, easy to abandon via the remote control though, like a black hole, it continues to exert a powerful gravitational force. "Something Empty in the Sky: 9/11 after X" articulates these issues in fiction by and about members of Generation X (the chapter's title is borrowed from Don DeLillo's influential essay "In the Ruins of the Future"). I discuss 9/11 novels by X authors—Frédéric Beigbeder's *Windows on the World,* Claire Messud's *The Emperor's Children,* and Jess Walter's *The Zero*—and novels in which Xer characters respond to the events and aftermath of 9/11: Jay McInerney's *The Good Life,* Ken Kalfus's *A Disorder Peculiar to the Country,* and DeLillo's *Falling Man.* I pay special attention to lies and infidelities (both marital and mimetic), eliciting from these novels an X attitude. This attitude refuses the affective charge of trauma theory, patriotic fervor, and bellicose rhetoric, even when what's right and what's true are, like the bodies of the World Trade Center victims in Manhattan, available only as dust and scraps and smell, invisible and pervasive, present and absent, here and disappeared.

These six 9/11 novelists, who evince a transnational attitude and employ a range of styles, underscore my X approach that refuses traditional fidelities and alliances and points the way to a future, after X. Chapter 5, "Not Yes or No: Fact, Fiction, Fidelity in Jonathan Safran Foer," is the first step in this book's move to trace Generation X's aftereffects. The chapter focuses on Foer's *Everything Is Illuminated* (set in Europe after the Holocaust) and *Extremely Loud and Incredibly Close* (set in New York City after the terror attacks of September 11, 2001). Born in 1977, Foer is the youngest author in this study: he is as much the product of X culture as he is a practitioner of the attitude associated with this demographic. Foer chooses international settings and transnational characters and, in keeping with the discourses of fidelity and media explored in the previous chapters, he figures violent history as available to be reworked, rewound, appropriated, and discarded. His novels allow me to pursue the ethical implications of this book's philosophical gambit: violence, itself real, is also the means by which reality is established; reality is inextricable from its constructed quality—that is, from fiction. Fidelity to nation, to the past, to trauma, and even to a generational cohort, does nothing but draw us apart. But if we turn our gaze from the object of fidelity to the trajectories that fidelity takes, the attitude associated with it, and the implications of its eschewal, we can begin to outline an ethic that is formed or fashioned from X ambivalence and disaffection.

My last chapter, "I Am Jack's Revolution: *Fight Club,* Hacking, Violence after X," focuses on the presence in cyberculture of the X text *Fight Club* (specifically, David Fincher's 1999 film adaptation of Chuck Palahniuk's 1996 novel). Both the film and the novel stage the migration of violence from fantasy to reality, from fiction to fact; they have been read through discourses of masculinity, terror, capital, and faith. I treat *Fight Club* as a hacker text, one that reflects crucial developments in computer science and industry in the 1990s. Adopted by hacker culture as early as 2002, *Fight Club* is formative of the "47 rules of the internet" developed on /b/, the birthplace of Anonymous; it figured in Project Mayhem 2012, Anonymous's call for massive corporate, financial, military, and state leaks, and in #OpIsrael 2.0, Anonymous's 2013 cyberwar against Israel.

The conclusion, "X Out," traces the reverberations of Xers' uniquely creative approach to violence, to reality, and to "real violence" in our contemporary global, connected, hypermediated world and reflects on the broader implications for my claims about complicity, media, mediation, and faith. As *Disappear Here* moves from text to film, from cyberspace to global politics, from U.S. slacker culture to the Middle East, X sheds its generational specificity. No longer a demographic but an attitude—anomic, affectless, extreme—X serves a silent, programming function in contemporary culture. Its presence is alternately visible and invisible, unlocatable and ubiquitous, a moving target and a promise of revolution.

The association of contemporary revolutionary movements with Generation X should come as no surprise. Since its inception X has marked the spot where the promise of social change and the absence of its realization, the lure and illusion of financial stability, and the urgency and futility of ethical action come compellingly into view and disappear. But as with all revolutions, reality—what the revolution will erase and violently bring into being, the values it will establish, the truths it will create—has as much to do with what we believe in as with facts on the ground. Facts are fickle, faith misplaced, and grounds contingent and contested. Follow the ones with faith in nothing on to this shifting terrain.

one
· · · · · ·

Why X Now?

Crossing Out and Marking the Spot

DISAPPEAR HERE

In Bret Easton Ellis's *Less Than Zero,* the narrator, Clay, notices a bill-board: "Disappear Here." The enigmatic message haunts him as he wanders through the glitzy world of the young, rich, and privileged in mid-80s L.A. As his Northeast paleness fades in the midwinter sun, Clay, like a photographic negative, registers the violence of his world. He is present at the screening of a snuff film, invited to participate in a gang rape, witnesses one friend's descent into prostitution and addiction, another's descent into madness, and notes reports of murder and predation. But he does not oppose, critique, or remedy. He is a detached, affectless observer, counting down the days until he returns to college in New Hampshire. The novel's concluding pages pursue this alignment of disaffection with negativity, of detachment with disappearance: Clay recalls a piece of music with "words and images so harsh and bitter that the song would reverberate in my mind for days" (207).[1] The images, he later learns, are unique to him; no one else has seen them. Private,

---

1. Though the song is not identified in the novel, Baelo-Allué suggests that Clay is referring to "Los Angeles" from the 1980 album by the punk rock band X (60).

unshared, unbidden, they haunt him, accruing agency and volition, becoming "violent and malicious" (208). They are images of "people being driven mad by living in the city. Images of parents who were so hungry and unfulfilled that they ate their own children. Images of people, teenagers my own age, looking up from the asphalt and being blinded by the sun" (207–8). These images replace the song, the words, and, in the novel's concluding sentences, they may even replace Clay as the narrative's focalizer. "These images stayed with me even after I left the city. [. . .] They seemed to be my only point of reference for a long time afterwards. After I left" (208).

Disappear Here: Violence after Generation X takes as its starting point this departure, or detachment, of body from world, image from ground, presence from representation, violence from the real. It probes the atomism and disaffection that began to be articulated in the 1980s and 1990s by young writers commonly associated with Generation X and explores the implications of this disaffection for violence today. Before Ellis's *American Psycho* (1991) made his name synonymous with extreme, gratuitous violence that bursts the bounds of fiction, *Less Than Zero* was touted as a defining novel for the MTV generation, its author described as the poster boy or spokesperson for Generation X. He shares this role with fellow Brat Packers Jay McInerney and Tama Janowitz (though Ellis is the only Xer in the group) and with Xer Douglas Coupland, author of *Generation X: Tales for an Accelerated Culture* (1991). Coupland's book, like Ellis's, is grounded in ambivalence toward presence, perception, and parrhesia. The book, typeset in such a way as to interrupt immersion and comment ironically on its self-avowed contemporaneity, opens with an account of a complete solar eclipse in Canada, and elaborates a "mood of darkness and inevitability and fascination" among young people, as they "crooked their necks, stared at the heavens, and watched their sky go out" (3–4).

What can such a generation teach us about violence? This question has not yet been asked of Generation X, though, in the 1980s and 1990s, callous, careless young people were taken to task by pundits and sociologists for their casual attitude toward drug use and sex, and their notorious youthful disaffection was the subject of much vexed chatter. Xers were scolded for being apathetic and for listening to heavy metal, policed by NEA legislation and rap lyric warnings. This censure was understandable. To adults at that time, haunted by the horrors of the mid-twentieth century (two world wars; the atom bomb; genocide; apartheid; partition) the GenX catchword "whatever" seemed disturbingly dismissive of real, traumatic violence. Boomers, who claimed the great social revolutions of the 1960s and 1970s, were left uneasy by the nihilistic refrain "Nevermind" from the grunge band Nirvana's anthem "Smells Like Teen Spirit" (1991). But "Gen X" is no longer a buzzword for youth culture. Xers are now entering middle age and assuming key positions as parents, teachers, politicians, authors, filmmakers, and arbiters of culture and society. Have Xers shed their apathy, their groundless antagonism, and learned to properly care? Or have they revised the values in which those judgments were invested, and changed the terms in which these debates are couched? (Yes, this is a leading question.)

Disappear Here measures the impact of Generation X's notorious youthful disaffection, an impact that reverberates globally today. It reverberates in the images and narratives that are the means by which the vast majority of people on this planet experience violence, as drone warfare, media ubiquity, and online activism scrim or screen long-standing antagonisms and loyalties and trouble what we mean by perception. In what follows I argue that with the rise of home media, personal computing, and reality TV, and with the fall of the Berlin Wall and the USSR, the relation between violence and the real—violence's premise of reality and violence's utility as a means by which reality is established—began to be revised. Consequently, Generation X initiated a move away from the twentieth-century approach to violence as a founding trauma that fiction, film, and media images reflect and respond to. But this book is not a generational study, an empirical survey, or a sociological work. It is instead a form of theft: one that acknowledges and erases origin, affirms and disavows or denies it. Generation X and its Xers, 1980s and 1990s fiction, film, and popular culture, are the ground and scope of this work. But I take X in all its permutations—opposition, erasure, multiplicity, precision, intersection, and a variable (an unknown value, a moving target)—for my own, broader purposes: to articulate the nature of violence, the real, and "real violence" today. *Violence after Generation X* looks at representations of real and fictional violence *after*—both subsequent and according to—the decades Xers came of age. What's real, and the role of violence in defining it, looks different after Generation X, and X marks the spot where "real violence" presents, appears, is represented and disappears here, in the world that Xers have brought into being.

A BRIEF HISTORY OF X

In his seminal "Generation X: A (Sub)Cultural Genealogy," John M. Ulrich traces the origin of "Generation X" from its first appearance in Hungarian-born Robert Capa's photographic project on the lives of young people after World War II to its contemporary association with white, middle-class, generally male subculture. *Generation X,* as Ulrich points out, was also the title of Charles Hamblett and Jane Deverson's collection of interviews with young people published in the UK in 1964 and the name of Billy Idol's 1970s punk rock band. The term's contemporary appellation is generally aligned with Coupland's 1991 novel (Coupland, who is Canadian, took the term from Paul Fussell's sociological study, *Class).* For Ulrich, Generation X takes much of its oppositional ethos from its status as a subculture or youth culture, derived from the Beats in the 1960s and from punk in the 1970s. "Generation X" received quite a bit of media attention in the 1990s and was quickly made voguish, mainstream, and discarded.[2]

With the new millennium, as Xers turned forty, "Generation X" received renewed attention. Serious scholarship like Ulrich and Andrea L. Harris's edited *GenXegesis: Essays on Alternative Youth (Sub)Culture* (2003), Daniel Grassian's *Hybrid Fictions: American Literature and Generation X* (2003), Christine Henseler's volumes on Generation X (*Generation X Rocks,* co-edited with Randolph Pope, 2007; *Spanish Fiction in the Digital Age,* 2011), and her edited collection and digital project, *Generation X Goes Global* (2013), joined publications designed for the mass market like Jeff Gordinier's *X Saves the World: How Generation X Got the Shaft but Can Still Keep Everything from Sucking* (2006), and Touré's *I Would Die 4 U: Why Prince Became an Icon* (2013), which claims the "gen X meme" for black culture. Recent demographic studies like *The Generation X Report* (published by the Univer-

---

2. Ulrich gives an overview of the books and articles, mostly mass-marketed, devoted to Generation X since the term came into vogue in 1991: "Cover stories in *Time, Newsweek, Atlantic Monthly, New Republic, Business Week,* and *Fortune*; demographic histories (*13th Generation*); anthologies of fiction and personal essays by Xers (*Next* and *Voices of the Xiled*); articles and books for advertisers on how to capture the Generation X demographic (*Marketing to Generation X*); political handbooks (*Revolution X*); satires (*Generation Ecch!*); personal memoirs (*Prozac Nation*); religious studies (*GenX Religion*); sociological studies (*Masks and Mirrors: Generation X and the Chameleon Personality*); film criticism (*The Cinema of Generation X: A Critical Study of Films and Directors*), television criticism (*Gen X TV: The Brady Bunch to Melrose Place*), the requisite anthology of excerpts from articles, books, and interviews (*The GenX Reader*)" (4; see also 32 notes 3 and 4).

sity of Michigan's Longitudinal Study of American Youth) and reports by Pew Institute for Research portray Xers as all grown up: peaceable, hardworking, dedicated parents and caring, responsible citizens: "active, balanced, and happy" (Dawson); confident in their ability to achieve the American Dream (Pew).

X has, it seems, been exonerated from its youthful alienation. It has also begun to shed its association with the white middle class: as Touré puts it, "Tupac and Snoop are just as good at expressing the gen X sense of dystopia and dislocation as Nirvana and REM. The gen X psycho-graphic is larger than racial or class boundaries, even if the media por-trayals are not" (63).[3] Henseler, writing "Short-*Changed*," agrees; she also stresses the centrality of Generation X for online culture. Claim-ing U.S. President Barack Obama for this globalized, media-savvy demographic, she describes Xers as parents of Millennials, as media entrepreneurs, and as literal and philosophical nomads whose worldview is a definitive, but neglected, aspect of the present moment. "We were the generation of change," writes Xer Henseler, "changing the dynamics between the self, society and technology, between the fixed and the fluid, the local and global as determined by the fall of walls (the Berlin Wall) and political powers (Communism), and the erasure of (technological) borders. We became some of the greatest agents of change on individual, cultural, social, political, and economic levels. We were at the center of the technological ®evolution" ("Short-*Changed*").

But change and revolution, the rise and fall of walls and empires, the emptying and crowding of neighborhoods, are unsettling as well as liberating. They are always accompanied by violence, and violence—as

---

3. X, of course, has origins in African American tradition. It aligns political resis-tance with a demarcation of language's limits. The X marks the loss of a name, lan-guage, culture, heritage, and social and familial structures, all violently wrested away by slavery; it also, and simultaneously, articulates presence and survival through a vexed relation to the language designed to erase and oppress. Ulrich notes this simi-larity, describing parallels between Generation X and the Nation of Islam's use of X. He hints that Generation X's origins in punk culture may attest to punk's assertion of alterity, an assertion that took racial otherness as its model (33n20). Here, Ulrich's approach to Generation X as a subculture limits his otherwise excellent analysis. Ulrich is strongly influenced by Dick Hebdige's work on subculture, and Hebdige's model is 1960s UK. In the United States, the limits of language and the ambivalence around naming emerge from a different tradition, one colored by the Middle Pas-sage, slavery, and Jim Crow and defined, in the 1990s, by scholars and artists like Toni Morrison ("Unspeakable Things Unspoken") and Henry Louis Gates (*Black Lit-erature and Literary Theory*). Articulating identity through language's limits was the topic of much discussion in African American studies in the 1990s—precisely when "Generation X" was becoming mainstream.

brutal manifestation or as subtle, insidious creep—is always accompanied by claims for the real, and by statements about the truth. These claims and statements take various forms: broken buildings, open bodies, updated maps, blood test results, revised history books, facts on the page and facts on the ground. As that grim list indicates, real violence and its mediated image perform similar truth-making functions. Xers were not the first to confront images of violence. But they were the first with the power to surf toward or away from them, to seek them out or to screen them. Further: Xers, attuned to the curricular debates of the 1980s and the discourses of postmodernism and poststructuralism (mainstream by the 1990s), were schooled in the power of representation and taught to dwell on the resonance of silence, absence, and omission. Consequently Xers were given to reflect on media, to think creatively about the susceptibility of reality to manipulation, censorship, silence, and control, even as adults worried about their disaffected, dispassionate, apathetic attitude. Turning to the future, after X, we will need to consider the formative role of that attitude to X culture, and the role of X culture for young people today. But before we can do so, we need to rewind, and understand what brought us to this point.

GROWING UP X

Though precise birthyears vary, Generation X, most broadly defined, refers to the generation born between 1960 and 1980. Also called the Blank Generation, the Thirteenth Generation, the post-Boomers, the Baby Busts, Xers came of age in the 1980s and 1990s, in a West marked by the ascendency of the New Right, defined by the Prime Ministry of Margaret Thatcher in Britain and Ronald Reagan's presidency in the United States. In France, François Mitterrand's economic policies caused widespread disenchantment with socialism in the 1980s, and led to the rise of Jean-Marie Le Pen and the far right; China, under Deng Xiaoping, had begun to move toward capitalism in 1979. As the economic function and social significance of the commodity replaced the commitment to liberal causes that characterized the '60s and '70s, Xers witnessed the vanishing of '80 glitz with the Black Monday stock-market crash of 1987, the collapse of the last great ideology with the fall of the Berlin Wall in 1989, and the dissolution of the Soviet Union in 1991. The 1990s ushered in the Lost Decade in Japan, after the strong economic growth that characterized the 1980s vanished and the asset price bubble collapsed.

This revision and evacuation of value was not lost on the young people. In contrast to their predecessors, the Baby Boomers, Xers are unswayed by the political values of the 1960s and notoriously unwilling to enlist on behalf of a cause or *ism*. Boomers are presumed to possess resources, material and ideological, denied to Xers, who, as Howe and Strauss put it in their seminal study *13thGen: Abort, Retry, Ignore, Fail?*, are reportedly "consumed with violence, selfishness, greed, bad work habits, and civic apathy" (17). A whiney mood, a pervasive sense of disenfranchisement, of defiance, underscores articulations of X identity; theirs is a register of dissatisfaction, of complaint. Assets, ideals, interests have disappeared; "We Don't Even Have a Name" is the title of the first chapter of Howe and Strauss's book.

This interstitial quality has been X's from the start. "'Generation X' has always signified a group of young people, seemingly without identity, who face an uncertain, ill-defined (and perhaps hostile) future," writes Ulrich (3). Henseler echoes this epochal distress, this sense of being historically belated or premature: X is a synonym for being "in-between," "after," and "lost" (*Spanish Fiction* 10). Martine Delvaux stresses X's unease with presence, in the present; she dwells on "the oxymoronic X which both eliminates it semantically and signifies its existence, the X that makes this generation's presence a thing of the past" (178). For Delvaux (who is French Canadian) and Henseler (a Hispanicist), "Generation X" is a useful moniker for a globally conceived set of attitudes. Like self-proclaimed X manifestos by Coupland, Douglas Rushkoff (editor of *The GenX Reader*), and Jeff Gordinier (author of *X Saves the World*), they alternate between claiming to be invisible and invincible, taken for granted and dismissed, targeted and ignored. Xers are poised between presence and absence, disappearing here.

Generation X lacks a definitive vast and violent event, a generational trauma like World War II or Vietnam, or a defining cultural moment like 1968. Unlike their predecessors who mobilized around—or against— great national conflicts or disasters, youthful Xers experienced violence as paralysis (the 1980s were ushered in with the Iran hostage crisis), menace (Reagan's play on the looming specter of the Evil Empire), and complicity, wherein violence is battled—or not—with the pocketbook. Though the 1990s saw a rise (or perceived rise) in youth violence globally, it was a violence that, Hans Magnus Enzensberger wrote in 1993, seemed strikingly divorced from ideological justification. Francis Fukuyama, writing of this "goalless new violence," underscored its "nihilistic character," its "strange abnegation of self" ("The New World

Disorder"). Lacking the great ideological organization of the Cold War (the end of which had led Fukuyama, famously, to declare the End of History),[4] Xers could not fail to notice how the global campaign for disinvestment from South Africa, though initiated in the 1960s, achieved critical mass only in the 1980s. They cheered ironically when Gordon Gekko pronounced, in Oliver Stone's 1987 film *Wall Street*, that "greed is good," and were haunted by the image of a lone protester facing a tank in 1989 in Tiananmen Square. The Israel/Palestine conflict (the Intifada of the 1980s) and war in the Balkans (in the 1990s) presented competing, and compelling, claims for historical victimization. Ethnic cleansing in Kosovo (1998) confirmed, for those who needed confirmation, the persistence of bloody international conflicts after the 1992 Maastricht Treaty created the European Union. The genocide in Rwanda (1994) underscored the role of race in global definitions of humanity, as NATO mobilized in Europe but allowed the killing in Africa to proceed unchecked. Developments in media and satellite TV brought these faraway tragedies home, underscoring the limits of agency. Images of famine in Ethiopia and the Sudan perpetuated this sense of futility, defined by the controversy around South African photojournalist (and Xer) Kevin Carter's image of a starving child stalked by a vulture (Carter reported taking the photograph and leaving).[5] Something must be done, the thinking goes, and yet the world is too big, its problems too complex, the child too near death, for action.

---

4. Fukuyama's controversial essay appeared in *The National Interest* in 1989; his book *The End of History and the Last Man* was published in 1992. By "end of history," Fukuyama meant the widespread adoption of liberal democracy, which had at that point "conquered rival ideologies like hereditary monarchy, fascism, and, most recently, communism" (xi). Liberal democracy, Fukuyama argued in both the essay and the book, appears to be "the 'end point of mankind's ideological evolution' and the 'final form of human government,' and as such constituted the 'end of history'" (xi). Responding critically to Fukuyama's optimistic thesis, Samuel Huntington stressed the resilience of culturally specific values, especially religion; he imagined a multipolar, multicivilizational world. Huntington's thesis was first published as "The Clash of Civilizations?" in *Foreign Affairs* (1993) and as *The Clash of Civilizations and the Remaking of World Order* in 1996. The Fukuyama–Huntington affair, which received much attention in mainstream press, concretizes the tenor of debates surrounding global politics in the post–Cold War period.

5. This iconic image is referenced in *House of Leaves* (368), Mark Z. Danielewski's complex novel about an unseeable film, an unnavigable house, and an unmanageable manuscript edited by an unreliable narrator. Critical response to *House of Leaves* has recognized its mastery of postmodernism, post-postmodernism, poststructuralism and deconstruction. Danielewski, a GenXer, has also been described as "a spokesperson for disenfranchised, non-party-line youth" (Benzon).

FIGURE 2. Vulture Watching Starving Child. Sudan, March 1993. This photograph by the South African photojournalist Kevin Carter wor Carter a Pulitzer Prize and elicited much debate about whether the journalist's responsibility was to help the child or to document her plight. Carter committed suicide in 1994 at the age of 33. © Kevin Carter / Sygma / Corbis.

Violence is here—of this Xers have no doubt. But the traditional ways to engage with it seem to have disappeared. The Cold War battle with the Soviet Union, that dictated the rhetoric of the social contract through the 1970s and organized the world into West versus Rest, ended with the dissolution of the USSR in 1991; in its wake, Generation X's atomism and disaffection are importantly tinged with nostalgia. Evil, like Empire, is an organizing principle; the threat of nuclear annihilation that haunted many Xers' childhoods in the 1970s and early 1980s is a loss that must be mourned. Consequently, it is resurrected and battled in video games like *Castle Wolfenstein* (1981) in which the player battles Nazi guards and members of the SS; *Wolfenstein 3D* (1992), a first-person shooter game in which the player, who assumes the role of an Allied spy, attempts to escape from the Nazi prison; and the visually sophisticated multiplayer *Doom*. Released as shareware in 1993, *Doom* was seminal to the emerging online gaming culture (it pioneered the deathmatch mode, by which players could kill each other, and encouraged players to modify and contribute to the game scenario by designing their own game levels).[6] But *Doom* elicited some controversy because of its extreme and graphic violence, and the technoculture it represented was linked, in the public's imagination, to a generalized anxiety about violence and impressionable youth (*Doom* figured prominently in the national soul-searching after the 1999 Columbine school shooting). For Xers (the youth in question), the distinction between music, video, television, online, and real-world violence figured differently than for adults; the value of drawing a line between fact and fiction fades in the face of pervasive violence, threats, and menace.[7] Lacking Nazis,

---

6. In *Masters of Doom: How Two Guys Created an Empire and Transformed Pop Culture,* David Kushner describes the origins of the game, which was developed by id software (founded by Xers John Carmack and John Romero). Id developed *Wolfenstein 3D* as well as *Doom,* and Kushner describes the graphic imagery that accompanied both games as the direct product of popular culture. "As the id guys came of age, in the 1980s, the action movie genre—with films like *Rambo, The Terminator,* and *Lethal Weapon*—conquered the box office, just as horror movies like *The Texas Chain Saw Massacre* and *Friday the 13th* had done in the recent past" (79). Both *Wolfenstein 3D* and *Doom* reflected the ethos of the early 1990s, Kushner writes: "The Reagan-Bush era was finally coming to a close and a new spirit rising. It began in Seattle, where a sloppily dressed grunge rock trio called Nirvana ousted Michael Jackson from the top of the pop charts with their album *Nevermind.* Soon grunge and hip-hop were dominating the world with more brutal and honest views. Id was braced to do for games what those artists had done for music: overthrow the status quo" (94).

7. Journalist and technology expert Steven Levy, writing about the 1999 Columbine school shootings, describes "a violence-fixated cultural landscape" in which the internet, Hollywood, video games, and traditional media news coverage in thrall to the human

Communists, and imminent apocalypse, haunted by divorce, famine, drugs, global warming, and AIDS, the real world appears to Xers too random, its violence too diffuse, to be an effective battleground for Evil. The self that battles is similarly diffuse, and can easily be simulated (especially online).

This is not to say that violence is absent from X experience of the world. On the contrary, Generation X originates from disaster. A "reaction against human atrocities, fallouts, and corruption," as Henseler puts it, X migrates to the marginal, the liminal, the virtual: a hypothetical, contingent space from which Xers "could reject the storylines written by others, especially by institutions, authorities, and politicians" (*Global* 11). This rejection, disavowal, and disenchantment informs X's designation as marginal (Henseler's term), hybrid (Grassian's), and interstitial: X is poised, as Delvaux puts it, between "the ambiguity of the 'what' and the everlasting 'ever'" (179). This awkward, tenuous balancing act contributes to X's self-image as the generation that is both uniquely privileged and robbed, abandoned, misplaced and missed-out. At the same time, it affords Xers a unique perspective. Just as violence is simultaneously, immediately, unbearably present and banished with a wave of the remote control, Xers learned to keep an eye on both the hope of change *and* the hypocrisy of promise, the attraction of solvency *and* the transience of value, the necessity of action *and* the resilience of personal, economic, and political interest.[8]

Such an attitude is of a piece with the postmodern philosophies articulated during this period. Jean-François Lyotard's *The Postmodern Condition,* published in France in 1979 and translated into English in 1984, articulated the distrust of master narratives as a defining paradigm of the age; by the 1990s, the works of Michel Foucault, Jacques Derrida, and Gilles Deleuze and Félix Guattari were established as the shibboleths of contemporaneity. Xer Jeffrey Eugenides' *The Marriage Plot,* set at Brown University in the early 1980s, describes what attracted young people to this work: "It drew a line; it created an elect; it was sophisticated and Continental; it dealt with provocative subjects,

---

drama create "a vicious cycle where even the examination of a disaster reinforces the violence-obsessed culture that may have helped trigger it" ("Loitering").

8. An example is the phenomenon of Band Aid, the charity supergroup founded in 1984 to raise money for the victims of famine in Ethiopia with a "Feed the World" logo and record-breaking single, "Do They Know It's Christmas?" Even before its release, Band Aid was widely derided by critics, who took the project to task for its presumed self-righteousness and implicit colonialism. Hebdige discusses the phenomenon in *Hiding in the Light.*

with torture, sadism, hermaphroditism—with sex and power" (24). The appeal of theory points at how, for Xers, traditional youthful activism was unavailable. For Eugenides' characters, college "lacked a certain radicalism"; the work of scholars like Derrida "was the first thing that smacked of revolution" (24). Xers are less inclined to engage than to deconstruct, to dwell in the aporia of irreconcilable opposites. They linger, as Xer David Foster Wallace's characters so memorably do, in the restless, counterarticulate logic of addiction, anxiety, neurosis, and depression. Depression, as Elizabeth Wurtzel writes in her memoir *Prozac Nation* (her "author's note" references deconstruction and Derrida), is an appropriate designation for her generation's "low-grade terminal anomie, a sense of alienation or disgust and detachment, the collective horror at a world that seems to have gone so very wrong" (302). Writing in 1994, Xer Wurtzel describes an emergent "depression culture" (the music of Nirvana, Nine Inch Nails, Pearl Jam, Beck, The Cure, Depeche Mode, The Smiths, Richard Linklater's film *Slacker*, Coupland's *Generation X*, and the rise, in fashion, of grunge and heroin chic) and muses that depression may well be a generational response to a world "perilously lacking in the basic guarantees that our parents expected: a marriage that would last, employment that was secure, sex that wasn't deadly" (301–2). Of course, depression itself is deadly: a fatal marriage of culture and clinic, symbol and act, something "in the air" in the mid-1990s and unutterable, unshareable, unspeakable despair. David Foster Wallace, who had struggled with clinical depression for decades, committed suicide in 2008.

This period also saw the rise of Critical Race Theory, which urged reflection on the deep complicity of narratives and institutions in structural violence. The movement held annual workshops in the 1990s, and published readers defining the field and outlining approaches to racism that focused on its invisible, entrenched, interested forms. Richard Delgado and Jean Stefancic, writing of the premises of Critical Race Theory, underscore its directives to look both *at* and *through* what presents as ordinary in order to uncover the invisible violence enshrined in everyday life. "Racism is normal, not aberrant, in American society," write Delgado and Stefancic. "Because racism is an ingrained feature of our landscape, it looks ordinary and natural to persons in the culture. Formal equal opportunity—rules and laws that insist on treating blacks and whites (for example) alike [. . .] can do little about the business-as-usual forms of racism that people of color confront every day and that account for much misery, alienation, and despair" (xvi). Together with postmodernism and poststructuralism's ethos of radical critique, the rise of Critical Race Theory formalized a general distrust of identitarianism and an ethical investment in ambivalence. Xers, who attended college in record numbers,[9] were well schooled in this kind of work. At the same time, witness to the rise of identity politics and political correctness, aware of the structural injustices deeply engrained in the status quo, Xers—of all colors—are profoundly suspicious of institutional authority, identity, and ethos. As Lila Mae, the protagonist of Colson Whitehead's complex racial allegory *The Intuitionist* (1999), realizes: "Don't believe your eyes. [. . .] There will be no redemption because the men who run this place do not want redemption. They want to be as near to hell as they can" (240).

Lila Mae is an African American woman elevator inspector in a Jim Crow–style city who, alone of all her colleagues, works by intuiting, rather than empirically verifying, elevators' functioning and who must fight to clear her name from a mesh of schemes designed to frame her. In the course of her travails, she learns that John Fulton, her mentor in the theory of Intuitionism and author of her personal bible, *Theoretical Elevators,* was a black man who passed for white. In the concluding pages of *The Intuitionist* Lila Mae, whose first encounter with Fulton's work is described as "a conversion experience" (59), has dedicated herself to completing it. No longer his disciple, she is his ghostwriter, or his medium, "filling in the interstitial parts" of his design for the perfect elevator that will destroy existing cities and establish new ones, a vision of revolution that is inseparable from violence: "They're all doomed anyway, she figures. Doomed by what she's working on" (254). Solitary, messianic, she thinks, "It will come. She is never wrong. It is her intuition" (255). But despite the novel's bewitching conceit, by which Intuitionists like Lila Mae have a 10 percent higher accuracy rate than Empiricists in their analysis of elevator functionality, Whitehead's reader cannot abide in the prophetic certainty of this assertion. Lila Mae is not never wrong. The novel has recounted her inaccurate hunches, mistaken convictions, and misplaced trust. Just like empirical verification, which Intuitionists disdain, accuracy and certainty are evoked and dismissed in this book. All that remains is faith—in nothing. The vision Lila Mae is in thrall to—the promise, from Fulton's writings, of "*another world*

---

9. Sixty-four percent of Generation Xers had completed four years of college in 2007, compared with 54 percent of Baby Boomers. See Carlson 5 (table 2). Note that Carlson uses a relatively narrow birthyear range for Generation X: 1965–82 (page 3 box 1).

beyond this one" (63)—is, she learns, a black man's venomous disillusionment with a world that will not let him rise, but Lila Mae keeps faith with this promise, knowing its origin is a lie.

Mistrust and ambivalence have functioned, historically, as productive attitudes, elaborated by postmodernism's and poststructuralism's hermeneutics of suspicion. But for Lila Mae, and her X creator Whitehead (for whom Intuitionism may well be a cipher for Critical Race Theory which, like Critical Legal Studies, feminism, and postcolonial studies, drew on the work of Foucault and Derrida to articulate the deep complicities of power with knowledge), this equipoise of creation and destruction, cynicism and idealism, engagement and passivity presents unique challenges to action and critique. Despite her revolutionary messianic certainty, Lila (whose name means "night") Mae is not an actor but a medium, a placeholder; her story is one of a path-breaking, capable woman who submerges herself in a great man's work. By the end of the novel Mae ("may"), balanced between possibility and probability, is transient ("she writes a sentence and then scratches it out" [254]), mobile ("She likes this new room. [. . .] There's time to move on and find another room" [254]), and contingent: though Fulton had described her, earlier, as "the one" (211), she realizes that "it didn't have to be her, but it was" (255). With its protagonist writing, erasing, on the move, interstitial, replaceable, and expectant, Whitehead's novel confirms, to the reader, this earlier, bleak, X intuition: nothing tells the truth; mistrust is as useless as trust (227). To this simultaneous quality of being and not being, of effecting great change by remaining uncommitted, of holding on tightly to nothing, an atheist keeping the faith, the music of the 1990s spoke loud and clear. Writing of the X anthem, Nirvana's "Smells Like Teen Spirit," Gordinier states: "that duality, that stuckness between a desire for change and profound doubts about how to achieve it, would come to define the philosophy of X. If the boomers had shot their wad by trying to forge a utopia, Kurt Cobain was saving the world by steering his generation away from that delusion" (15–16). On the other end of the 1990s music spectrum, arcane Indie folk icon (and Xer) Vic Chesnutt intones: "Free of hope, free of a past / Thank you God of nothing, I'm free at last."[10]

---

10. "Free of Hope" first appeared on Chesnutt's fourth album *Is the Actor Happy?*, released in 1995 and rereleased in 2004 with liner notes by poet Forrest Gander. Gander highlights "Free of Hope," calling it Chesnutt's "great elegy to our culture at the end of the last millennium," a "haunting refrain that inverts Martin Luther King's dream for our future and catches our emptiness and irony at the century's demise." Chesnutt, who had attempted suicide multiple times, died in 2007 at the age of 45.

X ON THE MOVE

Any study of Generation X must account for its uneasy situation between precision and elision, specificity and negation. X crosses out *and* marks the spot: it is a demographic and a philosophy, a local subculture and a diverse global manifestation. True, the persistent association of X with slacker, grunge, youth, and white male subculture in the United States makes it an unlikely player in a postnational world dominated by the images of the spectacular attacks on the World Trade Center on September 11, 2001, the fallout from the global recession of 2008, and the reverberations of the Occupy movement and the Arab Spring. Further, the term's function as a demographic marker for people born between 1960 and 1980 aligns it with somewhat empiricist claims, according to which Xers are more or less likely than Boomers or Millennials to bank or date online. As its title implies, *Disappear Here* embraces this epistemic unease, drawing on the philosophical tradition of writing about violence in the twentieth and twenty-first centuries *and* studies of Generation X that treat it as a youth or popular culture phenomenon, analyzing literary works, film, and cultural artifacts by members of Generation X, but situating these in the cultural contexts from which they arose and to which they contribute.

X, "the defiant demographic" (Gordinier xxi), dislikes categories, categorization, and the rhetoric of identity generally. Ian Williams or "Crasher," the reluctant X spokesman of Howe and Strauss's *13thGen*, puts it thus: "Why do we have to be a generation at all? Why can't we just peacefully take up our place on the great palette of time without people like you coming along and calling us 'post-whatever' and 'neo-pseudo-classical-glurb'? [. . .] I like being nice and undefinable, you're taking the fun out of everything" (13). Twenty years later X has become so established that, Touré notes, its persistent association with the white suburban middle class unfairly excludes African Americans. "Can the Black community be said to have escaped the key touchstones that shaped gen X: divorce, latchkey kids, AIDS, crack, hiphop, MTV, and widespread economic troubles? No. These things are absolutely part of the experience of Black people who grew up in the 1970s and 1980s. So how can Blacks not be part of the gen X meme? Of course we are" (63). At the same time, Touré is ambivalent about the term: "It's not a great name," he concedes, "but we're stuck with it" (64).

Touré's attitude, like Crasher's, is typical X. To a considerable extent, X *is* attitude: negation, defiance, disaffection, dislike—not least of the term "X" itself—and a penchant for the underground. Coupland, whose 1991 *Generation X* was seminal for the moniker, rejected the term soon after, in 1995, writing that X is "not a chronological age but a way of looking at the world," and lambasting the generational appellation as "demographic pornography" ("Generation X'ed"). But pornography (as the "porn wars" and the rise of Third Wave Feminism in the 1980s and 1990s made clear) can be useful, interesting, and even pleasurable and enabling. So can demographics. Read in retrospect, Coupland's declaration, in 1995, that "X is over" is, itself, of a piece with X 'tude, a metaphorical instrument smashing in the style of punk and grunge (bands like The Clash and Nirvana, like their predecessors in The Who, were famous for smashing their guitars onstage). As Xers, hardly "over," approach middle age, and in light of more recent work on commodity culture and global capitalism (not to mention the success of post-grunge bands like Nickelback and Creed), I propose we revisit this attitude, even embrace it, and think about the contemporary *after*—the preposition means both subsequent to and in accordance with—Generation X. Both as an object to study *and* an example to follow, an aging demographic *and* a beacon or guide, X marks the spot of multiple emergences and vanishings.

Not least of these is the real: a principle, an experiential category, an aesthetic quality, and something Xers were expected to *get*. "Are you down for the real?" raps the hip hop band Brand Nubian in their 1994 album *Everything Is Everything*. "If you down say you down, if you scared say you scared / This is the real don't fuck around and come unprepared." But even as Sadat X and Lord Jamar (both Xers) warn, "This ain't no TV show or a song from the radio / Murder on the streets, yo, is at a high ratio," the idea of the real as something to be down for, (psyched) up for, checked, or fetched is inextricable from the image that enraptures, exposes, and betrays. As David Foster Wallace, reflecting on the formative impact of the Watergate scandal for his generation, puts it: "When even the President lies to you, whom are you supposed to trust to deliver the real?" (36). The TV coverage of Watergate offered Xers a primer in the fabrication of the real, taught young people to gaze both at and through the image, and instructed them in the unique X dyad of detachment and immersion: "Television," writes Wallace, "got to present itself as the earnest, worried eye on the reality behind all images. The irony that television is itself a river of image, however, was apparent even to a twelve-year-old, sitting there, rapt" (36). For a wide spectrum of Xers (from rappers to writers), reality—commodified, sensationalized, marketed; evacuated, ambivalent, mobile—is both an unarguable presence *and* an unappealing investment.

X's unique relation to the real is captured in Howe and Strauss's *13thGen: Abort, Retry, Ignore, Fail?*, the first formal study of Generation X (what they call "the Thirteenth Generation"). A spinoff of "The New Generation Gap," a popular article in *The Atlantic*, *13thGen* is sized like a textbook; its argument (a rather conventional depth model by which Howe and Strauss essentially suggest that contemporary youth culture functions as a discursive site for the projection of national anxieties and desires) is interrupted by graphs, cartoons, sound bites, and (expanding the book's conceit, by which the Boomer authors upload the text to an online chat room which is then "crashed" by the Xers themselves) a discussion among Xers who log in and debate the argument's points and merits. *13thGen* thus straddles sociology and fiction; both an important cultural document and a self-conscious commodity, it is designed to appeal to the demographic it defines and describes. In an early review of Howe and Strauss's book, Sue Gardner accurately sums up its marriage of commodity and critique. *13thGen,* writes Gardner, "puts forth its thesis literally by design, in that the layout of the book appears to be a reflection of the authors' vision of the 20-something mind—fragmented, infested with trivia and ultimately incoherent." Gardner dismissed the book as one more exploitative move performed on young people by aging Boomers: "by profiling the 20-something niche market, [Howe and Strauss] have simultaneously created a potentially quite profitable market for their own services." This analysis by Gardner (a self-proclaimed Xer) illustrates X's unique combination of superficiality and depth. Early positioned as a marketing target, Xers' eyes were open to marketing's pitfalls and potential, to the mediated quality of perception, and to the fact that there is no outside to power. Consequently Xers dropped out *and* sold out, opted out *and* bought in. "X got hypermarketed right from the start, which was harsh," Coupland complains ("Generation X'ed"); and yet, I submit, this severity invites clarity. Harshness frees Xers from illusion, even as, visually figured in the grainy aesthetic that came to signify authenticity in film, advertising, and music videos in the 1990s, it is itself a media product. Xers could hold both in view. The generation with no cause to fight for, with nothing to believe in, alert to image manipulation and chronically suspicious of empirical certainties, is uniquely poised to articulate the changing nature of the real in the decades that preceded, and established, our increasingly virtual world.

Violence is commonly presumed to call a halt to the virtual. It represents the real—not least, an Evil real, one that demands response, ethics, critique, action, and that is historically suspicious of simulation. But X marks the spot from which to think of violence *after* the mainstreaming of opposition described by Nancy Armstrong and Leonard Tennenhouse in *The Violence of Representation*. Reflecting on the state of literary criticism in the late 1980s, Armstrong and Tennenhouse wonder about the efficacy of critique. "What can it mean," they ask, "that such belligerent terms as 'patriarchy,' 'resistance,' and 'subversion' are now cant phrases?" (1). Indeed: How do you respond to violence when the position from which you take your stand has been, essentially, deconstructed? You turn your gaze to the ground beneath your feet and see it vanish. Generation X expresses this dis-ease, a fundamental suspicion of being present, of being there, of *Dasein*, familiar to anyone schooled, as many Xers were, in poststructuralist and postmodern thought. Writing of X ethics as opposed to Boomers', Douglas Rushkoff notes wistfully, "It must be nice to have something external to believe in. Something that doesn't move. Something absolute" (7). Xers experience reality as a moving target, less an event to witness than an opportunity to believe in a world devoid of *isms* ("I want to believe" is the mantra of the popular 1990s TV show *The X-Files*).

Although throughout what follows I contend that *violence is real*—and the following chapter pursues the implications of this contention—I recognize that reality, for Xers, is mobile, appropriable, subject to revision, rewriting, rewiring, and reworking in a digital age. Given this mutability, we need to examine the role that violence (and "violence") plays in navigating reality's shifting terrain, that unquiet ground on which, as Marc Augé put it in 1999, "the global relationship between human beings and the real is altering under the influence of representations connected with the development of technologies, with the globalisation of certain key issues and with the acceleration of history" (7). Generation X's association with movement, with acceleration, with time running out at the millennium's edge, is also the question of certainty's shifting terrain under the spell of velocity, and concretizes the challenge that contemporaneity—the here and now—poses to study. ("I don't like giving names to generations," Crasher complains in *13thGen*, "it's like trying to read the song title on a record that's spinning" [23].)

Augé's reference to "the acceleration of history" is apposite. From its inception, X has been on the move, a generation defined by acceleration. Ulrich notes that Coupland's subtitle to *Generation X*, "Tales for an Accelerated Culture," echoes Charles Hamblett and Jane Deverson's characterization of 1960s youth culture in their sociological collection of interviews, *Generation X*. Writing in 1964, Hamblett and Deverson reflected on the unique problems facing young people after World War II. "Things, people, ideas get used up more quickly—yet are cast aside with the same old primal ruthlessness. This is one of the problems the young must face and conquer: the problem of social and scientific acceleration at the expense of biological time" (5). These problems have only increased in recent decades, with the advent of social media, the proliferation of user interfaces, and the omnipresence of technological devices with built-in obsolescence. For Xers, who have always dwelt in the tension between the specific and the universal, the document and the hypothesis, the demographic and the point of view, reality's mobile, mutable quality poses unique challenges to idealism, judgment, and action—especially in the context of violence.

To capture my topic—violence, the real, and "real violence" today—from these moving, shifting paradigms, *Disappear Here* brings together two bodies of work: the philosophical tradition of violence and representation in the twentieth and twenty-first centuries and studies of Generation X that treat it as a transient youth or popular culture phenomenon. (*Disappear Here* is thus a departure from the majority of Generation X scholarship that relies more on sociology than aesthetics, and that privileges an empirical approach over a philosophical one.) To bring these two traditions together, I turn to fiction—both in its sense of molding, making, and forming (from the Latin root *fictio*) and in the more conventional sense of prose narrative associated with the rise of literary realism in the eighteenth century. Fiction, in this, its broadest sense, echoes X's affiliation with uncertainty and elision, its ethos of creative, mobile engagement with the real, and its association with specificity and demographics.

In choosing fiction to approach violence, my methodology, again, echoes Armstrong and Tennenhouse's *The Violence of Representation*. Noting that traditional studies of hegemony and power "have lost their oppositional edge" (1), the authors draw a theory of violence from a reading of Charlotte Brontë's *Jane Eyre* (3–9).[11] With this move, Arm-

---

11. Armstrong and Tennenhouse defend their recourse to fiction, rather than the "masculinist social sciences," as a gesture beyond the oppositional dichotomous thinking that perpetually "others" and subordinates in order to name and define. They conclude their defense of their methodological choice by affirming the pervasive quality of violence in the United States at the end of the 1980s: "As American academics at this moment in history, we feel it is somehow dishonest to speak of power and violence as something that belongs to the police or the military, something that belongs to and is practiced by someone somewhere else. For clearly the subtler modalities of modern culture, usually classified as non-political, keep most of us in line, just as they designate

strong and Tennenhouse affirm the reciprocal relation of cultural construction and material experience that Richard Slotkin articulates in his monumental study of violence in twentieth-century U.S. culture, *Gunfighter Nation* (1992): literary fiction, popular history, film, and other commercial culture work together with political events and social crises to articulate the terms by which reality is perceived (*Gunfighter* 24). Like these important predecessors (published at the time Xers were reaching maturity and beginning to engage critically the culture around them), *Disappear Here* finds in fiction, film, and media a useful site from which to mine the truth-claims made by violence in the "new regime of fiction" that Augé calls for (6), a regime defined by acceleration, by the evacuation of affect, and by a general rethinking of representation. I claim for Xers the wistful attitude of the nameless narrator in Brat Pack author Jay McInerney's *Bright Lights, Big City* who, as he ricochets around New York City in a fruitless flight from grief, reflects: "You don't want to be in Fact. You'd much rather be in Fiction" (22).

ALL A GASH

Although this book is about violence *after* Generation X, *Bright Lights, Big City* is an important precursor and worth some attention. Published in 1984 (a year designated by *Newsweek* as "The Year of the Yuppie"), McInerney's debut book underscores the problem that violence poses to representation in this period. The opening lines offer a meditation on presence. "You are not the kind of guy would be at a place like this at this time of the morning. But here you are, and you cannot say that the terrain is entirely unfamiliar, though the details are fuzzy." Having both set and blurred the scene, the narrator continues: "You are at a nightclub talking to a girl with a shaved head" (1).

The girl with the shaved head (so central to the narrative that she appears not once but thrice in the 1988 film adaptation, with a screenplay written by McInerney) poses a challenge to reading and interpretation that is directly connected to violence in the glitzy world in which the novel is set. She has, the narrator notes, "a scar tattooed on her scalp. It looks like a long, sutured gash" (3). With this tattoo (itself a subversive signifying regime) a number of signifying regimes are evoked and subverted. The tattoo references violence as both sign and symbol, both

---

specific 'others' as the appropriate objects of violence" (4).

physical and (as head trauma) psychic, but does so through an image that is incoherent: a scar that looks like a gash. A gash implies depth—a point highlighted by the sutures, which lend the closed edges of the wound an additional dimension. A scar, on the other hand, is the mark of healed tissue. A scar that *looks like* a gash both testifies to wounding and disavows it, and the fact that this is a tattoo, a wedding of skin to sign, invites a reading that refuses reading of the body in pain.

In the book, the narrator will find and choose Vicky, a blueblood cousin of his friend Tad Allagash and graduate student in philosophy at Princeton. Vicky has hair "somewhere between strawberry and gold" (91) and a voice "like gravel spread with honey" (92)—unlike the bald girl whose voice is "like the New Jersey State Anthem played through an electric shaver" (3). She recalls to the narrator "Plato's pilgrims climbing out of the cave, from the shadow world of appearances toward things as they really are" (93), and she does not appear in the film adaptation. By omitting Vicky, the film remains true to the novel's preoccupation with the "problem" to the narrator that the bald girl represents. "The bald girl is emblematic of the problem. The problem is, for some reason you think you are going to meet the kind of girl who is not the kind of girl who would be at a place like this at this time of the morning" (3). Because she is emblematic, suggesting something other than what she is, the bald girl invites interpretation. She demands to be read.

In the exchange the narrator has with the girl about the tattoo, reading is very much in question. The narrator, attuned to the language of "Kings James and Lear" (8), tells the girl that the tattoo is "very realistic. She takes this as a compliment and thanks you. You meant as opposed to romantic" (3). The drive toward depth, the sublime, and the unpresentable, associated with the Romantics, is countered, here, by a discourse of resolute superficiality. The girl's inability to distinguish between presentation and the unpresentable, figured by the literary traditions of realism and romance, attests to her cultural illiteracy. "I could use one of those right over my heart," says the narrator of the tattoo. The girl misses the metaphor. "You want I can give you the name of the guy that did it. You'd be surprised how cheap" (3).

But the bald girl is not merely a problem of reading, an expression of nostalgia for bygone femininity, a yuppie joke, or a language game. Her presence in the novel testifies to what made it so popular: the lacerated quality of the narrator's existence, his perpetual disavowal of a very real pain, his fundamental desire to be elsewhere or otherwise. "How did you get here?" the narrator wonders. "It was your friend,

Tad Allagash, who powered you in here, and he has disappeared" (2). The surname Allagash (coined before the founding of Allagash brewery in Portland, Maine, in 1995) speaks to the violence that pervades the narrator's world. When all's a gash, even tattoos—not to mention scars—present as unhealed wounds, and Tad's relentless superficiality betrays the fragility of surface and the menace that lurks beneath it. Tad is the narrator's alter ego: he "is either your best self or your worst self, you're not sure which" (2). Relentlessly womanizing, perpetually drunk, continually partying, Tad is "a figure skater who never considers the sharks under the ice" (32). In the course of the novel the narrator, abandoned by his wife, who chooses a career as a model over domesticity with him, and failing at his job as a fact-checker for a prestigious magazine, wanders from bar to bar, party to party. He accepts and then rejects various offers (mostly by women) of help and care. Toward the end of the novel, he reaches out to Vicky and, in the course of their telephone conversation, the reader learns that what appeared to be behavioral (a manifestation of yuppie malaise) or reactionary (a response to the abandonment by his model wife) is, in fact, a symptom of a more abiding trauma: the slow and painful death, one year earlier, of the narrator's mother from cancer. Now, the bald girl is cast in yet another light: she must remind the narrator of his mother after chemotherapy, a fact that the attentive reader may intuit, but that the narrative never acknowledges.[12]

The bald girl sets the scene, establishes a problem, and disappears. Her tattoo—the incoherent image of a scar that looks like a gash— speaks to violence that is simultaneously spectacular *and* structural, but refuses both surface *and* deep reading.[13] Such an image underscores the interpenetration of violence and its signs, bodies and their meanings, presence and its absence. The bald girl, who demands to be read, refuses reading and eludes analysis. She is both a simulated diversion *and* an indicator of underlying psychic and social complexities. To the narrator, whose life is in tatters, she is one more gash: both the object of misogynistic predation *and* the repressed, disavowed incitement for traumatic repetition.

---

12. McInerney's mother Marilyn died of cancer in 1981, the same year McInerney's first wife, Linda, who worked as an international model, filed for divorce and McInerney was fired from the *New Yorker*'s fact-checking department. McInerney highlights these points on his website's biography.

13. I return to contemporary discussions of surface reading in this book's conclusion.

I linger on the image that opens McInerney's 1984 debut because, like Ellis's—published the following year—it is so emblematic of X. It demands a careful reading and eludes definitive interpretation. Just as X crosses out, marks the spot, and is perpetually on the move, the bald girl's tattoo, which testifies to a wound and conceals it, enacts the movement of the entire narrative: its perpetual, and simultaneous, affirmation and disavowal of the lacerated quality of existence. *Less Than Zero* moves similarly; like McInerney, Ellis concretizes this narrative style by turning to tropes of the feminine: Muriel, the anorexic/addict, whose wordless screams echo throughout the book (I discuss Muriel in more detail in chapter 3). The centrality of young women to the works of these young men, the tendency by female X authors like A. M. Homes, Donna Tartt, Jennifer Egan, Gillian Flynn, and Laura Albert (a.k.a. JT LeRoy) to choose male protagonists in their meditations on violence and predation, and Ellis's and Palahniuk's later self-identification as gay, call a halt to any easy dismissal of X culture as exclusively male or straight. X's politics of representation might best be described though the discourse of negativity—one that combines the medium of photography and an ethos of refusal ("Not!" was Word of the Year in 1992).[14]

That said, the differences between McInerney's 1984 debut and Ellis's 1985 one are worth noting. *Bright Lights, Big City* ends as the narrator, having confessed to Vicky, trades his Ray-Bans (that emblem of distance, detachment, and Brat Pack superficiality) for a roll of bread. The smell of bread evokes the past, home, domesticity, and his mother. The imagery is of redemption, rebirth: down on his knees, bread in his mouth, the narrator realizes, "You will have to go slowly. You will have to learn everything all over again" (182). Clay, in contrast, consumed by the discourse of negativity that dictated *Less Than Zero*'s representational and narrative ethos, disappears into his own hellish fantasies. The violent images from the song replace his point of view: his "only point of reference" (208), they orient without direction. The difference between these two novels could be attributed to the fact that McInerney was born in 1955 and does not fall within the Generation X demographic. I value more the insight it offers into how the relation between violence and the real was beginning to be redefined in the volatile mid-80s. Like Clay, who, despite the impressionability that his name connotes, functions

---

14. The annual "Word" is chosen by the American Dialect Society and widely reported in mainstream press. The 1992 selection included the exclamation mark ("Words").

as a negative, Generation X exposes violence, but not to confront, correct, or condemn it. The following chapters explicate how this quality grounds Xers' disinclination to identify, a disinclination that extends to the logic of representation and will come to dictate the critique of mimesis that developed in the literature of this period. By focusing on Xers' affectlessness, their disaffection, and their dislike of causes, truths, and ideals, I hope to underscore the role that fiction and faith (in nothing) play in determining how, in a world without *isms*, where fervor is uncool, Xers find that reality "bites." The reference is not only the title of the 1994 romantic comedy *Reality Bites* (directed by Ben Stiller and starring a host of X actors). It underscores the conflation of fragmentation ("bytes") and aversion ("bites") that leads one of the narrators in Coupland's *Generation X* to conclude, "It's not healthy to live life as a succession of isolated little cool moments." Another agrees: "Either our lives become stories, or there's just no way to get through them" (8).

CROSSING OUT AND MARKING THE SPOT

"Generation X" is, in its origin, multiple and migratory. Its movement— from Capa's photographic project, through Fussell's and Hamblett and Deverson's sociological texts, Billy Idol's music, and Coupland's fiction—attests to the concept's global appeal. Coupland's *Generation X: Tales for an Accelerated Culture* begins in Manitoba, is set primarily in the Mojave desert, and ends in Mexico, and Coupland's lone reference to "Generation X" in his book posits "X" as a translation from the Japanese *Shinjinrui* —"new human being," a term used in the 1980s to denote people in their twenties. In *Generation X*, the narrator Andy, who has lived in Japan, reflects, of *Shinjinrui*, that "we have the same group over here [in North America] and it's just as large, but it doesn't have a name—an X generation—purposefully hiding itself. There's more space over here to hide in—to get lost in—to use as camouflage. You're not allowed to disappear in Japan" (56). Noting this early alignment of the X with both a global cohort and that cohort's inclination to disappear, I find the appeal of "Generation X" is that, as Daniel Grassian puts it in *Hybrid Fictions,* an early study of U.S. literature after Generation X, "it aptly describes a diverse generation that cannot be simply defined" (14). Like Grassian, I am less interested in delimiting Xers by birthyears or nations, finding more value in the "media-focused historical and political events, as well as television shows, films and music that

frequently serve as [Generation Xers'] common frames of reference"
(Grassian 14).[15] For many X scholars, this frame of reference extends
to a globally conceived popular culture that is in vibrant dialogue with
U.S. (and British; but mostly U.S.) television, film, and music. Nonetheless, U.S. culture is prominent in this study, as it is for Generation X
generally, a point that deserves some attention.

I am an Xer and I lived in the Middle East until 1994. There, I was
attuned to national and ideological economies in which culture circulates. Some of the music, movies, TV shows, and books discussed in this
study were exported to the Middle East and I learned about them in
the 1980s and early 1990s. Of these, some were translated, subtitled,
and broadcast in prime time. Some were mistranslated, or broadcast
without key scenes, or in select cities, or with alternate endings. Others
were pirated, illegally copied, translated, and disseminated. Still others
remained for me to discover when I came to the United States for postgraduate work. For me, the attraction of U.S. culture has always been
tinged with recognition of these global complexities. A cultlike reverence
attached to the "American" appellation (both above- and underground)
during the Cold War; U.S. films and music albums differed, sometimes
crucially, from their exported versions; telling mistakes were revealed
in the subtitling, translation, or dubbing processes, or in the marketing campaigns; television series were broadcast on nationally run stations, without reruns, commercial breaks, or teasers, eliciting a different
kind of watching than in the West. These are just some of the sites of
productive dissonance that reverberate in my perception of U.S. culture,
and they inform my readings of this culture to this day. I note my personal experience in this context because it echoes in the work of Generation X scholars who share my transnational perspective. Christine
Henseler, who specializes in Spanish youth culture, makes liberal use
of Bret Easton Ellis, Coupland, and The Clash in her co-edited volume
Generation X Rocks; her current project, *Generation X Goes Global*,

---

15. Although Grassian self-identifies as a member of Generation X, he also clarifies
that his is not a study of Generation X literature but rather of "hybrid fictions" by
authors born in the 1950s through the 1970s. This demographic range allows him to
include some important X authors (Sherman Alexie, Douglas Coupland, David Foster
Wallace, Dave Eggers, and Michele Serros) as well as authors born just outside the X
demographic: Neal Stephenson, William T. Vollmann, and Richard Powers. Grassian's
approach to "hybrid fictions" claims for literary engagement a mode of critique that is
politically efficacious: hybridity, he suggests, allows these novels to agitate for socially
responsible action and political change (Grassian's models are Bhabha and Bakhtin).
Consequently, he dismisses Ellis and the Brat Pack authors who are, he suggests, insufficiently critical of the culture in which they write.

documents X's global relevance. Tara Brabazon, an Australian cultural studies scholar, articulates Generation X identity with recourse to Irvine Welsh's *Trainspotting,* Joss Whedon's *Buffy the Vampire Slayer,* and Quentin Tarantino's *Pulp Fiction,* rightly adding Baz Luhrmann's *Moulin Rouge.* For these scholars, as for Martine Delvaux, who is French Canadian, Jeff Gordinier (who recalls fondly the formative role, for Xers, of the Velvet Revolution in Prague), and Howe and Strauss (who note the impact on Xers of corporate globalization), "Generation X" is a useful moniker for a globally conceived set of attitudes. Like them I find in U.S. popular culture a useful tool for critical work in a global context.[16]

The centrality of violence to this culture has often been noted. In *Gunfighter Nation,* Richard Slotkin argued that violence plays a unique role in U.S. national identity, not because the United States is a uniquely violent society but because fiction plays so crucial and formative a role in it: "What is distinctively 'American' is not necessarily the amount or kind of violence that characterizes our history but the mythic significance we have assigned to it, the forms of symbolic violence we imagine or invent, and the political uses to which we have put that symbolism" (14). Slotkin argues that symbolic violence began to accrue "real" import and impact during Reagan's presidency in the 1980s (a crucial decade for Xers). Since *Gunfighter Nation* was published (in 1992) the reciprocal movement between literary fiction, popular culture, journalism, and mass media and political and cultural events that Slotkin traced in that early book has developed into a lively critique of mimesis in studies of violence and aesthetics by Joel Black, Mark Seltzer, Art Redding, and Elana Gomel, who have traced an involution of the relation of reality to representation. But *Disappear Here* departs from this (however recent) tradition in an important respect: Black's work on murderers (1991), Seltzer's work on serial killers (1998), Redding's on anarchists (1999), and Gomel's on killers (2003), all take, as their object, the perpetrator of violence. Despite the diversity of their approaches to the means by which violence manifests (through writing, in narrative, as art), and despite their eschewal

---

16. Henseler (*Spanish Fiction*) offers a survey of global X authors, including Victor Pelevin (Russia), Christian Kracht (Germany), Hallgrimur Helgason (Iceland), Andrew McGahan (Australia), Irvine Welsh (Scotland), and Amélie Nothomb (Belgium) (18–20). I would add to this list: Etgar Keret and Michal Zamir (Israel), Samir El-Youssef (Palestine/Lebanon), Hari Kunzru (British Indian), Mohsin Hamid (Pakistan), Marie Darrieussecq (France), Nelly Arcan (Canada), Lauren Beukes (South Africa), Wei Hui (China), and Chris Cleave and Tom McCarthy (UK). I discuss global X literature and film in the conclusion.

of a moral or prescriptive agenda in their discussions of it, their focus on perpetrators retains them in a somewhat stable realm, one defined and prescribed by judgment. The realm of judgment has two crucial qualities: it assumes temporal progression (by which a violent act *precedes* its grisly aftermath, and judgment follows) and the law's instantiation, which, in the form of judgment, determines the distinction between the perpetrator and (generally, his) victim. Consequently: for scholars who focus on violent perpetrators, the critique that violence demands must perforce occur *after* the fact of violence and *within* the realm of law.

But violence cannot always be captured by the sensemaking mechanisms of critique. Violence *does*—it destroys, constructs, and transforms—but it also *is*: a pure, immediate manifestation of force that cannot be captured by legalistic or even epistemic categories, by judgment, by "right" or "wrong." Violence signals this epistemic unease: the great criminal, as Walter Benjamin reflected in 1921, elicits "the secret admiration of the public. This cannot result from his deed, but only from *the violence to which it bears witness*" ("Critique of Violence" 281; emphasis mine). With this image of violence that is outside the law, Benjamin articulated, decades before Foucault, "the law's interest in a monopoly on violence." Benjamin knew that "violence, when not in the hands of the law, threatens it not by the ends that it may pursue but by its mere existence outside the law" (281). However taken we may be by Hannibal Lecter (and we are taken indeed!) our point of view remains with Clarice Starling's: capable but limited, fascinated but frustrated, and always, as Kathryn Hume puts it (discussing violence in fiction by Brian Evenson, Bret Easton Ellis, Cormac McCarthy, Samuel R. Delany, Dennis Cooper, and Kathy Acker), required to worry about "the nature of law and about which laws seem justified" (*Aggressive Fictions* 116). I explicate this argument in more detail in chapter 2. For now, know this: work on murder, killers, and perpetrators (real and fictional) remains within the somewhat secure realm of justice, legality, and judgment: of right and wrong. *Disappear Here* seeks less stable ground.

This is not to say that these scholars' important work on violence is not crucial for my own focus on violent images and images of violence in fiction, film, and popular culture. In the 1980s and 1990s, these images were the object of much debate (recall the NEA controversies in the United States and the criminalization, in Europe during those decades, of Nazi images and symbols). These debates revolved around judgment, value and values, and the potential of an aesthetic object to do harm.

Growing up in those decades, Generation Xers saw the representation of violence and the violence of representation intersect. *Disappear Here* probes the implications of this coincidence.[17]

My focus on violent images in fiction and film requires attention to developments in media during these decades, developments that left Xers with unique control over the images they saw. The ability to rewind and replay left Xers in a different relation to temporal progression, the inexorable one-two of cause-and-effect that is violence's grammatical core. This assumption of temporal inevitability has begun, in recent years, to be rethought, replaced by logics of affect, addiction, repetition, and accrual. In his important *Violent Affect: Literature, Cinema, and Critique after Representation* (2007), Marco Abel suggests that we revisit temporal inevitability (the idea that violence always occurs *prior* to critique) and the limiting nature of judgment that this temporal construct imposes. Borrowing from the language of masochism (articulated by Deleuze in *Coldness and Cruelty*), he envisions an encounter with violent images and events that is accompanied not by swift judgment but by judgment's delay. He proposes that we remain suspended—as if on pause—*before* judgment, *before* the law, and dwell in the affective intensity of sensation. Openness to this affective intensity is, for Abel, an ethical act, one that "requires a giving over of oneself to the Other, to becoming-other, to the process of being affected and effectuated by and from the future" (25).

X is notoriously affectless, though, a point to which I will return. It is also a generation accustomed to revisit crime scenes, reinterpret evidence, and reverse or refuse convictions. In addition to the public trials surrounding O. J. Simpson and the Rodney King beatings by the members of the LAPD—cases that revealed the pervasive racial violence of American society, and in which conviction, or lack thereof, was per-

---

17. My approach is thus directly different from the work of James R. Giles in his 2000 study *Violence in the Contemporary Novel: An End to Innocence* and his 2006 *The Spaces of Violence*. Giles opens *Violence in the Contemporary Novel* with an account of the 1994 murder of Robert Sandifer, an eleven-year-old victim of racial and urban violence that permeates inner-city life. Sandifer's tragic story represents, for Giles, the "plague of violence" that contemporary writers document and attempt to explain. Giles concludes his book with another account, also "ripped from the headlines," of the death of Girl X in foster care in 1997. By framing his study of violence in fiction with real-world accounts, Giles puts fiction in service of real violence (fiction witnesses violence, records it, and thus engages with it—but only between the covers of the book!). *The Spaces of Violence* further underscores the difference between real violence and fiction: Giles limits fictional texts to being mere "reporters of social and human conditions" (9). In contrast, *Disappear Here* treats real-world violence and fiction as reciprocal and recursive. I expand on this point in chapter 2.

ceived as a violence in itself—the 1990s also saw the public trials of Michael Jackson and Bill Clinton, media circuses that revolved around allegations of abuse of trust. Violence, judgment, and justice seem strikingly confused; prosecutor and defendant might easily change sides. Confession culture, wound culture, and reality TV all concretized, as Seltzer put it in his 2007 book *True Crime,* "the intensified turn of interiors, bodies, and acts into communication (the media apriori)" and "the radical entanglement of violence and technical media (the violence-media complex)" (7).[18] Given this entanglement, distinctions, assumptions, and classifications that are traditionally at work when we talk about violence need to be revisited. The first is the premise that there is a difference between real violence and fiction, or, as Seltzer puts it, "real and fictional reality" (*True Crime* 2) and, more importantly, *that this difference matters.* If we relinquish our affective investment in fact/fiction (a distinction that violence is repeatedly called upon to navigate, as the image of violence is commonly presumed to call a halt to such cynical speculation), we will be in a zone where, as Abel puts it (channeling Bret Easton Ellis's *American Psycho*), judgment is "not an exit" from the multiple challenges that violence poses—not least, to ethics, judgment, and justice.

This is why, in what follows, you will read about violence in media, philosophy, fiction, and cyberspace, but you will not learn much about the sociopaths, psychopaths, or otherwise ill individuals who become violent predators in real life. Indeed, the link between mental illness and serial killings or mass murders (which are extremely rare) should not be drawn casually. Most people with mental illness are not violent, and are far more likely to be the victims of violent crime or suicide than they are likely to perpetrate criminal homicide.[19] In the United States in the

---

18. Seltzer's book is subtitled *Reflections on Violence and Modernity,* and for Seltzer, modernity extends from the late nineteenth century into the twenty-first. But Seltzer's own turn from "the trauma thing" (in his 1998 *Serial Killers*) to the "fact/fiction thing" in his 2007 *True Crime* (38) confirms, to me, an increased interest in the extent to which, as Seltzer himself puts it, "modern violence has become inseparable from the mass-mediated relaying of violence" (*True Crime* 39).

19. "Asking whether mental illness causes violence is a bit like asking whether political dysfunction causes war. The two correct answers are 'sometimes' and 'it depends'" (Swanson). Levin quotes this statement by Thomas Insel, M.D., director of the National Institute of Mental Health: "Most people with mental illness are not violent, and most acts of violence are not committed by people with mental illness [. . .] People with untreated psychotic illness are at increased risk of irrational behavior, including violence, especially directed at family and friends. This usually happens at the onset of illness and before diagnosis or treatment. However, once treatment starts, these people have no higher risk of violence than the general population and are more often victims of crime."

1990s, a number of media events underscored the limits of affect as a gauge for human accountability in the media age of which Xers are a product. One is the case of Louise Woodward, or "the British Nanny." Woodward was a British teenager employed as a nanny in the United States by Sunil and Deborah Eappen. On October 30, 1997, she was found guilty of the murder of eight-month-old Matthew Eappen and sentenced to life imprisonment after a three-week trial that received extensive coverage in the U.S. and British press. Ten days after the conclusion of the trial, the judge Hiller Zobel revised the jury's decision from guilty to involuntary manslaughter and commuted the sentence to time served. Media coverage of the case made much of Xer Woodward's problematic affect both during and after the trial. "In the courtroom Woodward was seen to giggle or, alternatively, to sit calmly and silently. Her actions were interpreted by media commentators as insolent and an obvious sign of her lack of compassion" (Holohan 33). Even after her return to the UK, Woodward "appeared without remorse, sadly lacking in gracefulness and arrogant in her dismissal of the parents of the child she is convicted of killing" (Antonowicz). A cover story in *Time* magazine by Roger Rosenblatt includes the Woodward case in his characterization of an affective instability that defined the period: "With the notable exception of religious fundamentalism, the past 25 years have seen an aggressive pursuit of depersonalization, a shutting off of the emotions at once so purposeful and complete that many people, the young especially, speak of envying machines." Echoing much of the contemporary terminology around Generation X (though he does not use the term), he writes: "There was no Vietnam War to protest, no sexual revolution or drug culture to adopt (live free and die), no generation gap worth exploiting. The Gap had become a clothing store, the counterculture reduced to a few average hysterics who thought it exciting to proclaim God dead and the family expendable." Rosenblatt concludes by encapsulating the link of affective instability with ontological uncertainty and spectral menace that is the subject of *Disappear Here*: "the presence of absence, which eats at the mind quietly and which can, when touched by one last straw, incite a riot" ("Year Emotions Ruled").

And there's the case of the West Memphis Three: Xers Damien Echols, Jessie Misskelley, and Jason Baldwin, who, as teenagers, were arrested and, in 1994, convicted of the 1993 murder of eight-year-olds Steve Branch, Christopher Byers, and Michael Moore in the Robin Hood Hills of West Memphis, Arkansas. The children had reportedly been raped and tortured as part of a Satanic ritual. Here, too, media coverage made much of the reported affectlessness of the defendants, even as the authors of *The Blood of Innocents* (a sensationalist true-crime account of the murders) describe reported ringleader Damien Echols as fairly typical of the "antisocial, antiestablishment preoccupations of a teenager in the early 1990s," listing the music of Metallica and Ozzy Osbourne and the novels of Anne Rice and Stephen King as evidence of his obsession with death and horror (Reel, Perrusquia, and Sullivan 91). Subsequent to investigative journalism by Mara Leveritt (*Devil's Knot*), two HBO documentaries (*Paradise Lost* [1996] and *Paradise Lost 2: Revelations* [2000]), the outreach and fundraising efforts of the website www.wm3.org, and the public advocacy of a number of Generation X artists (including Henry Rollins, Eddie Vedder, Johnny Depp, and Natalie Maines), the West Memphis Three reached a plea bargain with prosecutors that neither affirmed nor denied their innocence. Their sentences were revised to time served and they were released in 2011, after eighteen years in prison.

If these sad stories have a lesson to teach, it is that to take X attitude as evidence of criminality is, quite simply, to torture sense. Indeed, mass murders at Columbine, Virginia Tech, Aurora, and Sandy Hook have underscored how, especially in the United States, combining easy access to firearms with prohibitive costs of health care yields a deadly brew. Like the assumption of a causal link between cultural tendencies and pathological actions, the discourse of rights, freedoms, and blame that proliferates around such tragedies obscures dysfunction that is far more systemic, costly, and tragic. The affectlessness I explore in the following chapters is of a different breed: not a psychiatric diagnosis but a cultural ethos, one deserving of thoughtful examination rather than condemnation, correction, or cure.

Abel, of course, means something else by "affect." For him, Deleuzian affect theory provides the terms for a relocation of the site of ethical engagement with violence: from the abstract realm of judgment to the concrete site of the body where violence is registered. Viewed as affective impact, violent images on TV and film are not different, Abel argues, from violent events that we witness, experience, or read about in the world. I value Abel's important critique of the representationalist logic that is brought to bear on violent images, his approach to the reality of violence as a question of intensity, and his willingness to forgo judgment. But I cannot share his faith in the body as a site of affective register and ethical engagement. "The body"—whatever that means—is, at best, a noisy system, an unruly control, a moving target; I am unsure of its reliability as a register, and distrust the accuracy of its affect as a gauge. Together with Rei Terada, I suspect that affect theory—broadly defined to include work by Teresa Brennan and Sara Ahmed—participates in poststructuralist anxiety according to which emotions articulate concerns about ethics that haunt poststructuralism after the "death of the subject." The dead subject, memorably described by Terada as a zombie, "unable to make decisions or to refute Nazis, likely to praise bad poetry or rip your lungs out" (154), is a construct that is more useful as an incitement for claims about values and demands for judgment than it is a vehicle for critique (the zombie will return to *Disappear Here* at the end of chapter 6).

The undead, moving *en masse,* is an apt figure for a world in which, as Hans Magnus Enzensberger reflects (writing from Germany), "violence has freed itself from ideology"; its perpetrators appear "autistic," striking in their "inability to distinguish between destruction and self-destruction" (20). But if the zombie is our *de facto* image for the posthuman, that image is not devoid of hope—not despite its inherent violence but because of it. Detached from affect, conviction, justice, and ideals, violence, in all its problematic potential, is revealed: it establishes connections, demarcates differences, and transforms personal and political lives. Violence challenges representation and undoes the difference between presence and absence. It incites affect and thwarts it, and all too often it destroys the very body that would register its impact. Given this ferocious fragmentation, invasion, and ruin, from the site of the collapse of destruction and self-destruction, being and appearance, presence and absence, fiction and the real, an X critique of violence can be forged: formed from disaffection, founded on faith in nothing, searching for what disillusion brings to light.

two

· · · · · ·

Nevermind

An X Critique of Violence

VIOLENCE IS

Violence: anything and everything can be conceived in terms of it. On one hand, violence seems self-evident—like pornography, we know it when we see it. On the other hand, violence inheres precisely in what is *not* known, *not* seen, and *not* self-evident: like pornography, its nature, and its danger, is subject to dispute.[1] Menacing, threatening, vicious, spooky; inevitable and preventable, promise and premise, an ineradicable presence, a fact of power, a force of nature, and a specter—elusive, ominous, a glance, a snigger, a furtive movement in the shadows, vanishing or materializing in the corner of your gaze. As fantasy, reality, and voiceless fear, violence is everywhere and nowhere. Visible and invisible, it disappears here.

Precisely because of this range and volatility, violence has been utilized to claim attention for a wide array of issues, including the violence of speaking, the violence of silence, of the normal and the abnormal, the violence of subjectivity, of affect, of critique. This breadth and variety speaks to something fundamental about violence: its utility as a means

---

1. Giles (*Spaces*) makes this analogy between violence and pornography as well (5). "I know it when I see it" is from Justice Potter Stewart's opinion in a 1964 pornography case (Gewirtz).

to stake a claim to the real. Violence always connotes urgency, emergency. It points to a problem that must be solved, a phenomenon that must be addressed, a presence that must be banished (though erasure or banishment is a site of further violence). Conversely, to violence's object, or victim, accrues political value and ethical weight, a coming-to-presence that is imbricated in its own complex logic of representation. Violence grants visibility even as it perpetrates erasure. How are we to grasp this breadth of functions? The one thing they have in common is that violence *is*. Violence *happens*: it is what takes place, though that place may be on the page, the screen, the couch, or the battlefield. It is this, the broadest sense in which violence signifies, that I take as my starting point for an X critique of violence: *Violence is real.* It follows, then, that violence in fiction (that is, violence that is fantasized or faked) is not real, or, it is not "really" violent.

Those quotation marks around "really" refer to reality's tenuous nature; they underscore how the reality that founds the definition of violence is always, already, in question. My goal here is to investigate the reality associated with violence. I focus on the 1980s and 1990s, a period in which, I argue, the epistemic validity of violence (its quality as "real") disappears; I pursue the implications of this disappearance for judgment, critique, and action. In what follows I trace how developments in film, media, and high and popular culture in the United States propelled Generation X to redefine the relation of representation to its object, initiating a move away from the twentieth-century approach to violence as a founding trauma that fiction reflects and responds to. With the vanishing of the premise that violence is real, questions about the function and utility of violence as a means by which reality is established come to the fore. When reality is produced for television and marketed for consumption, it is, I posit, fiction—in the sense of fashioning and fabricating, as well as illusion and delusion—and faith—an attitude of fidelity in the face of vanishing economic and epistemic certainties—that move to center stage in the creation, construction, and preservation of "real violence."

VIOLENCE IS REAL

Since Samuel Johnson countered George Berkeley's philosophy of immaterialism—the idea that the material world does not exist independently of our ideas about it—by kicking a stone (an anecdote related in James

Boswell's 1791 *Life of Johnson*), the simulated, mediated, virtual, and relative nature of reality has haunted assertions of its empirical, given quality. In *Connected, or What It Means to Live in the Network Society*, Steven Shaviro refers back to Berkeley's philosophy, suggesting that immaterialism most perfectly anticipates our present-day existence. Writing in 1997, citing similarities between Berkeley and cognitive scientists Andy Clark and Richard Dawkins, Shaviro stresses that "our sense of reality is the product of a simulation. It only remains for the cognitive scientists to follow Berkeley all the way and jettison the 'outer world' altogether as an extravagant, unnecessary hypothesis" (84). Traditionally, such flirtations with the virtual halt, respectfully, at the threshold of violence. The body in pain presents an immediacy that decries postmodern play. History—defined, in Fredric Jameson's memorable phrase, as "what hurts"—calls a halt to speculations about simulation.[2]

In X's mediatized, detached, dissociated world, how are we to think of the relation of violence to the real? Rather than embrace Berkeley's philosophy of immaterialism for our digital world, as Shaviro urges, I suggest we revisit Johnson's eighteenth-century refutation of it, as recalled by his biographer Boswell. "I shall never forget," writes Boswell, "the alacrity with which Johnson answered, striking his foot with mighty force against a large stone, till he rebounded from it, 'I refute it *thus*'" (1:431). This anecdote is commonly posited as an argument for the existence of things in themselves.[3] But in Boswell's account, violence functions not as

---

2. Jameson's statement appears at the conclusion of his chapter "On Interpretation" in his 1981 *The Political Unconscious*. It is his answer to the criticism leveled against Marxist methodology by the then growing field of semiotics (represented by Eco and Habermas). Semioticians, and, later, poststructuralists, argued that for Marxists, "History" functions as an unthematizable force, an immutable fact that eludes analysis. Jameson responds by articulating History formally, as an effect of what Louis Althusser (borrowing from Baruch Spinoza) termed an "absent cause." "Conceived in this sense," Jameson concludes, "History is what hurts, it is what refuses desire and sets inexorable limits to individual as well as collective praxis, which its 'ruses' turn into grisly and ironic reversals of their overt intention. But this History can be apprehended only through its effects, and never directly as some reified force. This is indeed the ultimate sense in which History as ground and untranscendable horizon needs no particular theoretical justification: we may be sure that its alienating necessities will not forget us, however much we might prefer to ignore them" (102).

3. For evaluations of this argument, see Patay and Silver. Most discussion of this phrase centers on the stone from which Johnson's foot *rebounds,* not the impetus toward violence (though Patay discusses the phrase "mighty force" [140–41]). Natoli, who notes Johnson's refutation of Berkeley in *This Is a Picture and Not the World,* underscores its "scripted" quality (7).

a check to meditations on virtuality but as a tool for navigating the relation between the material and the immaterial. With Johnson's kick of the stone (why not caress it? smell it? taste it?) something crucial about the relation of violence and reality comes clear: it is not the stone but the *violence directed against it*—the "mighty force" with which Johnson strikes—that establishes the reality of things in themselves. Violence, itself real, also works to lay claim *to* the real. Violence is the means by which reality is defined and redefined and, ultimately, produced. It is both tenor and vehicle, though what it lays claim to is hardly metaphorical.

Activists in the 1960s and 1970s relied on this world-defining power to legitimize violence as a tool for social change. Schooled by Jean-Paul Sartre and Frantz Fanon, they wielded violence to establish a new reality, one formed and fashioned by faith in a cause. In contrast, for Xers, the role of violence in constructing reality underscores causality's artificial nature and lays bare the fictive quality of faith. Xers were schooled not by Sartre and Fanon but by Atari and VCRs. Accustomed to the power to freeze, rewind, and replay images, Xers early began to chart the extent to which "truth" is not an issue of verification or veracity but an assemblage. They began to lay bare the relation of violence to its representation, and to explore how fiction—forming and molding—participates in the construction of the real, and of the reality of violence. In an age of mass simulation, stimulation, and media saturation, violence renders reality malleable, precarious; by violence reality can be made and unmade, claimed and dismissed, created, uncreated, deconstructed, and erased—X-ed out. Fiction may well be the term that best reflects this amorphous quality, a point familiar to literary critics, who will not fail to note the mediated nature of Boswell's narrative, or the fact that it was written at the birth of narrative realism in the eighteenth century. Johnson's kick of the stone, this iconic assertion of the reality of the thing in itself, is, after all, *Boswell's* tale. Probably embellished, possibly apocryphal, it speaks to the role of fiction in troubling Johnson's claim—"troubling," in the sense of productive dislodging of conventional certitude *and* in the sense of the moral disquiet that inevitably accompanies such work.

VIOLENCE IS FICTION

For Xers, the relation of violence to its reality was never a given. Violence haunts Generation X, but it is a violence that is both there and not there, palpable and ephemeral. The first generation conceived when birth control was widely available, whose parents paid for a babysitter and went out to see Evil-Child movies like *Rosemary's Baby* (1968), *The Exorcist* (1973), *The Omen* (1976), and *Halloween* (1978),[4] presented the worry of the latchkey child, orphaned by divorce, subject to predators and predatory music. The 1980s saw a rise of regulations to control teenage behavior, as Baby Boomers became convinced that their children, Xers, are the very threat that Boomers were accused of being.[5] The 1990s saw a spate of cases in which repressed memories of trauma and abuse were brought to light, accompanied by increased debate over psychiatrists' methods for eliciting such memories; the subsequent "recovered memory debate" raised questions about the validity of testimony to trauma and abuse and concerns about the fabrication of memories of violence.[6] Horror films and conspiracy theories play a crucial role in this generation's self-image. Wes Craven's 1984 *A Nightmare on Elm Street,* in which violence emerges from dreams, was formative; the explicit, grindhouse-style violence of the *Friday the 13th* franchise produced nine films—almost a decalogue—between 1980 and 1993. The TV series *Twin Peaks* (1991) and *The X-Files* (1993) elaborated compelling discourses of paranoia. Both horror films and conspiracy theory are sites where violence combines with fiction—where violence is most real *as* fiction. This is the case not only for fantasy but for reportage. Writing in 1983, Robert Stam states that "all of television, including the news, is inflected by fiction. [. . .] At times, the news has more than the attributes of fiction: it literally is fiction" (31). In the United States, the rise of CNN (founded in 1980) made the established networks compete for national attention. CNN carried the only live footage of the Challenger explosion in 1986, and that network's coverage of the rescue of Jessica McClure in 1987 drew the nation's attention with compelling, real-time storytelling. The effect was an erasure of the temporal lapse between the

---

4. These titles are included in *13thGen*'s "A Brief Chronology of the Evil-Child Movie Era (1964–1984)" (Howe and Strauss 66).

5. In *Decade of Nightmares,* Philip Jenkins writes: "So enormous was the generational gulf that by the mid-1980s, even many boomer parents were prepared to believe that their offspring were being assailed by a rock music culture awash with images of rape, violence, and devil worship, very much like the devil music that they had been accused of listening to twenty years before. [. . .] Through the 1980s, teenagers found themselves the subject of parental campaigns to regulate their behavior, to restrict the influence of gratuitous sex and violence. [. . .] Fears about threats to the young forced a definitive cultural change, ordained by families and enforced by police" (197).

6. See Porter, Yuille, and Lehman for an account of the recovered-memory debate in the 1990s.

happening of an event and its reporting, with crucial implications for the relation of reality and fiction. "Facts all come with points of view," as The Talking Heads put it in "Crosseyed and Painless," and Xers, write Howe and Strauss in their seminal study of Generation X (they call it "the 13th Generation"), "don't draw the division between fiction and reality the way older people do. In this age of participatory techno-culture—of hand-held video cameras and digital editing—13ers know that anyone can reveal the news and, conversely, that anyone can lie" (181).

During this period the changing face of war (traditionally, as Elaine Scarry stresses, a site for the establishment of reality in the form of opened and broken bodies) further marks the revision of the relation of violence to the real. For Xers in the United States, who were never subject to the draft, battle is something to watch on TV—or, more precisely, it is something seen on TV in childhood: the Vietnam War footage from the 1960s and 1970s, interspersed with sitcoms, reruns, and issue-driven "movies of the week." "As children, members of Gen X might watch *The Brady Bunch* after school, and then watch the fall of Saigon on the news with their parents over dinner," writes G. P. Lainsbury. "Each seemed equally real or unreal, each had the same truth content" (191). Lainsbury's characterization underscores Vietnam's mediatized quality that Coupland describes in *Generation X*: "Growing up, Vietnam was a background color in life, like red or blue or gold—it tinted everything. And then suddenly one day it just disappeared" (151). The Gulf War of the 1990s underscored this vanishing: increased government control over the images broadcast ensured the virtual disappearance of battle footage from television screens. Reflecting on this shift, Margot Norris describes Vietnam as "a television war, its gritty images of close-up combat and injury brought into the American living room every night for more than a harrowing decade." In contrast, she continues, "the Persian Gulf War of the early 1990s was different: video within video, representations not of carnage but of technology, a media production of media that looked more like simulation than representation" (234). Once war is derealized, Norris concludes, it no longer serves to anchor issues; it no longer serves the reality-making function of traditional warfare.[7]

---

7. Norris writes, "Precensorship's pre-editing of representation places not only the phenomenological events of the fighting but also the political and historical significance of the enterprise under erasure. The war passed through the public imagination and memory like a video phantom, unable—in the absence of any national pain or suffering—to imprint a lasting inscription on either the national conscience or the national self-image" (248). Norris is interested in how "the Persian Gulf War's hyperrealities were

If we are all, as good Lacanian subjects, haunted by a lost or inaccessible Real, this inaccessibility takes a peculiar form for Xers: they are haunted by the loss of the real *as image,* the loss of the real *on TV,* as well as the loss of the real *as violence.* In Xer Gillian Flynn's 2012 bestseller *Gone Girl,* a clever crime novel that probes the presumptions of veracity that surround intimacy, violence, and confession, the antagonist Nick, a self-described Xer, reflects on his generation's unique relation to the real: "We were the first human beings who would never see anything for the first time. We stare at the wonders of the world, dull-eyed, underwhelmed. [. . .] Jungle animals on attack, ancient icebergs collapsing, volcanoes erupting. I can't recall a single amazing thing I have seen firsthand that I didn't immediately reference to a movie or TV show. [. . .] I've literally seen it all, and the worst thing, the thing that makes me want to blow my brains out, is: The secondhand experience is always better. The image is crisper, the view is keener, the camera angle and the soundtrack manipulate my emotions in a way reality can't anymore" (72).

The rise of reality-based television in the 1980s and 1990s further underscored the extent to which "reality" is available to be produced and marketed, and the attractions of violence (both the uses and abuses of power and the positive irruptions of the natural world) were evident in early reality TV shows like *COPS* and *When Animals Attack*—both property of the new network Fox. Established in the mid-1980s, Fox staked out its identity as the "fourth network" in the terrain of reality-based TV, rightly wagering that reality promises good ratings and attracts desirable demographics. Reality TV captured the nature of television which, as James Friedman puts it, "does not simply portray a window onto a real world 'out there' but frames the world, contextualizes the narrative, and argues for the integrity of the reality it depicts" (16); studying the nature of these arguments in Europe in the 1990s, Arild Fetveit suggests that the popularity of reality TV in the digital era—specifically, reality TV that stresses disaster and violence—underscores a change in the "credibility" attributed to the image, credence that, at the end of the twentieth century, is "less dependent upon technology and more based on institutional warrant" (131). Reality TV thus figures reality as credibility and warrant, a contractual exchange in the currency of trust and faith; banking on "a longing for a lost touch with reality," reality TV reclaims the evidentiary

---

constructed out of a military press censorship whose agenda was to derealize casualties, to strip them of the impact of 'reality' and thereby make Operation Desert Storm murderously destructive yet simultaneously corpselike" (236).

power for the image and, with that image, re-establishes a sense of connectedness to the world (Fetveit 132). But this fact-defining quality is not a given: it is fashioned by televisual devices like graphic overlays, replays, and reenactments that overwrite immediacy, rendering it legible, the product of narrative, and network, convention.

If this erosion of the distinction between reality and fiction was always characteristic of television (and Xers commonly describe themselves as raised by TV), technological developments in production in this period traced the evaporation of the human perspective and of the judgments generally associated with that perspective. "The murders reported on Eyewitness News (forever playing the B-film to the high-art seriousness of Network News), murders that amount to narrativized visualizations of statistics, differ from the murders in police or mystery shows mainly in the fact that they happened to occur in the three-dimensional world," writes Stam (33). As the distinction between fiction and reality dissolves, so do other distinctions, like between perpetrator, victim and bystander, and the distinction between censure and approval. "Subjective shots suture us into the perspective of rapists and assassins. The viewer becomes voyeur and accomplice, domestic private eye, subconsciously applauding a spectacle of death and abuse" (Stam 33). Films of these decades articulated what Peter Hanson identifies as a "new morality" in the X directors David Fincher, Tarsem Singh, Quentin Tarantino, and Spike Jonze (9): "mired in mixed messages, undefined anger, inarticulate declarations, and visceral impact" (12). Like most Xers, these directors' approach to violence was informed by their experience of network television, home media, and cable: CNN and MTV—specifically, MTV's aesthetic of quick cuts, speeded-up storytelling, and fragmentation.

Television production in the 1980s saw a rise of motion-control technologies: the Steadicam, Camrail, and other robotically controlled studio cameras. This "gang of new and automated motion-control devices" (as John Caldwell describes them) redefined the realism posited by the televisual image; by replacing the human perspective promised by the manually controlled, pedestal-mounted camera, they "automate an inherently omniscient point of view and subjectivize it around a technological rather than human center"; the camera eye "floats like the eye of a cyborg" (81). As the digital began to replace the analog, electronic and nonlinear editing underscored this elision of human perspective, detaching film from human time as well as from human space: these editing systems "helped shatter the *sequential and temporal* straitjacket necessitated by conventional forms of editing" (Caldwell 81). As cause and effect lose their purchase on reality, veracity and certainty present as special effects of technology. Man, measure of all things, like the fictional '80s veejay Max Headroom, flickers, stutters, and disappears. Since the birth of cinema, the camera's mechanical eye has claimed access to a truth otherwise invisible; but for Xers, who grew up on '80s TV, "*nothing visual was set in stone*" (Caldwell 82).

Violence strikes that stone, laying claim to its empirical quality, so it is no coincidence that, concurrent with these developments, violence in film and television was a subject of much agonized discussion that revolved around a few highly publicized examples that galvanized debates about appropriate representation (mostly of pornography) (Slocum 8). Such debates posited Xers as a worrying audience, one that could not effectively distinguish between representation and reality. Teenagers and young adults were condemned as culturally illiterate by E. D. Hirsch Jr. in *Cultural Literacy* (1987). They were dismissed as closed-minded by Allan Bloom in *The Closing of the American Mind* (published the same year). They were derided as stupid, unable or unwilling to distinguish violent actions from violence on screen, in song lyrics, and in the media. They laughed in a screening of *Schindler's List*.[8] "DUMB," write Howe and Strauss, rehearsing the generalized sense of dismay around young people during this period. "They can't find Chicago on a map. They don't know when the Civil War was fought. They watch too much TV" (18). For Xers—the subjects of these agonized debates—the 1993 Congressional Hearings that cited MTV's iconic show "Beavis and Butt-head,"[9] the legislation around Parental Advisory labels for music albums in the 1980s and 1990s, and the discussions around the NEA's funding of Robert Mapplethorpe's photography (in 1989 and 1990) underscored the imbrication of all violence

---

8. On January 17, 1994, approximately 70 students of Castlemont High School in Oakland, California (the school has a mostly Black and Latino/a student population) were taken by their teacher to a screening of the film. Some laughed at a scene of casual shooting. The event propelled much public debate, a visit by Steven Spielberg to the school, and multiple crisis forums, evidence of what Yosefa Loshitzky, writing of *Schindler's List* in 1997, describes as "the way the film has been used as a 'weapon' in the multicultural wars dividing the contemporary ethnic landscape of American society" (6). The general adulation surrounding *Schindler's List* was parodied in "The Raincoats," a two-part episode of the hit TV show *Seinfeld*. "The Raincoats" aired on NBC in April 1994.

9. See Cynthia A. Cooper's *Violence on Television: Congressional Inquiry, Public Criticism, and Industry Response*, especially pages 127–30, for an analysis of these debates.

in the instrumental logic of power, and the disappearance of the real into the chatter of judgment. True to their characterization by Douglas Rushkoff as ignoring the products advertised in commercials and focusing instead on the marketing devices (5), Xers tuned not to the arguments in these debates but to the urgency and emergency with which their rhetoric was couched. Relinquishing their stakes in the very reality that violence, in these discussions, is wielded to establish, Xers change the channel.

The effect of this divorce of affect from critique should not be underestimated. As violence is deemed all-pervasive, and its readers or viewers stupid, its reality becomes mobile, contagious; it migrates from the content of the text to the context of its reception, from the page or the screen out into the world. Witness to concerns about copycat killers and to worries about the real-world effects of violence in cinema, in music, in video games, and on TV, Xers find fiction to be both cause *and* effect of violence. This is not only the case for notorious literary texts like Ellis's *American Psycho* and A. M. Homes's *The End of Alice,* both of which, published in the 1990s, elicited public censure and controversy, as if the predation the authors depicted was real, not fiction.[10] For Xers, real predation takes its cue *from* fiction, just as predation in fiction copies the real, and literary works like Ellis's and Homes's were a logical extension of a general cultural atmosphere. Writing of the Columbine 1999 school massacre, James Alan Fox and Jack Levin describe Dylan Klebold and Eric Harris's actions as part of the copycat phenomenon in which killers took their inspiration from real-life killers, from the portrayal of killers in fiction and film, *and* from video games (213).[11]

---

10. Homes's *The End of Alice* is narrated by a convicted pedophile who corresponds with a nineteen-year-old girl about her plans to seduce a twelve-year-old boy and reminisces about his rape and murder of a twelve-year-old girl named Alice. Reviewing the book for *The New York Times,* Michiko Kakutani compared *The End of Alice* to Ellis's *American Psycho* and described it as "a novel that proves that a woman can write as badly, violently and misogynistically as a man." In the UK, the NSPCC (National Society for the Prevention of Cruelty to Children) condemned the book, which was banned by bookseller W. H. Smith. In contrast to *American Psycho* (which I discuss in chapter 3), *The End of Alice* has received very little attention from critics since the initial controversy surrounding its publication.

11. Several very popular films in this period explicitly thematized the copycat phenomenon: Michael Mann's *Manhunter* (1986), Jon Amiel's *Copycat* (1995), and Jonathan Demme's *Silence of the Lambs* (1991). Concern about copycat violence accompanied the release of Oliver Stone's *Natural Born Killers* in 1994. Reflecting on the copycat phenomenon, Mark Seltzer writes: "Fact and fiction have a way of exchanging places here: virtual reality, after all, has its own reality. [. . .] The distinction between fact and fiction and bodies and information vanish, along the lines of an identification without reserve" (*Serial Killers* 16).

The widely publicized copycat phenomenon illustrates a general disintegration of causality, as real events, imitating fiction, become fictional, with crucial implications for the truths constructed about them. Rather than an unqualified reality that calls a halt to fiction, or an evil that demands and determines judgment, violence is alternately object and agent, means and end. The relation of image to action is an open switch, a reciprocal loop, alternating between immediate somatic sensation and discursive epistemes.[12]

In a departure from much of the tenor of public discourse around violence that posits it as a problem to be resolved or a scourge to be eradicated, some scholars have explored the implications of the interpenetration of fiction and reality that I have been describing. Writing of the 1980s, Joel Black reflects on how "the very activity by which we represent or 'picture' violence to ourselves is an aesthetic operation whereby we habitually transform brutal actions into art. We are greatly assisted in this by the mass media, which expose us, liminally and subliminally, to artistic representations of violence" (5). The 1980s produced what Mark Seltzer, in 1998, calls "*wound culture*: the public fascination with torn and open bodies and torn and opened persons, a collective gathering around shock, trauma, and the wound" (1).[13] Stressing that trauma figures both the wound *and* its absence, Seltzer defines trauma as "an effect in search of a cause" (257), and consequently trauma becomes a site where the basic intimacy, even involution, of fact and fiction, event and repetition, bodies and signs, the virtual and the real is revealed. Elana Gomel, who traces the emergence of the violent subject from the nineteenth century into the twenty-first in her 2003 book *Bloodscripts*, sees a similar involution of story and action, fiction and real: "Literary

---

12. Concrete example: David Koresh, founder of the Branch Davidian sect, whose Mount Carmel ranch in Waco, Texas, was raided by the FBI in 1993 after a fifty-one-day siege (the raid, which was televised live, left seventy-six cult members dead, including seventeen children), modeled the Waco siege on TV coverage of the 1992 L.A. riots. For Koresh, Caldwell writes, "the fires that raged when Los Angeles burned in 1992 provided not a sense of simultaneity or realism, but rather a powerful and codified template for stylized and horrific spectacle. The alienated televisuality of the L.A. rebellion could be appropriated and choreographed for the benefit of the mass audience, even by those in other places and with very different apocalyptic ends" (31). An apt pupil of this reciprocity of violence and its televised image, Xer Timothy McVeigh cited the Waco incident as a motivation for the Oklahoma City bombing on April 19, 1995, timed to coincide with the second anniversary of the Waco assault.

13. Seltzer notes "less an opposition between bodies and representations than their radical involution: a basic entanglement of bodily processes and technologies of reproduction and visualization, reproduction and mimesis, that is not simply reducible to, or contained by the order of representation" (*Serial Killers* 36).

murderers are not pale reflections of some essential violent psyche. On the contrary, actual murderers are stories of violence made flesh" (xiv).

This revision of classical mimesis's ancient hierarchy of image and event, fact and fiction is explicitly articulated in the Video Backpacker scene of Richard Linklater's iconic X film *Slacker* (1991).[14] Surrounded by televisions that broadcast images of pornography, media violence, and disaster, and wearing a television as a backpack, Video Backpacker (none of the characters in *Slacker* have names) elaborates on the erosion of the privileged position traditionally accorded to the experience, or witness, of violence. "Back when I used to go out," he says, "when I was last out, I was walking down the street, and this guy, like came barreling out of a bar, fell right in front of me, and he had a knife, right in his back. Landed right on the ground. And . . . well, I have no reference to it now, I can't refer back to it, I can't press rewind, I can't put it on pause, I can't put it on slo-mo and see all the little details. And the blood was all wrong, it didn't look like blood, and the hue was off, I couldn't adjust the hue, I was seeing it for real but it just wasn't right." Video Backpacker's affectlessness (which echoes an earlier character's affectlessness as he publicly murders his mother, then sits calmly in front of the TV set waiting for the police) is characterized by a dismissal of the values that violence is traditionally called upon to establish. He does not express fear or pity, or call for justice. Nor does he care about the distinction between reality and fiction, the real and its image, real and "real" violence. This vignette offers the foundation for a critique of violence after Generation X, one that takes, as a given, the identification of image as violence and its detachment from the real: as Video Backpacker puts it, "a video image is much more powerful and useful than an actual event."

---

14. Radwin's reading of this film claims for *Slacker* an articulation of Generation X's philosophy, values, and attitude, which he aligns with postmodern cinema. Radwin identifies in *Slacker* four ideas central to Generation X: questioning master narratives, anarchy, conspiracy, and the value of images over reality (36). Because Video Backpacker, writes Radwin, is a relatively static moment in a film marked by fluidity and open framing (he is limited to just three feet of space), he redefines space and mobility: "While he does not have mobility in the usual sense, he can see far beyond the rest of us and virtually go anywhere the televised image can take him" (45). For Video Backpacker, "the image is not a source to be conquered with revolutionary force. On the contrary, it must be courted. [. . .] Video Backpacker has come to share substance with the sets, not merely cohabitating with them, in exchange for access to and control of images and the powers they possess" (46).

FIGURE 3. *Slacker* (1991). Screen grab. Video Backpacker (Kalman Spelletich) shows off his collection. Note the texts broadcast on the screens ("TV IS," "WE ARE," and "IMAGINE YOUR SELF"). Throughout the scene, the screens, as if in symbiosis with the speaker, display images that reflect on and underscore his points. © Linklater/Orion.

A HISTORY OF VIOLENCE

We should step back and consider the bodies of work that have left us at this point. Studies of violence in the twentieth century can be divided into two streams. The first brings together approaches to violence that treat it as mediate or mediated, a means (justified or not) to an end: mediate violence is instrumental, structural, or systemic. The second brings together approaches to violence that stress its immediate manifestations: violence that is excessive, unspeakable, sublime. These two approaches to violence differ in their conceptions of power, causality, agency, and temporality. For the tradition of mediate violence, violence serves a purpose; its clearest articulation is in Hannah Arendt's and Michel Foucault's thinking on power, which employs violence to discipline, regulate, subdue, and create docile bodies. In her 1969 book *On Violence,* Arendt distinguishes between violence and power. Violence, she writes, "is by nature instrumental; like all means, it always stands in need of guidance and justification through the ends it pursues" (51); consequently, violence cannot be viewed in isolation but is always in dialectical relation to power that legitimizes or justifies it. For Foucault, the modern era is defined by the dissemination of violence into a myriad of disciplinary mechanisms by which power, invisibly, painfully, produces its subjects (his 1975 *Discipline and Punish* is, of course, the seminal text for this tradition). This type of violence (mediate violence) is at base creative and generative, though we may dislike or decry its methods and objects, and it is intimately linked to law and justice, the instruments of the State. Because of its intimacy with institutions and other mechanisms of discourse in which it inheres, mediate violence is difficult to tease out of the logic of power that grounds the law; discussions of mediate violence inevitably turn on evaluations of the end to which it serves as a means. Mediate violence may be just or unjust, legitimate or illegitimate, but it cannot be observed independently of the institutions and systems through which it operates.

In the realms of sociology, politics, and theories of power, mediate violence tends to be approached with recourse to a logic of causality. Its critique focuses on the presence or absence of a causal link between violent images and violent behavior, and privileges terminology of sight, spectacle, and the subject. At the time Arendt and Foucault were writing, these terms were very much in dialogue with concepts of power that, as Michael Hardt and Antonio Negri have since pointed out in their monumental *Empire,* now need to be rethought in terms of monadism, multiplicity, and movement. The tradition of mediate violence proved quite fruitful for literary criticism in the 1980s and 1990s: mediate violence inheres in language, articulating the deep structure of culture, as well as the bodies and minds that culture produces. These attributes make mediate violence an attractive topic for poststructuralist thinkers for whom the decentered nature of power, like the absent transcendental signified, defies and defines discourse. The temporality of articulation, the diachronicity of speech, and the means-to-ends logic all anchor mediate violence to causality and temporal progression—in other words, to history—and make writing a useful site from which to identify and critique it. For many of the authors in Nancy Armstrong and Leonard Tennenhouse's influential collection, *The Violence of Representation* (1989), *all writing is violence*—a logical but somewhat empty conclusion to the tradition from which Derrida writes of the violence of the letter. Reflecting on this tradition in 1998, Art Redding writes that "*Violence* points to what critics not so long ago were fond of calling a transcendental signified, hollowed of precise meaning yet necessary to structure our language into a series of ideologically sensible and value-ridden binaries" (*Raids* 14). These methods of critique are unavailable to Generation X. Like Redding, Xers dislike binaries and are suspicious of the values they represent. Literacy is a product not of writing and reading but of viewing and re-viewing popular culture. The ability to rewind and replay undermines causality at its core. Authority is absent, evacuated, ineffective. Institutions like the state are perceived as being too deeply complicit in extensive networks of power to be efficaciously critiqued.

In contrast to this instrumental tradition (mediate violence) is a more positivist one for which violence inheres in the stark fact of destruction. I call this type of violence immediate violence. Immediate violence is predicated on the pure instantiation of somatic sensation, itself inarticulable or alien or hostile to language. The ancient tradition of the sublime elicited the compelling nature of an immediacy that refuses representation; Georges Bataille, in the 1950s, elaborated on a violence that exceeds reason, mastery, and the law of taboo, "that which can never be grasped, but we are conscious of being in its power" (40). Building on this tradition in the 1980s, Jean-François Lyotard outlined a postmodern discourse of the sublime, an admixture of pleasure and pain at the encounter of the somatic and the nonsensible: "not a pleasure, it is a pleasure of pain: we fail to present the absolute, and that is a displeasure, but we know we have to present it, that the faculty of feeling or imagining is called on to bring about the sensible (the image)" (126). Lyotard's elision of the distinction between sensation and sight (the sensible / the image) underscores how the purview of immediate violence is not legitimacy but representation, not law but art—aesthetics, from the Greek *aistheta,* meaning that which is available to perception, and which, Joel Black has pointed out in his important book *Aesthetics of Murder,* entered English through the macabre (3). Unlike mediate violence, which is aligned, through its means-to-ends logic, with chronological progression, the temporal mode of immediate violence is not progression but repetition—hence its association with trauma. In recent decades, this affective charge of the unpresentable (Lyotard's "faculty of feeling") has been vested with ethical weight in the discourse of unspeakability that surrounds genocide and torture and terror, a discourse richly informed by trauma theory. Elana Gomel, writing of violent perpetrators, brings together the discourse of trauma with the discourse of the sublime in *Bloodscripts: Writing the Violent Subject.* "The ellipsis of the violent subject's life-story is a scar of the sublime. Violence both wounds the narrative and stimulates its recovery. [. . .] The initial trauma shatters the plot of the self, producing gaps, lacunae, silences, and inconsistencies; but the sublime sense of power generates a narrative reconstruction, which, nevertheless, bears the traces of the initial fragmentation" (xxix).

By virtue of its location outside discourse, immediate violence promises the possibility of a site of resistance and transformation. This promise has, of course, historically proved fatal—both literally and metaphorically. Consequently, critiques of immediate violence are deeply concerned with the ends to which immediate violence may prove to be a means. Such critiques are interested in who evokes the power of purity, *heimat,* or faith; how these promises are put to work, in what arenas, and to what purpose. In other words, critiques of immediate violence subject immediacy to the criteria (instrumentality; temporality; means and ends) that define, and determine, *mediate* violence. Dominick LaCapra, writing of these disparate types of violence, walks straight into this trap: "The concern becomes acute when violence is not only seen (however contestably) as useful or necessary to achieve certain results [. . .] but is also transfigured in sacred, sublime, redemptive, or foundational terms" (*History and Its Limits* 7). Mediate violence (itself debatable and contestable though potentially justifiable if it results in a greater good) is always a means to an end: it is employed for the purpose of ultimate reform, transformation, or cure. *Immediate* violence is not employed but, as LaCapra puts it here, "transfigured." It presents as the inviolable: the sacred, the sublime, the realm of aesthetics or art. Precisely because of this departure from the means-to-end logic and that logic's juridical, political, and scientific realm, immediate violence is worrying: it elicits "acute concern." Musing on immediate violence's destructive potential, LaCapra stresses empirical research that serves as a "reality check" (*History* 8). But this critical gesture is, itself, in need of critique. It treats the empirical as a stable, constant quality. Reality is wielded to control, or to check, the fantastic excesses of the immediate. Immediate violence is thus posited as, at worst, a fantasy, a child's tale, a tragic lie; at best, it is a disguise with which real power masks its operations. Critical work, so goes this logic, tells the truth, pulls the mask off, and shows by whom, how, and why the fantasy of redemptive violence is produced. It draws back the curtain to reveal the faceless men in suits.

This is the challenge that immediate violence poses to critique. Critique folds immediate violence into a logic of mediation: the immediate is interrogated about the ends to which it serves as a means. Its historicity is evaluated, the ethics of its actors are weighed and judged. But aren't the men in suits employed by other men in nicer suits, themselves in thrall to some deeper, darker force? Indeed, the idea that immediate violence can be checked—that is, that its fictional quality can be ascertained, and that its transformative power can be restrained—is predicated on the assumption that critique can unveil a more or less reliable and stable distinction between reality and fiction, between historical fact and its guises. It is predicated on the assumption that the buck stops. Generation X is distrustful of precisely such work. Unwilling to incline toward the immediate in their media-saturated world, unlikely to align with critique over the promise of presence, Xers, with characteristic ambivalence, refuse to choose. Awake to the operations of mediate violence, the pervasive quality of power (corporate, ideological) that controls what presents as real, aware but wary of immediate violence, the lure of total destruction, revolution, holocaust, apocalypse, reluctant to take a stand, loath to judge, inclined to see positions as deeply vested and interested, simultaneously compelled by and weary of the narratives produced around the videotaped police beating of Rodney King in 1991 and the O. J. Simpson murder trial in 1994, Xers view causality as just one more narrative, affect as one more attitude, and judgment as a somewhat arbitrary cessation imposed on the mobility and nomadism that drive this "accelerated culture."[15] Cessation presents as a wishful fantasy, an arbitrary pause, and the distinction of agent from object, cause from effect, emerges as a construct, grounded only in faith.

BODIES IN PAIN

But wait: it bleeds. It screams. It's broken. For many scholars and critics, the body in pain is ground zero for thinking about violence. Pain figures as certainty: its pure unmediated somatic sensation is a firm site

---

15. From its inception, "Generation X" has been associated with acceleration. Ulrich has pointed out that Hamblett and Deverson use the term "accelerated culture" in their 1964 *Generation X*, a collection of interviews with young people in Britain, and that Coupland borrowed the phrase for his 1991 *Generation X*, subtitled *Tales for an Accelerated Culture* ("Generation X" 9–11).

for the location of violence's reality, set in stark opposition to its simulation or fictionalization. "We are truly convinced of the *thingness* of the body when we see it open—and red," writes Gomel. "Outside language, locked in the brutal *thingness* of physical suffering, the victim confronts—and becomes—the Real" (5). The traditions of mediate and immediate violence approach the body in pain differently. For the former, it is a means to an end in the logic of power. For the latter, it is an end, the end of all ends; here all logic stops. Two seminal theories of violence and the body in pain—Foucault's *Discipline and Punish,* first published in English in 1977, and Scarry's *The Body in Pain,* published in 1985— straddle the period I am discussing and inform the kinds of conversations that literary discourse produced around violence in this period. Taking the two together underscores how the body in pain presents both as absolute certainty *and* as void of all certainty. Generation X is poised at the crux of this intersection.

In Foucault's seminal articulation of mediate violence, the harrowing account of the torture to death of the body of the condemned that opens *Discipline and Punish* is designed to underscore the *vanishing* of immediate violence from the public sphere. The memorable opening pages, a collection of graphic accounts of the execution of Robert-François Damiens, vividly demonstrate the stakes of his study, set in the wake of "the *disappearance* of the tortured, dismembered, amputated body, symbolically branded on face or shoulder, exposed alive or dead to public view. The body as the major target of penal repression *disappeared*" (8; emphases mine). For Foucault, modern power renders the body in pain invisible; its absence is the condition of possibility for the production of the modern subject and the mediated reality in which she lives. Like Foucault in *Discipline and Punish,* Elaine Scarry's *The Body in Pain* takes as a starting point pain's vanishing. Pain, Scarry stresses, is invisible; its very somatic plenitude ensures that it eludes the epistemic certainty that it is wielded to establish. "Vaguely alarming yet unreal, laden with consequence yet evaporating before the mind because not available to sensory confirmation, [. . .] the pains occurring in other people's bodies flicker before the mind, then disappear" (4). In contrast to Foucault, who disappoints many a bloodthirsty undergraduate after those vivid opening pages, Scarry dwells repeatedly on—one might say she returns obsessively to—the unarguable reality of the human body in pain, the pure untrammeled physicality of which is the site from which, she argues, power fashions culture through specifically *aesthetic* work: making and unmaking the world. Indeed, it is pain's very invisibility—

its unspeakable, unrepresentable quality—that ensures, for Scarry, its perpetual presence: "pain comes unsharably into our midst as at once that which cannot be denied and that which cannot be confirmed" (4). Both Foucault's tortured body and Scarry's body in pain figure as the site of unmediated physical sensation, a Real untouched by fiction. But the one disappears, the other is here.

The co-presence of Scarry and Foucault reflects an intersection, in the 1980s, of the two traditions of thinking on violence: the mediate violence of discourse and power and the immediate violence of unspeakable sensation. As the mediate and immediate intersect, the specific challenge that immediate violence poses, not only to critique but to presence *for* critique, becomes clear. The challenge is this: by virtue of its uneasy presence—it both compels and repels, it both disappears and is here—the immediate qualifies and forecloses mediate violence. It is its outside or its core, available only by mediation, which raises questions of media and transmission, and with them, questions of verification and certainty. Like mediate and immediate, speculation and action, fiction and history, pain's radical unknowability and its fundamental thingness coexist, two lenses that resolve into a single stereoptic image. For Foucault and Scarry, the body in pain is such an image, and like all images it flickers; both here and not here, its indexical function is determined as much by its absence as by its presence. This flickering should put us in mind of the contingent relation to the real that, historically, has haunted all images, a contingency that comes to the fore as images become increasingly available to manipulation. Walter Benjamin's meditations on photography and film in the 1930s (in "The Work of Art in the Age of Its Technical Reproducibility") stressed the liberatory implications of a medium that can construct reality; Jean Baudrillard, in the 1960s, celebrated the murder of the real by the image. Continuing this development, Joel Black argues for an approach to violence as an aesthetic experience—"rather than moral, physical, natural, or whatever term we choose as a synonym for the word *real*" (3). Aesthetic violence, by which Black means murders that are *actes gratuits,* claims the immediate as its objective and thus collapses the distinction between being and appearance on which the classical idea of mimesis is predicated. Black traces the aestheticization of violence from Romantic philosophy and literature, through Thomas De Quincey's 1827 essay "On Murder Considered as One of the Fine Arts," into the nineteenth and twentieth centuries, but the inspiration for his book is, he states explicitly, *the 1980s:* "a time when 'reality' is mediated to an unprecedented degree by the visual mass media," and the distinction between reality and appearance is available to be seized by terrorists, killers, and film directors alike (17).

Writing of the same decade, Richard Slotkin identifies Ronald Reagan's administration as a moment in U.S. culture in which "the myths produced by mass culture have became credible substitutes for actual historical or political action [. . .] The substitution of myth for history serves not only as an advertising ploy for electing the candidate but as an organizing principle for making policy" (644). This revision of the relation of fiction and fact, according to which fiction precedes, organizes, and explains the "facts" that it produces, was perfected, Slotkin concludes, by Reagan: "At the height of his powers he was able to cover his actions with the gloss of patriotic symbolism and to convince his audience that—in life as in movies—merely symbolic action is a legitimate equivalent of the 'real thing'" (644). These symbols, myths, or anecdotes took very real form in the continental United States and Central America in the 1980s; George H. W. Bush's War on Drugs and the 1991 Gulf War further attest to what Slotkin describes as a tendency, within the politics and media at the time, "to think mythologically about policy questions, substituting symbol and anecdote for analysis and argument" (652).

The slacker is the wise child of this development, and offers a perspective on the body in pain that is less invested in safeguarding its reality than in exploring its potential for the creation of new realities—aesthetic, epistemic, and political. "We all know the psychic powers of the televised image," says Video Backpacker in 1991, "but we need to capitalize on it and make it work for us instead of us working for it." As the technology to fabricate images was increasingly available in the 1990s, Xers assumed a detachment of image from a documentary role; the relation of the image to the real is an opportunity for mischief, and mischief, as Tyler Durden instructs us in *Fight Club,* is an anomic site from which violence can work revolution or devolution, saving or ending the world.

This identification of violence with its image, and the detachment of image from document, has long elicited concern about verity and documentation. Such concern is predicated on the assumption that there is a distinction between real and fake, and that that distinction matters. And yet, as Susan Sontag writes in *Regarding the Pain of Others,* the image's evidentiary function is inextricable from the stories told about it. Musing on the medium of photography, Sontag stresses that the photograph's unique claim on reality renders the real vulnerable to fiction. Precisely because "photographs of atrocity illustrate as well as corroborate, [. . .] the illustrative function of photographs leaves opinions, prejudices, fantasies, misinformation untouched" (*Regarding* 84). Writing of the Abu Ghraib torture photos in 2006 (when Xers are in their 30s and 40s), David Simpson is struck by the paucity of suspicion in their reception. "One might at least imagine that these photos were faked. [. . .] We live in a world in which the accusation or assumption of faked evidence is almost normative. But no one raised this question about Abu Ghraib. [. . .] The staging of these incidents as pranks rather than as formal spectacles provided exactly the touch of the real that might have been absent from more carefully composed images falling into the inherited genres of wartime reporting" (133). That "touch of the real"—the real as touch-up—is not exclusive to the visual image. It is part and parcel of any attempt to make sense of the world. Reflecting on the role of violence in literary visions of politics in her 2010 book *Binding Violence,* Moira Fradinger writes that even "the always new, material, untransferable experience of pain can only be metaphorized through our existing symbolic reservoir. This is to say that because of the gap between experience and our means to apprehend it, 'our reality' presents itself to us with the structure of fiction. Inseparable from the conventions through which we make sense of it, give it its consistency and coherence, reality results from the workings of fiction, even as it also always leaves a remainder of materiality that cannot be symbolized" (20). For Generation X, poised at the intersection of immediate and mediate violence, the reality premised by the body in pain is both undeniable *and* uncertain, both fiction *and* real.

This epistemic unease extends, for Xers, from the somatic certainty of the body and its experience to an existential discomfort with the fundamental categories of metaphysics: presence and being. With the social and media developments in the 1980s and 1990s, Xers bore witness to a uniquely modern kind of disappearing. Modernity, as Leo Charney notes, signals the loss of presence and of full sensation, and Charney finds in the spate of "ultra violent" films released in these decades a reaction to this loss and an anxious attempt to re-present presence in a world haunted by its lack. "The force of violence externalizes and renders as temporary kinesthetic effect the rolling hunger to face the present, to feel it and see it and re-present it," writes Charney; "Moments of violence aspire to restore, or at least to represent, the moments of tangible presence that are otherwise unachievable, as if their very force could hurtle them into the inside of a present moment" (49). J. David Slocum, surveying the history of violence in American cinema, also notes a tendency in this period toward elision of fact, fiction, and image.

"Especially in a modern society mediated by popular culture," he writes, spectators "los[e] track of the distinctions between representation and reality in everyday life" (3). In postmodern cinema, "even the most graphic instance of violence [. . .] potentially becomes like any other image, homogenized and empty of meaning or seeming originality" (Slocum 21). The assumption that violence is real, or not "really" violent, turns on this disappearance of presence; much depends, as U.S. President Bill Clinton notoriously put it in 1998, on what the meaning of *is* is. Clinton's equivocation did not come as a surprise to Xers. Schooled by David Cronenberg's 1983 *Videodrome,* which plots how the "real violence" on screen (the snuff TV that the protagonist pursues) stages the mutation of the human body and of the reality in which it acts, and his 1996 film *Crash,* in which broken human bodies assert the reality of staged scenes, Xers are inclined to think the reality of violence is possibly real, probably faked—the two options are not antithetical—and most likely produced for the camera, less of a bedrock of fact than a wager of faith. In Bret Easton Ellis's *Less Than Zero,* the screening of a snuff film produces these avowals: "I bet it's real. [. . .] It's gotta *be*" (154, my emphasis)—a protestation of certainty that betrays how, as Charney puts it, violence in this period works "to substitute and compensate for an actual presence of presence" (57).

CRITIQUES OF VIOLENCE (1):
Benjamin and Derrida

What, you may ask, are the stakes of this discussion? Is its author in thrall to a fantasy of transformative violence promised by revolution, crusade, or jihad? Violence is real; if the reality of violence disappears, how is violence to be critiqued? My discussion of the traditions of mediate and immediate violence lingered on the specific challenge each tradition poses to the work of critique. I now turn to Walter Benjamin's seminal 1921 essay "Critique of Violence," to Jacques Derrida's influential reading of this essay in "Force of Law" (1992), and to Giorgio Agamben's discussion of its fundamental stakes for contemporary culture and politics in *State of Exception* (2003). Benjamin's essay has been disquieting to many of his readers who see in its final move to "pure" or "sovereign" violence an embrace of the absolutist logic that characterized Fascism, evidence of immediate violence's complicity in totalitarian thought and its genocidal effects. The essay has come to represent a limit case for thinking on violence; it functions as a cautionary tale by which the tragic Jewish philosopher, in thrall to a fantasy of the immediate, produced an articulation of violence that replicates the logic of National Socialism. I turn to the essay and to Derrida's influential discussion of it in the 1990s to concretize my thinking on violence: the challenges it poses to critique, the tendency of violence's reality to disappear, the role of fiction in articulating this reality, and the limits this vanishing poses to judgment. Taking my cue from Giorgio Agamben and Alain Badiou, I suggest a new approach to violence and fiction, and to reality and faith. For me, that approach must take as its starting point Generation X.

Written as a thought experiment inspired by Georges Sorel's *Reflections on Violence,* "Critique of Violence" dissects mediate and immediate violence; its goal is to articulate a notion of violence that might lay claim to revolutionary force and create, as Sorel imagines violence will create, new conditions for existence. The original German (*Gewalt*) weds violence to force, legitimate power, and justified authority, identifying mediate violence as the site from which Benjamin begins his investigations. Benjamin identifies a circular logic in thinking on violence: whether violence is regarded as a fact of nature or a product of history, its critique takes the form of what Benjamin calls "this basic dogma: just ends can be attained by justified means, justified means used for just ends" (278). This tautology dictates discussions of violence and limits such discussions to issues of legitimacy, confining a critique of violence to the realm of violence's relation to the legal system, and retains violence firmly in the realm of the mediate. Critique (Benjamin means examination in the Kantian sense of identifying separations and distinctions, rather than the evaluative sense of passing judgment) is limited to determining whether violence by or against the system is *justified* (by the system that, with recourse to legality, determines what is and what is not legitimate).

Unlike Sorel, who speaks of violence as if he knows what it is, Benjamin does not presume that the object of his investigation is readily available. Much of his "Critique" reflects on the difficulty violence poses as an object of study. Violence, for Benjamin, is hard to find, and he ultimately locates the object of his study in fiction. The question of the critique of violence, he notes at the outset, is a question of whether the means or the ends to which violence is employed are just, that is, authorized as lawful by the state (hence the dominance of state power in his discussion). After pressing on the circular logic that the dogma represents ("just ends can be attained by justified means, justified means used for just ends"), Benjamin aims to exit it: his goal, after all, is to critique *violence,* not justice or law. So he moves, in the final pages of the essay, to nonmediate or immediate violence. Benjamin articulates two types of immediate violence: mythic and divine, or sovereign, violence. Mythic violence, illustrated by the Greek myth of Niobe, is, Benjamin concludes, deeply vested in causality (what Benjamin calls fate) and judgment. Niobe, condemned for the sin of arrogance, is punished with the deaths of her children. Apollo, who would have spared her last son, had already loosed the arrow that kills him, and the boy's death is dictated not by divine intention but by natural law (the laws of physics and the inevitability of temporal progression that dictated the trajectory of the arrow's flight). This pervasive quality of law in mythic violence renders this violence the site of judgment, unveiling and enshrining guilt. Niobe is spared, "more guilty than before through the death of the children" ("Critique" 295).

As an illustration of divine violence (and, perhaps, as a parallel to Sorel's recourse to Christian religious tradition in his reliance on accounts of the miracles of the saints), Benjamin turns to the Old Testament story of the judgment of the company of Korah. Korah and his associates attempted to disrupt the hierarchy of desert society, undercutting Moses's privileged relation to God by claiming that God may reside in all Israelites—a radical dissemination of divine presence and a challenge to the logic of representation that retained a privileged position for Moses and his family as sole representatives of God and God's law. The deliberate erasure of the distinction between the law and power advocated by Korah (which could also be seen as a dangerous reproducibility, and dissemination, of the divine) is corrected as God has the earth open and swallow the company. The supernatural quality of this violence underscores how the destruction of Korah is premised on a radical refusal of natural law (this is what Benjamin means by it being "bloodless" [297]). If Apollo's arrow was subject to a law that exceeded the god's intention, the God that strikes Korah manifests as pure power, distinct from the law and from justice as dispensed by law. The violence "strikes privileged Levites, strikes them without warning, without threat, and does not stop short of annihilation. But in annihilating it also expiates" (297). In contrast to Niobe, who remains as an emblem of guilt, "more guilty than before," Korah, expiated, disappears. Divine violence without law (and thus without justice or guilt), is, for Benjamin, pure or "sovereign": violence unavailable to judgment, that establishes the real without legislating it, and that is extracted from the logic of ends and means that governs mediate violence. Benjamin describes this violence in terms of the groundless image, one detached from causality and reference: it is "the sign and seal but never the means of sacred execution" (300).[16]

Such an approach to violence is not without risks. In "Force of Law: The 'Mystical Foundations of Authority,'" Derrida dwelt on those risks. The essay was first delivered as a lecture at Cardozo School of Law in New York City in 1989—soon after the revelations, in 1987, surrounding Paul de Man's World War II journalism, revelations that elicited much soul-searching in academia about the ethics of deconstruction—and participates in a movement, prominent in the 1980s and early 1990s, within literary criticism to articulate the relation of the present to violent, traumatic history. The essay's published form in 1992—coincident with Shoshana Felman and Dori Laub's seminal book *Testimony: Crises of Witnessing*, in which the de Man scandal also plays a significant role—remains a very loving reading of Benjamin's "Critique." But it includes a postscript in which Derrida parts ways with Benjamin, evoking Nazism and the Final Solution as the point at which Benjamin's essay makes available "a temptation to think the holocaust as an uninterpretable manifestation of divine violence" (62).[17]

Derrida's departure from Benjamin is couched as a series of intersecting concerns about violence, mimesis, and affect. The problem with "Critique of Violence," according to Derrida, is that it may be, or may be made to be, "about" the Holocaust, and the potential of this similarity produces a reading (or interpretation) of *history* that he finds unbearable. "When one thinks of the gas chambers and the cremation ovens, this allusion to an extermination that would be expiatory because

---

16. Put differently: violence rules. Generation X is well positioned to consider the implications of sovereign violence—violence that rules, with no specification as to what violence rules *over*. According to *The Oxford English Dictionary*, the first application of the intransitive verb "rules" to a specified activity or object (i.e., not a person) is in 1981 ("Rules"). Xer Mike Judge's popular animated show "Beavis and Butt-head," which aired on television between 1993 and 1997, appropriated the intransitive verbs "rules" and "sucks" as aesthetic criteria with which to rate music videos.

17. Derrida's reading of Benjamin has been authoritative (though Beatrice Hanssen seems to wish to distance herself from it). Hanssen, who notes that Benjamin is thinking about the logic of means to ends and trying to think of violence in terms of pure means, concludes that Benjamin's essay "fell short of providing an incisive differentiation between just and unjust uses of violence, and therefore, in the final analysis, of offering a credible critique of violence" (23). I discuss the function, in critique, of credulity—or faith—in the following section.

bloodless must cause one to shudder. One is terrified at the idea of an interpretation that would make of the holocaust an expiation and an indecipherable signature of the just and violent anger of God" (62). In the wake of the Holocaust—of any holocaust—only one reading is appropriate: one that is affectively laden, that causes shuddering and terror. Within these affects inhere assumptions about judgment, representation, and action. Derrida is concerned with the possibility that through interpretation, the unjustifiable may be justified—the immediate may enter the realm of the mediate, and function as a means to (unacceptable) ends. Or, more precisely, it may *look like* what it shouldn't: the text, Derrida writes, "seems to me finally *to resemble too closely,* to the point of specular fascination and vertigo, the very thing against which one must act and think, do and speak" (62; emphasis mine).[18] I linger on Derrida's reading of Benjamin because its assumptions about mimesis and affect, its impulse toward action (thinking, doing, speaking), and its reliance on the empirical validity of historical violence (emblematized by the Holocaust) evokes the logic by which critiquing immediate violence folds it into mediate violence and makes it disappear (this logic trapped LaCapra, too). Generation X puts this logic to question, and offers a way out.

Derrida's instantiation of genocide as a limit case for thinking about violence reverberates with the debates about the ethics of Holocaust representation, and the complexities of memory, in the 1980s (especially after the airing of the NBC television miniseries *Holocaust* in 1978) and 1990s (especially after the 1993 Hollywood blockbuster *Schindler's List*). Both *Holocaust* and *Schindler's List* represented a "mainstreaming" of an atrocity urgently designated, in the developing discipline of Holocaust Studies and by such as survivor-spokesman Elie Wiesel, to be unspeakable. The Holocaust's formal induction into popular culture was accompanied by much debate about the ethics of memory and of representation—echoed in the Historians' Debate in Germany—discussions that revolved around how these events would figure for future gen-

---

18. Derrida's turn to history (which is also a turn to politics and a critique of state power) is especially striking because Benjamin has, at this point in his essay, abandoned the sociopolitical realm. Though Benjamin briefly cites the image of an angry man as an example of immediate violence, and offers "the educative power" as an example of divine violence (a point noticed by Redding), it is fiction—Hellenic and Hebraic myth—to which he turns to articulate the tricky concept of immediate violence. Derrida finds this turn to fiction disquieting: he evokes history—as Holocaust—to counter it. Though I am, of course, sympathetic to the impetus behind Derrida's gesture, I linger on Benjamin's move to myth because it hints at the power of *fiction* in thinking on immediate violence.

erations (read: Generation X). In the course of these discussions, and in the wake of the de Man scandal, the Holocaust figured as a definitive real violence, an absolute evil, one irreconcilable with ethical relativism or constructivist theory, a forbidding warning to postmodern play, a uniquely unarguable—because uniquely and unarguably violent—reality.

Precisely because Xers are acutely attuned to the constructed nature of causality, the vagaries of justice, and the production of real violence for stage and screen; because of their acquaintance with confession culture, wound culture, and reality TV; and because of their awareness of the inevitability of complicity in acting, thinking, and speaking, they cannot hold to the assumptions about history, about justice, about trauma, and about reality that informed Derrida's reservations about "Critique of Violence" (reservations that were echoed in subsequent work on Benjamin by Martin Jay, LaCapra, and Hanssen). Derrida's "specular fascination," and the challenge it poses to action, are, for Generation X, a starting point, not a limit case; as for Video Backpacker in *Slackers,* specular fascination is something to be embraced, not eschewed. The slacker is unlikely to care about what may lie beyond representation's limits; she is more inclined toward situational ethics than the ineffable, and is notoriously unconcerned with history. "Generation Xers possess a media literacy which allows a celebration of an investment in the image that is not linked to the real," proclaims Xer Tara Brabazon (21). She continues to reflect on the implications of this detachment of the real from judgment: "Good Guys and Bad Guys no longer wear white and black hats. They look the same. Both use violence. Both justify the use of violence through religion" (28). She concludes by relinquishing the distinctions that violence and judgment are evoked to establish: "If any collective or community offers potential to be subjected to the vagaries of fact and fiction, truth and ideology, then it is Generation X" (55).

NOTHING TO BELIEVE IN

Dangerous relativism? No doubt, though to be dangerous, relativism must maintain a firm faith in the boundaries it aims to transgress. For a generation with nothing but faith in nothing, it is precisely faith—fidelity—that comes to the fore in understanding the relation of truth to fiction after the spectacular detachment of violence from the real. Especially after the terror attacks of September 11, 2001, both accounts of disaster that call on fiction to validate experience ("it was just like in the movies") *and* the more cerebral responses that urge us to safeguard violence from fiction testify to how violence renders reality precarious. The truth that violence is called upon to make presents as mobile, nomadic, a question of verification, attribution, and attitude. I use the term fidelity to describe this question and the work it asks us to do. In keeping with this book's self-description as a form of theft, I appropriate for this term its connotations of faith and trust (phenomenal, economic, and interpersonal). I also borrow from Alain Badiou's work on the subject. Badiou distinguishes the object of fidelity from knowledge, dissociates fidelity from conventional thinking on ethics, subjectivity, and religion, and posits truth as the product, not the object, of a "procedure" of fidelity. Because Generation X is so frequently characterized as the generation with no cause to fight for, nothing to believe in, the concept of fidelity is crucial to understanding how X rewrites the relation of violence to the real.

As a genre with particular claims on the contemporary, the novel's specific brand of realism is dictated by fidelity. Writing of the genre's inception in his study of Defoe, Richardson, and Fielding, Ian Watt states, "the novel's primary task is to convey the impression of fidelity to human experience" (13). With the development of postmodernism, this impetus to fidelity has only come more starkly into view. Precisely because of violence's inarguable facticity, fiction is enjoined to evince a particular kind of fidelity: it must, paradoxically, be true. "History is the record of *real human action and suffering,* and is not to be tampered with lightly," writes Brian McHale in *Postmodernist Fiction* (emphasis mine); departing from the historical record is commonly conceived of as "a betrayal" (96). When postmodernism meets fiction, "history and fiction exchange places, history becoming fictional and fiction becoming 'true' history—and the real world seems to get lost in the shuffle" (96). McHale's phrasing is a relatively mild articulation of the sense that fiction about violent events must be true to the known facts of those events. The violence of history, the record of atrocity, terror, genocide or abuse, commonly calls a halt to simulation, imagination, and fiction. In the 1960s and 1970s, postmodern texts that dealt with vast and violent historical events acceded to this logic by figuring violence and disaster as the limit case of discourse—what I have elsewhere described as the unspeakable (*Against the Unspeakable*). In her study of the figuration of history by postmodern texts, Amy Elias has pointed out that postmodernism is modeled on "a post-traumatic consciousness that redefines positivist or stadialist history as the historical sublime, a desired horizon that can never be reached but only approached in attempts to understand human origins and the meaning of lived existence" (xviii). The breakage of the frame associated with postmodernism, its distrust of certitude and coherence, is ultimately a gesture of fidelity to an unspeakable, unknowable history that must not be betrayed, a gesture that underscores the incommensurability of vast historical violence to the world in which these texts are written and read. (Elias notes a decrease in postmodern literary experimentation after the 1980s, possibly because of increased political conservatism with the rise of Reagan and Thatcher, and possibly because of a decrease in faith in the ethical and politically redemptive possibilities of experimental narrative form [75].)

We should reflect on this gesture of fidelity, the urgency with which it signals, and the subject and object it presupposes, in order to chart how Generation X, that faithless crew, figures the relation of violence to reality in its absence. Both injunctions to historical accuracy and gestures toward the limits of comprehension locate "real violence" in the realm of the unspeakable. But what lies beyond the limits of language is a vast, uncharted space; to locate historical certainty there is a supreme act of faith in our powers of orientation. When Saul Friedländer writes, in his introduction to the influential 1992 collection of essays on Holocaust aesthetics, *Probing the Limits of Representation,* "one cannot define exactly what is wrong with a certain representation of the events, but [. . .] *one senses* when some interpretation or representation is wrong" (3–4; emphasis mine), he presumes an affective, sensitive subject as the site for the determination of what is historically accurate *and* aesthetically sound, a subject that, like Derrida's, "shudders," and does so in all the right places.[19] In the 1980s and 1990s, when Generation X's reputation as uncaring, unschooled, irresponsible, and violent was becoming established (Howe and Strauss extensively, and indignantly, document this reputation in 1993), the ethics of this subject are of no small concern, and much is made of her responsibilities to the past, to history, and to the reality of violence. Studies of witness, testimony, trauma, and ethics in this period evinced what Amy Hungerford (*Holocaust of Texts*) has called a logic of personification, according to which texts are treated like people, with urgent injunc-

---

19. Derrida's "Force of Law" was part of a 1990 colloquium organized by Friedländer on the subject of his 1992 edited volume, *Probing the Limits of Representation: Nazism and the "Final Solution"* (Cornell, Rosenfeld, and Carlson 3).

tions toward memory and care—an extension of ethics from relations between people, to people's relations to texts, to history, to the real. Hungerford is quite critical of this logic, which valorizes fidelity to the facts of extreme historical violence. If facts are elided, forgotten, dismissed or denied, this erasure of the historical comes to stand for an erasure of the personal, as if to miscount, or discount, the victims murders them all over again. Fidelity to the unspeakable ensures that history's violence is both factually registered *and* affectively charged and guides us to the "right," and responsible, readings of silence.

For Xers, whose adult finances coincided with the establishment of the concept of the credit default swap (CDS) in the 1990s and who saw 401(k)s diminish when Enron filed for bankruptcy in 2001, "fidelity's just the name of a discount brokerage house." This statement is spoken by arch-plotter Bernard Melman—possibly a figure for Bernard (Bernie) Madoff—in Jay McInerney's novel *Brightness Falls* (168), which sets the stock market crash of 1987 and the AIDS crisis in a context of marital and professional infidelity. Like marriage and monetary trust, religious faith, for Xers, is predicated on incoherence and uncertainty and colored by irony.[20] In *Finding Faith: The Spiritual Quest of the Post-Boomer Generation,* Richard W. Flory and Donald E. Miller write of Xers that "there seem to no longer be any universal truths [. . .]. [W]hat is true for one person may not be true for another, and it is all based on one's own experiences, whether through religion, lifestyle, ethnicity, or 'whatever'" (10). In *Virtual Faith,* self-identified Xer Tom Beaudoin advocates "seriously attending to the revelatory significance of hesitation, ambiguity, ambivalence, and instability in the lives (and faith experiences) of many Xers" (141). "Xers have a sense of self that, in its fragmentation, simulates the real, undivided self that we were assumed to have," he writes (140). Such an approach to faith eschews any easy distinction between love and violence, fidelity and revolution. Cultural atomism and isolation drive Xers to violence as an expression of fidelity: they marry the sign to the somatic with piercings and tattoos. "In a sense," Beaudoin writes, "these bodily incisions love our bodies (and there is a great confusion between body and self) unconditionally. They will never leave, which is blessed assurance for our abandoned generation" (141). Violence as an expression of fidelity found another form in

---

20. This refusal of faith has characterized Generation X since its inception. Hamblett and Deverson's *Generation X* concludes, with fifteen-year-old Michael Jacobs, "we have done away with God and yet have found no suitable replacement" (191).

the explosion of Christian rock music in the 1990s, and churches soon saw the utility of harnessing the oppositional ethos of this music as a recruitment tool to undo the damage done by sex scandals surrounding televangelists like Jim and Tammy Bakker, media events that illustrated, for Xers, "the failure and hypocrisy of corporate, political, and religious institutions to act ethically," a failure that resulted in widespread "distrust and cynicism of large-scale institutions" (Flory and Miller 9).

But fidelity is not solely the realm of finance and religion. Faith underwrites truth claims, and "much depends," writes Barbara Herrnstein Smith in *Scandalous Knowledge: Science, Truth and the Human*, "on an untroubled faith in the simplicity and stability of truth" (36). Herrnstein Smith's reference to faith is of a piece with the terminology of dogmatism and orthodoxies with which her argument's contemporary stakes are defined. "The charge of 'postmodern relativism,'" Herrnstein Smith concludes, "when directed at those pursuing unorthodox lines of thought in epistemology, ethics and social and political theory, operates by the same rhetorical and institutional mechanisms as did the charges of cynicism, materialism and nihilism directed in the past (and, in some places, still) at secular, naturalistic challenges to received theological-humanistic accounts of the human. [It is] A scapegoat label" (38–39). Xers witnessed the holy wars of these epistemological debates. Precisely because it *is* so irreverent, taking Generation X as our starting point for thinking about the relation of violence to the real exposes the work that fidelity performs in writing this relation and in constructing the subject that defines itself accordingly.

Though its impact on Anglo philosophy was not to be evident until over a decade later, Alain Badiou's *Being and Event,* published in France in 1986, recaptured fidelity as a philosophical paradigm. Fidelity does not exist in and of itself, argues Badiou. Its presence or absence can't be verified. Rather, fidelity can be identified only in what it produces, and what it produces is truth. Thus, in a decisive break from the religious tradition, Badiou reverses the relation of fidelity to truth: not an eternal beacon or fundamental ground accessed by faith, not an object toward which the subject yearns, truth, for Badiou, is the product of what he calls a "procedure of fidelity" (*Being* 335). In other words: counter to established notions of faith as a pre-existing quality, possessed by the subject, that maintains a subject's integrity through a variety of situations, Badiou puts fidelity under the sign of the modernist erasure of presence. "There is no general faithful disposition," he emphasizes; fidelity is not an effect of mimesis or the manifestation of a person's unswerving faith in a god, ideal, or *ism*; it is, simply, "a functional relation to the event" (*Being* 233).[21]

Hypercritical, affectless Xers, for whom violence is real, reality is fiction, the body intersects with its image, and affective certainty is absent or disappeared, have much to gain from considering the theory of fidelity elaborated here, not least because of the version of the subject that informs this approach. Drawing on mathematics as well as philosophy, Badiou posits a subject that is *not* affectively impacted; in other words, a subject that is neither a physical body, nor a subject in the traditionally psychological sense. Such a subject, because it is not identified with a coherent body or psyche that can be violated or traumatized, offers an approach to violence from which the implicit moralization of affect— feeling or sensing what's wrong—is, in essence, subtracted. Furthermore, because Badiou divests fidelity of religious belief, his approach sets the stage for an articulation of contingent affiliations and alliances.

In his more accessible *Ethics,* Badiou expresses the stakes of this work for the decades in which Xers came of age. Written in the 1990s, *Ethics* was, Badiou reflects, "driven by a genuine fury. The world was deeply plunged in 'ethical' delirium. Everyone was busily confusing politics with the hypocrisy of a mindless catechism. [. . .] The presumed 'rights of man' were serving at every point to annihilate any attempt to invent forms of free thought" (liii). This confusion is an expression of what Badiou calls the ideology of human rights, which rallies around the image of the victimized human body to demand, in terms weighted with moral urgency, action that is assumed to be ethical, but that, in fact, prohibits new kinds of knowledge by urgent invocations of right, wrong, and the reality of violence. Rather than a moral gathering around the rights of human being conceived as the victim of violence, Badiou demands, in *Ethics,* a return to the antihumanist projects of Foucault, Althusser, and Lacan, and proposes an alternative conception of ethics, defined by mobility (the maxim "Keep going!") and characterized by persistence in a hypercritical stance and affective detachment (*réserve*) (*Ethics* 91). For Generation X, the attractions of this approach hardly need to be spelled out.[22]

---

21. An event, according to Badiou, exceeds the multiple situations that humans find themselves in. Fidelity describes a relation to this event that forms and re-forms someone into a subject. I return to Badiou, and his thinking on the event, fidelity, and ethics, in chapter 5.

22. Nonetheless, I spell them out in chapter 5. "Not Yes or No: Fact, Fiction, Fidelity

CRITIQUES OF VIOLENCE (2):
Agamben

We are not yet done with "Critique of Violence." Agamben revisits Benjamin's essay in his 2003 *State of Exception*. Writing with a sense of urgency propelled by the instantiation of the USA Patriot Act and the authorization, by President G. W. Bush, of indefinite detention in 2001, haunted by a history of totalitarianism in Europe and by the Nazi genocide, Agamben attempts to articulate the relation of law to life, and locates at the heart of this attempt the dialogue between the Jewish philosopher Walter Benjamin and the Nazi jurist Carl Schmitt on the nature of anomie—the zone outside of language or law. Benjamin's "Critique of Violence," Agamben writes, aims "to ensure the possibility of a violence [. . .] that lies absolutely 'outside' (*außerhalb*) and 'beyond' (*jenseits*) the law. [. . .] The task of Benjamin's critique is to prove the reality (*Bestand*) of such a violence" (53). Agamben's characterization of Benjamin's essay underscores what is at issue in *any* critique of violence: the reality that violence claims or is claimed by, the reality that violence is leveled against or that it brings about. How can this reality be accessed by critique?

Agamben mentions Derrida's "Force of Law" only briefly (37), treating its title as an opportunity to articulate the state of exception as "the separation of 'force of law' from the law" (38)—what Agamben calls 'force-of-~~law~~.' He writes: "Such a 'force-of-~~law~~,' in which potentiality and act are radically separated, is certainly something like a mystical element, or rather a *fictio* by means of which law seeks to annex anomie" (38–39). Agamben's term *fictio* is significant, and I turn to it below. First I note his staging of the issue through the conversation between Benjamin and Schmitt in their publications in the 1920s, a conversation that continued, after Benjamin committed suicide in 1940 while attempting to escape the Nazis, in Schmitt's citations and references to Benjamin in his published work and correspondence.[23]

Agamben approaches this material with a focus on Benjamin's and Schmitt's reflections on the relation of violence to law (remember: law is the realm of mediate violence). Schmitt, Agamben argues, is attempt-

---

in Jonathan Safran Foer" returns to Badiou's thinking on the event to pursue this argument's philosophical and ethical stakes.

23. For an account of the Benjamin–Schmitt dialogue, see Bredekamp. The *Stanford Encyclopedia of Philosophy* offers a good account of the controversy surrounding Schmitt's legacy ["Carl Schmitt"]).

ing to appropriate the immediate violence (or anomie) that Benjamin's essay articulates. In other words, Schmitt studied the logic that trapped LaCapra and Derrida, by which any attempt to critique immediate violence folds it into the mediate, names it as fantasy, fable, or falsehood. Schmitt, Agamben concludes, tried to capture anomie with law and inscribe it within the juridical (55). But note the imagery in which Agamben's work on anomie is couched: immediate violence is real; *inscribing* it turns it into fiction. Distinguishing between Benjamin's "real" state of exception (57–58) and Schmitt's "fictitious" one (59), Agamben stresses the "pure violence" that Benjamin articulates: pure violence refers to human action that is extraneous to the law, that neither makes law nor preserves it, that is neither end nor means, that is, indeed, unavailable to the logic of mediation. At issue (and here is where Agamben's critique of violence intersects with my own) is not only the distinction of reality from fiction but the question of whether violence can be assured an existence outside the law—that is, outside the realm of the mediate that folds immediate violence into the logic of the mediate, that worries about the ends to which it serves as a means, and by thus worrying makes it disappear. In Benjamin and Schmitt's dialogue Agamben sees the ultimate stakes of Western politics and metaphysics, stakes that are, importantly, imaged in terms of *language* and of *presence*. "Pure violence as the extreme political object, as the 'thing' of politics, is the counterpart to pure being, to pure existence as the ultimate metaphysical stakes; the strategy of the exception, which must ensure the relation between anomic violence and law, is the counterpart to the onto-theological strategy aimed at capturing pure being in the meshes of the logos" (60). At this point of his argument, as if startled by its extreme level of abstraction, Agamben offers this concrete analogy: the relation of law to anomie is like the relation of language to its limits, a relation on which real life depends. "Everything happens as if both law and logos needed an anomic (or alogical) zone of suspension in order to ground their reference to the world of life. *Law seems able to subsist only by capturing anomie, just as language can subsist only by grasping the nonlinguistic* (60; emphasis mine).[24]

---

24. Agamben often turns to language in *State of Exception* to underscore his study's metaphysical stakes. In a digression that reflects on this methodological tendency, Agamben reflects that "not only language and law but all social institutions have been formed through a process of desemanticization and suspension of concrete praxis in its immediate reference to the real. [. . .] The floating signifier—this guiding concept in the human sciences of the twentieth century—corresponds to the state of exception in which the

In the course of *State of Exception*, this analogy of law and language will solidify into a concern with *fiction*. Pure violence, Agamben will conclude, is bound to law by fiction, a term that appears seven times in the short book's final pages (86 88). "Fiction," for Agamben, under scores a departure from the brute facticity of bare life and illustrates the essentially fabricated or constructed nature of power. The state of exception, he writes, "*is founded on the essential fiction* according to which anomie [. . .] is still related to the juridical order and the power to suspend the norm has an immediate hold on life. As long as the two elements remain correlated yet conceptually, temporally, and subjectively distinct [. . .] their dialectic—*though founded on a fiction*—can nevertheless function in some way. But [. . .] when the state of exception, in which they are bound and blurred together, becomes the rule, then the juridico-political system transforms itself into a killing machine" (86; emphasis mine). The ultimate aim of *State of Exception*, Agamben concludes, is to make this fiction evident, "to bring to light the fiction that governs this *arcanum imperii* [secret of power] par excellence of our time" (86); "Life and law, anomie and *nomos* [. . .] result from the fracture of something to which we have no other access than through the fiction of their articulation and the patient work that, by unmasking this fiction, separates what it had claimed to unite" (88). Only thus, he stresses, can new conditions for existence be forged.

But how? And by whom? Throughout this discussion, I have held to this Generation X stereotype: "slackers, emotionally and intellectually stagnant and vapid, apathetic, brainwashed creations of popular culture" (Grassian 14). I do not propose that beneath this stereotype lurks an as-yet-untapped resource for transformative ethics. Instead, I propose to embrace it, to think of violence after—that is, according to—Generation X. The generation with no cause to fight for, with nothing to believe in, is uniquely able to articulate, as Agamben urges us to, the fiction that forms our world.

---

norm is in force without being applied" (37). Discussing the concept of "pure violence" that Benjamin advances in "Critique of Violence," Agamben turns to Benjamin's writing on *language*—in his 1931 essay on Karl Kraus—finding there a useful parallel to a tricky concept: "Just as pure language is not another language, just as it does not have a place other than that of the natural communicative languages, but reveals itself in these by exposing them as such, so pure violence is attested to only as the exposure and deposition of the relation between violence and law" (62).

NEVERMIND

The genocides and horrors of the twentieth century, the spectacular attacks on the World Trade Center in New York City that ushered in the twenty-first century, seem to call a halt to any easy equation of violence and fiction, as does the evidence of more private, pervasive violence on broken bodies, economies, ecosystems, and psyches. Together with religious extremism and patriotic fervor, fidelity's most murderous manifestations, this history reminds us that *violence is real*. And yet: as reality is mediated, digitized, disseminated in information and reconfigured as connectivity, its relation to violence needs to be examined, as does the role of violence in establishing reality, the role of reality in designating "violence," and the utility of the distinction of reality from fiction in the discussions that violence incites us to have. Precisely because *violence is real*, we might more usefully turn our attention to the forms this reality takes: it is the product of the work of molding, making, and forming in the Latin root *fictio*, the blurring of politics and bare life that transforms the state into a killing machine, and the tradition of prose narrative associated with the rise of literary realism in Boswell and Johnson's time, a tradition that, in the 1990s (as Xers were nearing maturity) reached what Joseph Tabbi calls "a crisis of reference and representation" (208).

Crises are traditionally resolved with judgment. Judgment distinguishes truth from lies, reality from fiction. It demarcates zones of agency, imputes culpability, nominates perpetrators and victims, and closes the book. And yet, as Agamben makes clear, judgment is the realm of law, of language; its claims to power are, quite literally, fictitious. For Xers, attuned to the construction of cause-and-effect, schooled in the media circus, justice presents as written by history, under the sign of the victors or the powerful; guilt and innocence are not stable categories, nor are they atemporal or absolute. Video Backpacker put it best: "I was seeing it for real but it just wasn't right." What's real and what's right do not coincide for Xers. Precisely because of the discourse of threat, fear, and menace that surrounds them, X marks the spot of multiple collapse: not only of such fundamental distinctions as reality from fiction, immediate sensation and mediated image, but of the categories that rely on them: prosecutor from defendant, real from right, right from wrong. For a generation that expects, even demands, to rewind, the idea that violence must align with sensation, precede critique, and dictate (just and righteous) action seems, at best, misguided. Victim and perpetrator intersect; X icon Kurt Cobain's suicide, both an expression of generational malaise and an act of self-inflicted violence, imaged as "the bullet that shot through a generation," posited X as its own victim/executioner.[25] Like Cobain, the rapper, the suicide bomber: both predator and prey, violence's agent and object, X offers a perspective on violence that is, crucially, divested from sensemaking mechanisms. The slacker is disinclined to fold the immediate into the mediate and make it disappear. Anomic, affectless, alyxithymic, a product of "a culture that has the unique distinction of being both hyper- and anaesthetic at the same time," as Joel Black writes of the 1980s (3), she is also disinclined to care about such work.

This is not to say that the very real questions that violence poses do not still resonate in politics, culture, and society today. These questions are familiar. They go like this: How do we distinguish real-world, bodily violence from violence that is fantasized, fictional, fake? How must we mobilize to safeguard the oppressed, without perpetrating further the damage wrought by centuries of hegemony? How can we respond, with appropriate affect, to images that teach to titillate? How do we oppose symbols and words that affirm and disown a history of oppression? To these questions, vibrant with urgency, freighted with weight, resonant with the horror that the questioner may be herself complicit in the very violence she so fervently wishes to end, the preceding pages have attempted to outline an alternative: an X critique of violence.

An X critique of violence expects us to eschew those familiar, ethics-laden verbs—distinguish, mobilize, respond, oppose, end. With causality, judgment, and faith Xed out, the generation with no cause or credo offers an exercise in subtraction: of affect from the unspeakable, of judgment from representation, of urgency from the distinction of fiction from fact. Tarry in the noncommittal, withhold judgment, do so without recourse to the promise of future justice or immediate affective response-ability. Rewind and witness, in your mind's eye, Johnson's foot abandon the stone. Forsake faith, not only in an ideal or a cause or a metajuridical outcome but in the perceiver's ability to feel her way or to "sense" what's "wrong," pause, and abide, like Clay in the final lines of *Less Than Zero,* in the flickering light of the unmoored images that orient without reference. In their bleak light, know only this: violence is real. *Or is it?* Minus affect, judgment, and urgency, in a world where disinformation is its own, privileged kind of knowledge, the reality of violence becomes a

---

25. Wurtzel and Delvaux both cite the phrase "the bullet that shot through a generation," ascribing it to *Newsweek*'s coverage of Cobain's suicide.

test of faith, a test that Xers will resolutely fail. Violence is real. But its reality, while hard, is also hard to find. *Is it real?* Does it matter? *What difference does it make?* At this point, Ground Zero of the twenty-first century, X changes the channel. X quits the program. X answers, "whatever." X says: Nevermind.

three

The Game That Moves

Bret Easton Ellis, 1985–2010

A VEST, A FLAG

"People are afraid to merge on freeways in Los Angeles." Thus begins *Less Than Zero*, Bret Easton Ellis's iconic novel from 1985. Like driving (its isolation, its dangers, its perpetual objectlessness) and freeways—the habits and hazards of unlimited freedom—the fear of merging speaks directly to the atomism and loneliness that pervade the scene of young, hyperprivileged, disaffected college students who drift aimlessly from party to party, in and out of each other's beds, toward and away from the desert, toward and away from the beach. In keeping with the novel's title, the opening paragraph proceeds through a series of "nots"—narration by subtraction. Reflecting on his friend Blair's statement that people are afraid to merge, Clay, the narrator, feels that nothing else seems to matter: "not the fact that I'm eighteen [. . .] not the mud that spattered on my jeans in New Hampshire [. . .] not the stain on the arm of my shirt [. . .] not the tear at the neck of my grey argyle vest [. . .]. All it comes down to is that I'm a boy coming home for a month and meeting someone whom I haven't seen for four months and people are afraid to merge" (9–10).

Clay is alienated—a Holden Caulfield for the '80s. His sense of isolation concretizes the more general isolation represented by the novel's opening sentence. But even though it's all it comes down to, the fear of merging gives way—it doesn't matter, or it matters less—in light of Clay and Blair's friend Muriel's anorexia. "It seems easier to hear that people are afraid to merge rather than 'I'm pretty sure Muriel is anorexic,'" he reflects (9). Both resistant to the dictate to be thin, fragile, and in control, and complicit in a society determined and driven by image, anorexia is an embodiment of the image: an inscription, on the body, of the dictate of subtraction. The series of "nots" that compose the opening paragraph point to more conceptual subtractions. Clay's sense of being out of place (his clothes, and especially his vest, feel "vaguely eastern" compared with Blair's outfit) falls away in the light of "people are afraid to merge." The fear of merging falls away when confronted by the reference to anorexia. The reference to anorexia is qualified or uncertain—Blair is only *pretty* sure Muriel is anorexic, and Muriel's thinness may well be the product of drug use. At the vanishing-point of these subtractions is "Disappear Here." Clay first sees the phrase on a billboard, and, like "people are afraid to merge," the image of Muriel shooting up, and the sound of her wordless screams, "Disappear Here" echoes through the book.

But it is Clay's vest, with its red diamond pattern, that sets the stakes for this chapter's discussion of violence and representation in fiction between 1985 and 2010. When Clay and Muriel meet at a party, she is immediately enamored of the vest. "It looks like you got stabbed or something," says Muriel, "please let me wear it" (82). What's attractive about this vest is not its preppy pattern or its chic ghoulishness but its image of a wound. In *Less Than Zero*'s culture of excess, signs of visceral immediacy are scarce commodities. Clay gives his vest to Muriel because he's "too tired to say no" and proceeds into a world of sex, drugs, clubs, television, and violence: a snuff film, a dead body in an alley, a young girl tied to a bedpost and gang-raped. In this world, signifiers are detachable and substitutable; emotions are displaced or misplaced. Like the other characters, who can't keep track of who is sleeping with whom, who interrupt a night of clubbing to cry for no reason, and who perpetually counter each other with shibboleths like "what do you do?" "what's going on?" and "wonder if he's for sale," Clay wanders toward and away from the land's end (the phrase refers to the beach, to a club, and, of course, to Los Angeles) before subtracting himself from the scene of the novel and returning to college and the East. Before he does he returns to the party house to reclaim his vest. He finds it in a pile of abandoned clothing by a wall where someone has written the alphabet with the letters out of order. Outside, by the pool, Muriel is still screaming (149).

Due to Ellis's immense popularity and Brat Pack marketability in the mid-1980s, *Less Than Zero* was immediately optioned for film, and the adaptation was released in 1987. Muriel doesn't appear in the film, but Clay's vest does: adapted to a white silk shirt with what looks like a blood-spatter over the heart that is worn by the character of his friend Julian (played by Robert Downey Jr.). In the novel, Julian's descent into prostitution and addiction was more or less dispassionately observed by Clay; in the film, Clay and Blair try hard to save Julian before he dies from an overdose in the desert outside of Palm Springs. Julian's character, his death, and the adaptation set the scene for Ellis's 2010 novel *Imperial Bedrooms*, which revisits the characters from *Less Than Zero*. "They had made a movie about us," *Imperial Bedrooms* begins (3), and Clay, now a screenwriter, recalls the screening of the film in 1987: "In the book Julian Wells lived but in the movie's new scenario he had to die. He had to be punished for all of his sins. That's what the movie demanded. (Later, as a screenwriter, I learned it's what all movies demanded.)" (8). *Imperial Bedrooms* goes on to recount what happened to the "real" Julian Wells:

> The real Julian Wells didn't die in a cherry-red convertible, overdosing on a highway in Joshua Tree while a choir soared over the sound track. The real Julian Wells was murdered over twenty years later, his body dumped behind an abandoned apartment building in Los Feliz after he had been tortured to death at another location. [. . .] His body was discovered by a group of kids who went to CalArts and were cruising through the streets off of Hillhurst in a convertible BMW looking for a parking space. When they saw the body they thought the "thing" lying by a trash bin was—and I'm quoting the first Los Angeles Times article on the front page of the California section about the Julian Wells murder—"a flag." (9–10)

In the 1985 novel, Clay's vest was detached not only from the body but from affect. Its promise to impart visceral urgency to the psychic wound was unfulfilled. The film restored the signifying function (the white shirt Julian wears that signals his punishment or sacrifice) and appropriated the sign of the wound for the purposes of judgment and justice—not out of affirmation of these values but because of the logic of images represented by cinema: "it's what all movies demanded." To these demands Ellis's 2010 novel responds with the image of an American flag—drenched in signification.[1] Like the vest, and like the wound, the flag signals and distracts. It compels reference and eludes it and interferes with the signifying order of text: coming across the word "flag," Clay has to stop reading the article and start again from the beginning (9). With this image—itself, of course, a simulation, as the students mistake the body for the flag—Ellis reappropriates the anomic amorality of *Less Than Zero,* and qualifies the logic of image, reference, and commodity appeal that dictated its adaptation.

This chapter examines how this happens and what it means for violence and its representation in fiction in recent decades. I follow the trajectory of Ellis's novels *(Less Than Zero, The Rules of Attraction, American Psycho, Glamorama, Lunar Park,* and *Imperial Bedrooms),* setting them in the cultural contexts through which they are read: Generation X, blank fiction (a literary mode that began to be developed and described in the 1990s), and the contemporary extreme. Ellis is a poster boy for Generation X and a formative figure for theorists of blank fiction; extremity best articulates the trajectories of his most recent works. Though in what follows I dwell on these terms and contexts, my goal is not to separate into periods or classify by genre but to provide a frame for my examination of the relation of violence to fiction; specifically, the mobility of violence that wanders from the content of the text to the context of its reception in the quarter century between the publication of Ellis's first novel and his most recent book. From the epistemic violence to which Muriel's anorexia mutely attests, to the casual racism and sexism that characters in Ellis's novels display (and of some readers to whom his works appeal), to the rapes, murders, torture, and terror depicted in such graphic detail (especially, but not exclusively, in *American Psycho*), to the virulence with which Ellis's work is derided or dismissed, "violence" disappears: so wide a range of manifestations and definitions pose significant challenges to critical work. Rather than separating real violence from its representation, extricating violence from "violence" or fact from fiction, I trace how Ellis's novels subtract epistemic certainty from violence and tease apart violence and the reality

---

1. For Colby, who also notes the similarity of Julian's corpse to an American flag, this image is a comment on the G. W. Bush administration. With it, writes Colby, borrowing terminology from Žižek's *Violence: Six Sideways Reflections,* Ellis "brutally establishes the novel's subjective violence as the underwritten counterpart to the objective violence of American neoimperialism" (171–72).

FIGURE 4. *Less Than Zero* (1987). Screen grab. Julian (Robert Downey Jr.), flanked by Clay (Andrew McCarthy, right) and Blair (Jami Gertz, left), before he dies of an overdose in the film's final scene. Julian's death, his white shirt with the blood-red patch, and Blair and Clay's attempts to save him depart from Ellis's more ambiguous 1985 novel. © Kanievska/Fox.

attributed to it. They blur distinctions between reality and fiction, object and agent, violence and "violence," underlining the mobile or unstable nature of the ground from which such judgments may be made.[2]

The care with which I treat Ellis's work may come as a surprise to readers for whom "Bret Easton Ellis" denotes a has-been wunderkind, a half-baked celebrity writer whose substanceless, flashy, trashy novels reflect the vagaries and superficialities of contemporary commodity culture and whose reputation, as his critics are happy to point out, is based on *Less Than Zero*. But the philosophical seriousness of Ellis's work was recognized early on—as early as 1988, David Pan (writing in *Telos*) set *Less Than Zero* at the center of his reflections on voyeurism, violence, aesthetics, and critique in 1980s culture. Ellis's value for critical work has been reaffirmed by a recent edited collection (Mandel, *Bret Easton Ellis*) and two book-length studies. Georgina Colby, in *Bret Easton Ellis:*

---

2. My approach to Ellis's work thus bears some similarity to Colby's recent, and excellent, *Bret Easton Ellis: Underwriting the Contemporary*. Colby approaches Ellis through the concept of underwriting, by which existing paradigms are both undermined and reinforced, and is attuned to the political and cultural scenarios with which Ellis's writing is in dialogue (she reads *Imperial Bedrooms* as a post-9/11 text [165–88]).

Underwriting The Contemporary, affirms Ellis's philosophical seriousness: his work underwrites—that is, both inscribes and guarantees—the
contemporary scene in which he lives.[3] Sonia Baelo-Allué, too, sees in
Ellis a new literary paradigm. In *Bret Easton Ellis's Controversial Fiction: Writing Between High and Low Culture,* she identifies Ellis as an
author who embraces celebrity status, combining high literary culture
and mass entertainment.[4] Both Colby and Baelo-Allué see in Ellis's work
a refusal of judgment, of convention, of value, and of the traditional status of literature.

For me, the revision of values that Ellis represents (both in recent
critical assessments and in the initial acclaim, and then censure, that
surrounded his work) is an opportunity to revisit the nature of value,
and values, in critical debate. In the controversy around his 1991 novel
American Psycho, the book's (and the author's) market value contrasted
with the values in the name of which critics derided the novel and its
author or called for a boycott of its publisher, Knopf. At the same time,
Ellis's work has been the grounds for serious meditations by scholars
like Walter Benn Michaels, David Punter, Elizabeth Young, and Marco
Abel who recognize the conceptual sophistication of his work and value
his prescience as a cultural touchstone. But the ambivalent nature of
Ellis's stature as an artist is not a question to be resolved or an illusion
to be dispelled. I do not want to suggest that his work has value hereto
unappreciated or unacknowledged. To do so would be to assume that
beneath the cool, disaffected, violence-is-chic ethos to which he appeals
lie more conventional literary depths. Ellis is both trashy and disposable
and innovative and deep. His work does and does not have value. In this
way it elicits questions about the nature of value—literary, market, and
moral. Precisely because of the dubious nature of Ellis's value and values,
and because the literary value of his fiction does *not* go without saying,

---

3. "Ellis transforms the contemporary into literature through a writerly act that inscribes contemporary conditions onto his surface narratives," writes Colby (4). "Through
resisting any imposition of moral authority and by courting hermeneutic variability," she
concludes, "Ellis's novels withstand the forces of cultural reification. As such, his narratives are not static but embody a dialectical space in which contemporary moments are
uneasily held in a topology of narratives. By this means, Ellis presents a new literary
paradigm" (187).

4. Baelo-Allué writes: "Nowadays corporations and the market have promoted the
entrance of authors into the entertainment industry, a phenomenon which will probably
mark their future role [. . .] Celebrity authors cannot be judged by past standards, according to which they have 'sold' themselves to the system and do not deserve any serious
attention" (21).

his novels set the stage for questions about violence: its relation to value, to judgment, and to the reality in which it figures.[5]

The previous chapter's closing gambit was that Generation X chooses not to care whether violence is real or not. Violence is real—or it is not "really" violent—but the reality of violence, I argued there, becomes hard to find in the decades that saw Ellis's rise to fame (and his swift descent to notoriety). The previous chapter also traced the ways in which the question of how to critique violence is bound up with judging whether the ends justify the means for which violence is employed; such judgment inevitably turns on questions of legality and justice. In evaluating works of art the logic of ends and means similarly applies, though it is value, not legality, that drives judgment: violence in art elicits questions of whether a work has "earned" its right to this material, and the answers revolve around the categories of justified and gratuitous. In the controversy over *American Psycho,* for example, assessments of the novel contrasted the violence in the text with its literary merits. Tara Baxter, who reports running Ellis's writing through a readability index calculator, dismisses the text's literary value out of hand in order to focus on the violence of an exploitative male fantasy that Ellis, she claims, indulges. Norman Mailer and Christopher Lehmann-Haupt considered the novel's function as critique of 1980s excess and concluded that the novel does not rise to the moral challenge posed by the violence it depicts. For all, the value of the work (and, for such as Baxter, the values of its author) is indexed by the ends to which violence is judged to be a means. "Is it worth it?" critics ask; the ambiguity of the pronoun both highlights this economy and obscures it.

Ellis's novels stage the detachment, or dislocation, of violence from value, from judgment, and from cause-and-effect that my previous chapter described, and explicate what it means, when confronted with "real violence," to turn away or say, "Whatever." Both the vest, and the flag, in different ways, fail or refuse to reference wounding. This failure initiates a detachment of wounding from pain, cause from effect, reference from signification, violence from the real. Clay, who owns the vest, disowns or disavows the pain it represents. Muriel, the anorexic who internalizes and performs society's crippling demands on femininity, appropriates the visual confirmation of wounding, but then abandons or is abandoned

---

5. Some recent scholarly work on Ellis's novels has taken up this concern with monetary value, focusing on the underlying violence of 1980s Reaganomics and contemporary deficit finance. See Godden, Heise, and La Berge.

by it (the disordered alphabet, the wordless scream). Julian's murder in *Imperial Bedrooms* reverses this process: red and white stripes are added to the broken body after the fact, simultaneously simulating and confirming the violence inflicted on it. Refusing the epistemic certainty with which violence is traditionally aligned, images are taken apart and put back together, revealing their quality as fictive—formed, fashioned, staged. Clay, who knows too much about this murder, notes that the white suit "belonged to [Julian] but it wasn't something he was wearing the night he was abducted" and that its red streaks are puzzling, because "Julian had been stripped before he was killed and then re-dressed" (10).

The vest in *Less Than Zero* failed or refused to signify violence. *Imperial Bedrooms* reconstitutes the sign, marks or flags it, and fashions violence from *trompe l'oeil*: "If they thought it was a 'flag,'" muses Clay, "then where was the blue? And then I realized: it was his head. The students thought it was a flag because Julian had lost so much blood that his crumpled face was a blue so dark it was almost black" (10). As violence is owned and disowned, invested and divested, flagging and flagged, detached and redressed, the criteria for its critique—judgment, value, volition—disappear. To begin to trace this erasure, its trajectories and consequences, I set Ellis's earliest work within the context of a generation defined by its *lack* of values, the people that consumed Ellis's fiction and figured in it, but who were not yet established enough, in the 1980s and 1990s, to worry publicly about its influence on them: Generation X.

"WHATEVER": GENERATION X

An absence of faith (because there is nothing to believe in) or relegation of faith to the invisible hand of the market (for which belief is everything or nothing) characterizes Generation X and its literature, both of which have been disparaged as more attuned to the clamor of advertising than to the nuances of art. In his introduction to *The GenX Reader*, Douglas Rushkoff lists some of the qualities commonly attributed to Xers: "illiterate, unmotivated, and apathetic couch potatoes [who] have no career goals, no cultural pride, no political ideology, no family values, and no discernable ambitions" (3–4). Rushkoff identifies two central characteristics of Generation X. The first is the centrality of images, particularly from advertising, that function as the main language of the postmodern cultural landscape. Xers view images not as transparent vehicles for meaning but as complex texts; their much-reviled passive spectatorship is but a guise for sophisticated dissection and keen, if detached, analysis. "Exposed to consumerism and public relations strategies since we could open our eyes," writes Rushkoff, "we GenXers see through the clunky attempts to manipulate our opinions and assets, however shrinking. When we watch commercials, we ignore the products and instead deconstruct the marketing techniques" (5). This cynical, ironic, hyperliterate spectatorship contributes to Generation X's much-commented-on disaffection—dropping out, or opting out, of culture and ideology—and leads us to its second characteristic: political and cultural apathy, a lack of commitment to the causes and agendas that characterized the '60s. As Kathryn Hume puts it in her discussion of Coupland, McInerney, and Ellis, "American culture is McDonald's and Nike, Microsoft and Armani, cellular phones and the World Wide Web. This is it, we live it, and they do not think we will find anything more worthwhile by looking further, looking backward, or trying to change" (*American Dream* 281). For Hume, these novelists and their characters "hardly celebrate this life, [but] they do not reject it in the name of some other values" (281). This is a world in which happiness is the product of Prozac, serenity is elicited by Valium, love is haunted by AIDS, and certainty is dismissed with "whatever."

Ulrich, who traces the term from Capa's early 1950s' photographic project through the Beats, punk, and into 1980s white male subculture, situates Generation X at the "paradoxical borderline status (inside and outside, within and against the mainstream), with 'X' capturing the dual sense of negation and freedom and 'generation' signifying a kind of hyperbolic assertion of subcultural, rather than demographic, solidarity" (19). Indeed, the X signals the atomism and disaffection that *Less Than Zero* expresses. But its alliance with negation also needs to be read in the context of a period—the 1980s—in which "not" signaled neither protest nor failure but a truly viable option. In fact, an emphatic "not" following a declarative sentence was a popular form of sarcasm for young people at the time ("Not!" was the "Word of the Year" in 1992). Read as counterpoise, not negation, "not" articulates X's existential mode that Gonzalo Navajas describes in terms of Continental philosophy: unlike Sartre, Derrida, Althusser, and Balibar, for whom critique operates through a struggle of the self with its historical and cultural context, "for the writers of the Generation X, negation is devoid of all attributes of ethical greatness and it has become a customary and banal *Lebensstil* that does not need further elaboration" (6).

If such a group could be said to have a literary manifesto, it might best be described by the "policy of storytelling" in Douglas Coupland's novel, *Generation X*:

> Inspired by my meetings of the Alcoholics Anonymous organization, I instigated a policy of storytelling in my own life, a policy of "bedtime stories," which Dag, Claire, and I share among ourselves. It's simple: we come up with stories and we tell them to each other. The only rule is that we're not allowed to interrupt, just like in AA, and at the end we're not allowed to criticize. This noncritical atmosphere works for us because the three of us are so tight assed about revealing our emotions. A clause like this was the only way we could feel secure with each other. (13–14)

The enforced apathy ("we're not allowed to interrupt") posits the characters as spectators to each others' performance; the abstention from critique ("we're not allowed to criticize") reflects Generation X's notorious postmoral or amoral stance. This attitude of apathy and abstention is often dismissed as disaffection, but as Coupland presents it, willed atomism and disinterestedness holds the characters together— this is what grants the book its coherence. The "policy of storytelling" thus has specific implications for narrative: *Generation X* is not quite a novel, not quite a collection of short stories; its structure is informed by repetition, not progression; by the policy's repeated instantiation, not the characters' development. Teleology—that traditional narrative engine—is replaced by tautology: the same thing happens, over and over.[6]

In such a context, violence serves no purpose: it just is, and its detachment from volition recasts the relation of violence to the world in which it functions as cause or effect. In *Less Than Zero* Clay recalls himself at fifteen collecting newspaper clippings of violent acts, some accidental and some purposely murderous, but his archive serves no testimonial or memorial function: "*I collected a lot of clippings,*" he muses, "*because, I guess, there were a lot to be collected*" (77; italics in original). The counterpoise of violence as a means to an end, and violence as unmotivated or

---

6. Delvaux reads Coupland's "policy of storytelling" differently: "Rather than constituting a means of escaping, the act of storytelling represents a way to keep reality in check. [. . .] Fragments of horror are woven into narrative threads to be shared with friends, in all security, away from the streamlining stories of media malevolence. The policy goes against the monovalence of the official discourse on Generation X, a discourse which dismisses its need for interaction, dialogue, security" (181).

misdirected, highlights the arbitrary nature of judgment. Invited to participate in a rape, Clay refuses, stuttering, "It's . . . [. . .] It's . . . I don't think it's right"—the only recognizable moral code in the entire novel, and a strikingly inarticulate one (189). Clay's friend Rip responds to this tentative gesture toward morality with an assertion of power: "What's right? If you want something, you have the right to take it. If you want to do something, you have the right to do it" (189). As the negative moral code (Clay can only articulate morality by defining it as what it isn't) is countered with a discourse of self-determination and enfranchisement (you have the right), the conflation of power and morality in the dual definition of what's "right" effectively undercuts *any* judgment of violence as means *or* end.

That violence must serve some end, if only a political one, is troubled in the 1980s with the emergence of "identity politics" according to which power is presumed to accrue to groups that can claim a history of disenfranchisement or victimization. The recognition of the value of such histories, however justified and belated, infuses X's plaints of disenfranchisement with agonistic affect (Douglas Rushkoff's defiance in *The GenX Reader*; Geoffrey T. Holtz's resentment in *Welcome to the Jungle*). Discussing these attitudes, Andrea L. Harris asserts that "the so-called alternative position of 1990s white male youth culture is in fact a position appropriated from the truly alternative or marginalized of American culture—women, African Americans, lesbians and gays, and the poor" (270). Harris's reading of X in terms of identity politics is itself notable: her distinction between the inauthentic ("so-called") alternative and the "truly" marginalized aligns authenticity with marginalization and posits, for the critic, the important task of distinguishing a false alternative from the true one. This logic is also evident in the curricular restructuring in the 1980s in which, as John Guillory puts it, "Canonical and noncanonical authors are supposed to *stand for* particular social groups, dominant or subordinate" (7), and in the debates around affirmative action in the popular press. "Self-righteousness has given way to situational ethics," writes Hornblower of Generation X in 1997. "Their parents fought attack dogs and fire hoses to desegregate lunch counters; now Xers struggle with ambiguous battles over affirmative action, where helping blacks and Hispanics arguably hurts Asians and whites."

This political and cultural context in which identity is wedded to what is culturally marked as marginal adds another dimension to the challenges of defining "Generation X." While the rhetoric of a disen-

franchised minority may well be inappropriate, the rhetoric of subculture (to which Ulrich appeals) is also limited.[7] Imagining X as a
subculture, battling for specificity within the context of commodity capitalism, clinging to the "alternative" nature of music broadcast on Top
40 radio, forecloses the more radical implications of what X signifies
(or refuses to signify) that Ellis's early novels articulate. To return to
my discussion of Clay's vest in *Less Than Zero*: the markers of identity and the visual signification of culture's assault on femininity are
urgently appropriated, but then abandoned, by Muriel; in the film version, these markers are reappropriated for the beautiful and doomed
emblem of Generation X, in the form of a commodity (Julian's fashionable white shirt) sported by Brat Packer and Xer Robert Downey Jr.
In Ellis's second novel, *The Rules of Attraction,* signification becomes
increasingly unreliable, the logic of the commodity extends out to high
culture and in to the body, authenticity fades away, and identity dissolves into repetition.

Set in Camden College in New Hampshire, a thinly disguised version of Ellis's alma mater Bennington College in Vermont, *The Rules of
Attraction* is structured as a series of monologues by a range of characters, including Sean Bateman (whose brother Patrick is the narrator
of *American Psycho*), Victor (the protagonist of *Glamorama*), Lauren
Hynde (who also appears in *Glamorama*), and Clay, who is referred
to as "that guy from L.A." (17, 18, 22, 84). As in *Less Than Zero*, the
characters in *The Rules of Attraction* drift from party to party and in
and out of each others' beds; unlike *Less Than Zero* of which Clay is
the sole focalizer, *The Rules of Attraction*'s decentered structure provides multiple takes on events. Sean's relationship with Paul Denton,
for example, is described in loving detail by Paul and explicitly denied
by Sean. This abandonment of epistemic certainty underscores the logic
of exchange, but unlike the commoditized world of *Less Than Zero*
(in which, as James Annesley puts it, characters drive BMWs, not cars,
and wear Ray-Bans, not sunglasses [*Blank Fictions* 7]), in *The Rules of
Attraction* characters commoditize themselves through academic dis-
ciplines—the inscription of knowledge on the body and its manifestation as affect. Characters have "Drama major arms" or "Social Science
major breakdowns"; in their quest for identity they are constantly
changing their major; true to the newer-is-better logic of the commodity, they (mis)identify to each other as freshmen (a more desirable position than senior).

---

7. See chapter 1 footnote 3 for a discussion of Ulrich's terminology of subculture.

Within this logic of exchange, epistemic certainty fades away. What happened is unimportant, as is who it happened to. The novel revolves around a case of mistaken identity (Sean's obsession with Lauren is based on his erroneous conclusion that Lauren has been putting anonymous notes in his mailbox), and in the novel's opening pages each of its main characters is introduced by a vignette that feature mistakes of affect and value. In the stream-of-consciousness account of a nameless girl (probably Lauren) who loses her virginity to someone she thought was from NYU but was really a townie, groans of pain are mistaken for groans of pleasure. Sean and Paul are introduced through mis-takes of high culture: stealing books. Sean, noticing a girl at a party, thinks "I've seen her stealing Dante in the bookstore" (17); Paul, choosing against a drunken random sexual encounter, steals a girl's copy of Gabriel Garcia Marquez's *One Hundred Years of Solitude*. For Paul, Sean, and the Dante thief (alternately named Deidre, Dede, D), literary value is not intrinsic but appropriable. Neither Dante nor Marquez have any value in and of themselves or for the characters who steal them; the act of stealing the book (generally associated with the logic that taste overrides the rights of ownership) undercuts the rights of ownership but not in the name of any value, aesthetic or otherwise. Indeed, none of the mistakes in the novel seem to merit correction or restitution. When Paul and Lauren determine that Sean's obsession with Lauren had been based on a mistake, they both conclude that "it doesn't matter" (280). In the final pages of the novel Paul chases after a motorcycle driven by a figure who may or may not be Sean. "I don't know *why* I was running after that motorcycle but I was. [. . .] I was running and I was running because it felt like the 'right' thing to do" (281). If, in *Less Than Zero*, what's "right" is the site of a confrontation of morality with power, in *The Rules of Attraction*, "right" is rote. "I wasn't acting on passion," Paul confesses, "I was simply acting" (281; Paul is a drama major).

Xers are commonly opposed to Boomers, and for Generation X, the political foment of the '60s provided a cause for every rebel, set forth clear choice of action, and promised for that action political and ethical consequences. Regardless what the '60s were really like, for many Xers the tie-dyed hippie stands in nostalgic contrast to the preppy Reaganite. "Our parents were rebels of the sexual revolution and Vietnam War veterans, hippies now turned yuppies," writes Martine Delvaux; in contrast, she laments, Xers "live through talk-shows, sit-coms and email, condoms, and anti-depressants" (171). In *The Rules of Attraction*, Ellis redefines this nostalgic relationship. *The Rules of Attraction* characterizes the '60s as a disaster: one of the characters claims the assassination of JFK as the origin of the generational malaise. "There was this . . . our mothers were pregnant with us when we . . . I mean, he . . . was blown away in '64 and that whole incident . . . screwedthingsup" (30; ellipses in original) (of course, Kennedy was assassinated one year earlier, in 1963).

The opposition of the '60s to the '80s is figured in this novel by the character of the hippie, and Sean's relation to the hippie has, at its center, the insecurity of violence's epistemic certainty and the challenge this uncertainty poses to judgment—aesthetic and ethical. The scene is set as a flashback: inspired by a graffito "Whatever Happened to Hippie Love?" Sean recalls a hippie, whom he describes as the first girl he liked at Camden. The hippie (she's never named) dissolves the generational contrast on which Generation X relies for its articulations of futility. She is both a fashion choice in the '80s *and* a residue of the '60s; she is defined by her carefully cultivated image *and* by her inherent hippiness. "This is the Eighties," Sean remembers thinking, "How could there be any hippies left? I knew no hippies when I was growing up in New York. But here was a *hippie*." Both generic and genuine, the hippie confirms and subverts expectations: "A hippie who was not too tall, who had long blond hair, features sharp, not soft like one would expect a hippie's features to resemble, yet distant, too" (94).

The hippie *is* sharp, and her acuity is the crux of her relationship with Sean, whose attempts to define himself uniquely in relation to the hippie are stymied by her designation of all people as "beautiful." This denigration of individualism (and especially white male individualism) goads Sean, who responds by pointing to other people in the room, and grows increasingly frustrated by the hippie's refusal to judge.

"What about him?" I pointed to a guy who it was rumored had actually caused his girlfriend to kill herself and everyone *knew*. There was no way in hell the hippie could think that *he*, this fucking monster, was beautiful.

"Him? He's beautiful."

"Him? Beautiful? He killed his fucking girlfriend. Ran her over," I said.

"No way," the hippie grinned.

"Yes! It's true. Ran her straight over with a car," I said, excited.

She just shook her lovely, empty head. "Oh man."

"Can't you make distinctions?" I asked her. "I mean, our sex is great, but how can everything, everyone be beautiful? Don't you understand that that means no one is beautiful?"

"Listen man," the hippie said. "What are you getting at?"

She looked at me, not grinning. The hippie could be sharp. What *was* I getting at?

I didn't know. (97)

The hippie's refusal to make distinctions sheds an unwelcome light on Sean's own neglect of the distinction between driving a girl to suicide and running her over with a car. Her generic affirmation of everything as "beautiful" undercuts Sean's craving for distinction and eviscerates his judgments—not just his moral judgments or his judgments of taste, but his judgments about violent acts and agents—and points to the epistemic uncertainty on which they are founded (the murder is confirmed and unconfirmed: both a rumor and something that "everyone *knew*"). Sean navigates this impasse by repeating, mantralike, "I fucked the hippie." Sean's characterization of the hippie as someone he fucks inflects their relationship with violation and in this way reintroduces distinctions: not between beauties and monsters or agents and victims but between the '80s and the '60s, himself and the hippie. Though she is the first girl he liked, he is not like her, so he redescribes his fascination as alienation, not just from the hippie but from the values she represents and from his own attraction to them. The sex is terrific, the hippie is cute, but fucking counteracts the fondness, protectiveness, and even tenderness with which he recalls their relationship; with a bravado that betrays his ambivalence and uncertainty, he concludes the vignette: "This little hippie girl with a wreath on her head, looked at me as I held her and said, 'The world blows my mind.' And you know what? I fucked her anyway" (98).

"STAB": BLANK FICTION

The inarticulate violence with which Sean resists the collapse of distinctions that the hippie represents demonstrates how the literary mode of blank fiction operates within the context of Generation X. For Generation X, a sense of an inevitable complicity presents as apathy: Xers' notorious reluctance to rally in the name of an agenda or a cause. Blank fiction resists this apathy, but not in the name of any cause other than that of resistance. Blank fiction invests X's sense of complicity with an ethos of resistance, and, as such, it forces questions about the nature of reality. It does so with violence: blank fiction focuses on the role of transformation and revolution and the necessity of violence to bring it about. Like Tyler Durden who, in Chuck Palahniuk's *Fight Club*, emerges from the narrator's malaise to wreak havoc on a corporate and commoditized world, blank fiction originates from Generation X and operates within it; also like Tyler Durden, whose existence apart from the narrator is ultimately in question (is he a fantasy or a reality that threatens to overtake the narrator's?), blank fiction's resistance to commodity capitalism, however futile, reads as a dissolution of the distinction between fiction and reality and underscores the role of violence in defining each. If Coupland's "policy of storytelling" best articulates X's literary ethos, blank fiction finds its most succinct articulation in Dennis Cooper's *Frisk*, in which an account of a sex game turned real concludes with one word: "*Stab*" (64). Simultaneously the act of wounding and the experience of it, "*Stab*" abolishes the distinction between cause and effect. It disposes of volition, effaces the difference between violence's agent and victim (or continues the blurring of this distinction initiated by the voluntary aspect of the BDSM scenario). Detached, by the italics, from the narrative point of view, it seems to ascribe point of view to the text itself—a coming into consciousness of the text as violence. Cooper's *Stab* marks a departure from Ellis's image of the vest with which I opened this discussion. *Less Than Zero*'s stab's value is its verisimilitude. Muriel was attracted to Clay's vest because, recall, "*it looks like* you got stabbed or something." Cooper's "*Stab*" is performative: it unites, in action, the characters, reader, and text. Like Tyler Durden's terrorism in *Fight Club*, the reality of its violence is simultaneously real and fiction: both given *and* debatable.

Blank fiction is associated with Ellis, Palahniuk, and Cooper's "flat, affectless, atonal prose and non-committed narrative voices" ("U.S. Literature: Blank Fiction"). But true to Richard Hell's punk anthem from which the term derives, "blank fiction" reverberates with the angst of a counterculture movement; it is informed by an ethos of resistance, however inarticulate or futile. Elizabeth Young and Graham Caveney in *Shopping in Space* appropriate Hell's phrase "blank generation" for the fiction of the New York literary scene in the 1980s. For Young and Caveney, the term provides what they see as a necessary association with punk but links this apathy to '80s excess and conveys the "flat, stunned" quality of the writing (iii). James Annesley in *Blank Fictions* extends the term to U.S. literature of the 1990s in which "there is an emphasis on the extreme, the marginal and the violent. [. . .] A sense of indifference and indolence. The limits of the human body seem indistinct, blurred by cosmetics, narcotics, disease and brutality" (1). Annesley approaches this fiction with an eye to its relationship with consumer culture, a relationship that is informed by capitalism's relentless dialectic of articulation and co-option.

Robert Siegle's *Suburban Ambush,* about the 1970s and '80s New York downtown scene, is an important recourse for scholars of blank fiction. Siegle's interest is in authors like Kathy Acker and Joel Rose whose "energetic reflexivity inevitably takes one deep into a critical engagement with the social, political, and economic structures of the culture" (xiii). For Siegle, the marginal, hip, underground, or cult status of these authors lends their critiques of power/knowledge an interventionist and oppositional edge. Though some of the authors Siegle discusses (Lynne Tillman and Dennis Cooper) figure prominently in Annesley's and Young and Caveney's studies of blank fiction, Siegle dismisses Ellis, who writes what he calls "the wrong fiction" (xii). But for self-identified scholars of blank fiction—for Young and Caveney and for Annesley—Ellis is central and crucial. His role, in their work, is similar to Althusser's and Foucault's in Siegle's study: Ellis's novels provide the theoretical scaffolding from which these scholars define the nature of this fictional mode's critical engagement, its vocal but inarticulate opposition.[8]

The privileging of Ellis in scholarship of blank fiction is in part an expression of impatience with high postmodernism and with the resolutely readerly products of creative writing workshops. Young writes that blank fiction texts "seem almost blind and stunned in terms of 'literary' qualities, as if surprised to have found themselves written at all" (239; she makes an exception for Cooper). Robert Rebein in *Hicks, Tribes, and Dirty Realists* privileges the work of Raymond Carver, William T. Vollmann, Thom Jones, Lorrie Moore, and Dorothy Allison over and against what he dismisses as the "self-reflexive, end-of-the-line works of fantasy and fabulation" represented by the canonical postmodernists John Barth, Donald Barthelme, Robert Coover, William H. Gass, and Thomas Pynchon (1–2). Carver, Vollmann, Jones, Moore, and Allison represent, for Rebein, the vitalization of realism, "a new realism that is more or less traditional in its handling of character, reportorial in its depiction of milieu and time, but is at the same time self-conscious about language and the limits of mimesis" (20). For Ellis and other blank fiction practitioners, this realism's coming-to-consciousness is fun-

---

8. Baelo-Allué surveys a number of terms applied to Ellis's work (Brat Pack, postmodern, minimalism, downtown writing) and chooses blank fiction as the term that best accounts for Ellis's style (22–35).

damentally Hegelian in its reliance on violence. True to the master–slave dialectic that Hegel outlines in *Phenomenology of the Spirit,* violence will realize—in the sense of making real—and requires realization: when its epistemic validity is uncertain, it must be granted by recognition.

Because blank fiction is characterized by the blurring of the difference between reality and fiction, mimesis floats free. "It's not dates that matter, nor is it situations or personalities, it's the commercial features of the environment that provide these novels with their reference points. Blank fiction does not just depict its own period, it speaks in the commodified language *of* its period," writes Annesley (*Blank Fictions* 7). This period is one in which, as Young and Caveney put it, "it is increasingly difficult to 'see' anything, let alone render it in text through the blizzard of fall-out from an uncertain, nervously apocalyptic world which seemed constantly poised, like a psychotic at bay with no hostages, on the brink of shooting itself in the head" (20). In Young and Caveney's image (that cannot but recall Ellis's *American Psycho,* as that novel plays a prominent role in their book) violence does not communicate *about* the real; it communicates the real, and communicates the real *as violence*; to paraphrase Annesley, blank fiction does not just depict violence, it speaks its language. Violence raises the stakes of resistance and underscores blank fiction's interrogation of a world in which, as Kathy Acker puts it, "language is always fiction and true" (4).

Like Generation Xers, blank fiction writers are haunted by the vagaries of identification where there is nothing to identify with, and troubled by the nature of resistance within consumer capitalism that co-opts opposition and markets it as "alternative." Their response is to resist this culture on the level of reference. In Hell's "Blank Generation" anthem, the refrain alternates "we are all a blank generation" and "we are all a ____ generation," drawing attention to the opacity of the blank, that signifies by its refusal to signify. Blank fiction does not reflect or represent the reality in which it is written; it is an attempt to communicate the real itself in a world where, as Young and Caveney put it, "there has been an inevitable erosion of the 'real'" (19) and in which "fiction is now the closest we're likely to come to truth" (iv). Here, too, blank fiction scholars take their cue from Siegle's book. *Suburban Ambush,* subtitled *The Fiction of Insurgency,* sets as its stakes the blurring of the distinction between fiction and fact, and raises the question of resistance or revolution within the context of this blurring. "Downtown writing is insurgent," writes Siegle, "but its alpha and omega reside in the other half of the double genitive—in its status as fiction rather than revolution" (3). By forcing together the urgency of resistance and the inevitability of its failure, and locating the effects of social and political reality in fiction, Siegle sets the stage for blank fiction's uneasy relation with realism, its eschewal of a depth model of representation, and underscores the stakes of the violence, subversion, and extremism that characterize many texts in this genre, and of which Ellis's *American Psycho* is Exhibit A.

Notorious for its descriptions of rape, torture, murder, mutilation, cannibalism, sexism, homophobia, and racism, *American Psycho* turns on the distinction between reality and fiction, surface and depth. The novel is narrated by Patrick Bateman, an investment banker in Manhattan. His lifestyle is defined equally by conspicuous consumption and gruesome murders—both the consumption and the murders are rendered in excruciating, and chilling, detail. In a world in which "surface surface surface was all that anyone found meaning in" (375), Patrick attempts to find meaning *in* surface by repeated penetrations *of* it—not just with his penis, but by cutting, biting, stabbing, drilling, and, in a notorious scene, with a hungry rat. But the novel remains resolutely superficial. Like the characters' perpetual confusion of referent and reference, words and what they mean, Patrick's victims blur, or bleed, into each other and become indistinguishable and interchangeable. In dreams lit like pornography he fucks girls made of cardboard (200), and even his confession of existential angst, like his confession of his multiple murders, means "*nothing*" (377; italics in original).

The critical reception of *American Psycho* underscores the crux on which it teeters: the violence of representation and the representation of violence. These are hard to tease apart because the novel itself undoes the fundamental categories on which mimesis is predicated: the distinction of appearance from reality, surface from depth, is subject to "a slow, purposeful, erasure" (282). In one of his rare addresses to the reader, Patrick clarifies that the grounds for comparison and contrast are absent: "There is no real me," he states. "Though I can hide my cold gaze and you can shake my hand and feel flesh gripping yours and maybe you can even sense our lifestyles are probably comparable: *I simply am not there*" (377). Indeed, though his first-person narration dominates the novel, Patrick does not emerge as a narrator until after a long rant by his mirror image and alter ego Timothy Price. Initially, the two men are indistinguishable: both wear an Armani overcoat, receive exactly the same greeting, appear interchangeable to Patrick's fiancée, and Timothy, Patrick stresses, is "the only interesting person I know"

(22). But Timothy disappears: "I . . . am . . . *leaving,*" he says to Patrick, "*Leaving. Disappearing*" (60), and proceeds to run along the train tracks of the nightclub Tunnel, "disappearing into blackness" (62). Timothy returns in the novel's concluding pages, distinguished from the other characters by a smudge on his forehead that only Patrick can see and by his evident dismay with TV footage of President Reagan. "How can he lie like that," Timothy complains of Reagan (396). "He looks so . . . *normal*. He seems so . . . out of it. So . . . *un*dangerous" (397). This dismay over Reagan's lies does not translate into an affirmation of the value of truth; Timothy does not illuminate Patrick's motives. Patrick's is a world where people find meaning in surface, and in which "the lines separating appearance—what you see—and reality—what you don't—become, well, blurred" (378). Timothy, having emerged from the vanishing-point where the parallel lines of the train tracks meet, cannot quite articulate this resolute superficiality, not to mention its implications. Speaking of Reagan, Timothy reflects: "He presents himself as a harmless old codger. But inside . . . [. . .] But inside . . . ." Patrick completes the sentence with the words Timothy cannot utter: "*doesn't matter*" (397).

Beyond the controversy surrounding its publication—the details of which are by now well known—*American Psycho* has spawned an extensive tradition of criticism, much of which turns on whether its violence is "real." There is evidence that the killings and tortures may be fantasized by Patrick: his hallucinations include fantastic scenarios reported in the same affectless detail with which he enumerates his victims and their gruesome fates. At the same time, the unnerving documentary quality of these scenarios compelled Tara Baxter to describe the book as a "'How-To-Kill-Women' manual for that ever-growing special interest group: the good ol', all-Amerikan misogynists" (246) and Roger Rosenblatt to title his review "Snuff This Book." Both Baxter and Rosenblatt locate the violence to which they are responding in the world into which the novel enters; to make their arguments, they claim that the violence perpetrated or promised by the book coincides with the violence Patrick describes. Whether fictional or not, a feature of the novel's prose or a fact in the world in which the book is bought or sought, it all comes down to this: violence—particularly, in this controversy, violence against women—is *real.*

In more sophisticated assessments of the novel, violence is not something the book promises but, rather, its premise. *American Psycho* figures not as a perpetrator who must be identified, judged, and condemned, but as a helpless collaborator in violence of a more diffuse, epistemic nature. Carla Freccero locates the "real" violence in the real-world context in which Ellis writes. Abel, discussing "the level of violence launched against Ellis's novel," focuses on "the inevitability of violence that criticism does to that which it encounters" (*Violent Affect* 33). Young dismisses the distinction between real and fictional violence in favor of the text's impact on the reader: "What difference does it make whether we believe Patrick committed some, any, or all of the murders, or not?" she asks. "We still have to read all the detailed descriptions of the killings and *the effect on us is exactly the same*" (116; emphasis mine). For all, the question of whether violence does or does not occur (in the mind of the narrator or the fictional world of the novel), and where violence might or might not take place (in the text, in the reader, in society, in criticism) does not matter, or it matters less, than the fact that violence *is*. The critical discourse produces, as C. N. Serpell puts it, a "blank space, limned by the competing discourses of whatever the critic has decided Bateman represents. [. . .] And yet this blank space acts" (52). It not only acts; it moves: as "real violence" wanders from the content of the text to the context of its reception, from the mind of the psychotic narrator to the impact of the text on the reader or the market, there is no outside to which violence can be consigned, no safe space to which it can be banished, no comfortable "real" to which the reader can retreat and from which she might praise or denigrate the novel's representational quality. The novel does not offer its reader any ground from which to distance herself from the point of view of its protagonist, and no position from which to condemn his violent actions. Consequently, the categories with which to critique violence or judge it disappear.[9]

Writing of the "blank" in blank fiction, Michele Aaron describes "the mapping of an empty space for the assumption and occupation by the reader" (126), what she calls a "grafting" of the reader into the fiction. But *American Psycho* does not graft the reader into the fiction. It grafts her into the reality of the violence by which the text is occupied. The extreme violence of this text cannot be dismissed, but the possibility that the violence in the novel may be hallucinated by its protagonist blurs the line between fact and fantasy, leaving the reader unsure whether, by registering the violence, she is affirming reality or departing from it. In

---

9. Like Abel, Serpell concludes that the text leaves the reader suspended between judgment and immersion, and locates within this zone of suspension the novel's ethical stakes: *American Psycho*, Serpell concludes, forces readers to recognize their complicity in the very horrors that the novel recounts (68).

contrast with the mobility of "real violence" (a violence that moves from the content of the text to the context of its reception, from personal psychosis to social problems in the 1980s, from the atomism and alienation of consumer capitalism to the "wet snapping sounds" of Patrick's hands in a victim's stomach before she dies [305]), the text is bracketed by literary references to a hermetic hell (*American Psycho* opens with the quote from Dante's *Inferno* and closes with a reference to Sartre's *No Exit*) and dominated by Patrick's narrative voice. The novel is sealed, inscrutable, and opaque, qualities that sit uneasily with its resolute superficiality and its deadly mobility. But it will migrate to other Ellis fictions and explode in the pages of *Lunar Park*.

"IN IS OUT": EXTREME

Though the trajectory of his novels sits well within the context of Generation X (for whom he has been claimed as a poster boy) and the literary mode, within Generation X, of blank fiction (for which his work functions as a condition of possibility), Ellis is, ultimately, an uneasy fit. The functional repetition of Coupland's policy of storytelling and the blunt impact of Cooper's "*Stab*" do not quite account for *American Psycho* or for Ellis's subsequent novels *Glamorama* and *Lunar Park*. For these, the genre of the contemporary extreme helps articulate how Ellis negotiates the reality of violence, and the violence of reality, in the wake of the disappearance of epistemic certainty and any stable criteria by which violence might be evaluated. Set in a world that both solicits our recognition and resists it, contemporary extreme novels are controversial, often violent, works that challenge the distinction between the world we live in and the words we use to describe it. Durand and Mandel define contemporary extreme novels as "set in a world both similar to and different from our own, a hyper-real, often apocalyptic world progressively invaded by popular culture, permeated with technology, and dominated by destruction" (1). Brian Richardson characterizes extreme narration as positing outrageous, impossible, experimental, and eccentric narrative points-of-view that reflect a disintegration of grammatical and psychic subjectivity. Discussing a movement toward "extreme realism" in art after the 1980s, Mario Perniola describes "a disturbing experience where repulsion and attraction, fear and desire, pain and pleasure, refusal and complicity are mixed and mingled. [. . .] The meeting place between human and machine, organic and inorganic, natural and artificial, impulse and electronics, people and commodities" (4).

Located at the intersection of GenX complicity and blank fiction's refusal, the extreme reflects the ethos and attitudes of each, by way of inversion. Rather than responding or re-presenting, extremity pursues; it enhances, rather than resists. The term's connotations of political extremism—a grotesque literalization of engagement—is the flip side of the reticence that causes Xers to dismiss ideological fervor as uncool. Similarly, blank fiction's affirmation of inarticulate refusal echoes the moral outrage that extreme situations elicit: resistance is justified, even necessary, though the categories with which to articulate it vanish into the *differend*. In the 1980s and '90s "extreme" proved a potent marketing device for which resistance to the system can be distilled into a slogan, stamped on a T-shirt, advertised, and sold. In the 1990s, X replaced the "ex" of "extreme," eschewing, with the elimination of that wimpy vowel "e," any connotations of negation or belatedness: "Urban Xtreme," initially the name of a youth advisory agency that articulated the fashion of urban hipness and grunge in the United States in the early '90s, is still a vibrant, global, logo. "Extreme" subsequently moved to sport (the term "extreme sport" entered the language in 1989; the X-games were established in 1995), and cinema: Asian extreme, a genre of horror films characterized by gore, violence, and the supernatural (especially the films of Xer Park Chan-wook). In common parlance, "extreme" serves as an interjection to denote radicalism (an evolution of the 1960s' "far out"). Finally: extreme describes a physical dissolution or explosion (the etymological origin of the term traces a trembling outwards).

It is in this final sense that extremity best articulates how Ellis's novels eliminate the categories by which violence can be critiqued. Unlike *American Psycho,* which takes as its aesthetic credo Patrick's lament, "surface, surface, surface was all that anyone found meaning in," *Glamorama* is motivated by the declaration by Victor Ward (a reincarnation of Victor Johnson in *The Rules of Attraction*) that "in is out. Out is in" (17); indeed, in a series of terrorist bombings, cars, buildings, and people explode. The novel's unlikely premise involves a series of ungainly plots, some political, some cinematic, some perpetrated by an unlikely group of terrorist supermodels. The prominence of film, fashion, and imaging technology in *Glamorama* certainly evokes Perniola's extreme realism, in which images, "endowed with the strongest emotional impact," "interact with images of fashion, cinema, television, internet, graphics, advertisement, design, making possible a social imaginary characterized by provocation" (10).

Because most, but not all, of the carnage is real (some of it is a prop, and most of it is staged for one or more of the novel's ubiquitous film crews), *Glamorama* challenges the fundamental distinction between diegetic and extradiegetic, setting as the stakes of this challenge mimesis and coherence. "I don't want a lot of description, just the story, streamlined, no frills, the lowdown: who, what, where, when and don't leave out why [. . .] what's the *story?*" (5), demands Victor in the novel's opening scene, but this gesture toward origin, motivation, and design dissolves into multiple, disparate movements. Unlike Patrick, who disengages from social situations with "I have to return some videotapes," Victor moves—or quits—by splitting; his exasperated mantra is "spare me," and, in the course of the novel, he disappears, replaced, it seems, by the machinations of the political forces that are orchestrating his politician father's rise to power and have demanded, of playboy Victor, "a new you" (90). But Victor's disappearance is not, merely, the effect of violence; he has always, already, disappeared. In the novel's originary scene (a pool party at a house on Ocean Drive), Victor recalls: "The future started mapping itself out and I focused on it. In that moment I felt as if I was disappearing [. . .] floating above the palm trees, growing smaller in the wide blank sky until I no longer existed" (545).

Victor's desire for coherence ("who, what, where, when and don't leave out why") is a response to specks that he has noticed on the wall of a nightclub he is opening in the novel's first section. Like the "body parts—legs and arms and hands, *most of them real,* skidding across the platform" in the aftermath of an attack on a Paris métro station (364; emphasis mine), the specks are not reliably organic or inorganic. Nor can their presence be established unequivocally. "Everyone's acting like there's a question as to whether these specks are an illusion or a reality," declares Victor, "I think they're pretty goddamn real." But he is informed that "reality *is* an illusion" (10). The specks' reality is ultimately irrelevant, as the more important question is whether they are *in*—in the sense of being fashionable, and hence present by design—or *out* (that is, unacceptable to the up-to-the-moment hipness of the club). Initially Victor thinks the specks are part of a design: "They don't look accidental but like they were somehow done by a machine" (5). At the same time, he recognizes the distinct possibility that the specks are biological: "Specks, man, look at these fuckers. [. . .] I think they're *spreading.* I don't think that patch was here before!" (7). Both real *and* illusion, in *and* out, somatic or not, specks or specs, the specks prefigure the novel's decoupling of narrative from coherence, coherence from volition, and violence from the real so as to stage what Perniola calls "a veritable irruption of the real in the rarefied and highly symbolic world of art" (3).

Despite Victor's demands for one, *Glamorama* lacks an overarching narrative; instead of a story, there are multiple designs. Victor's own projects and schemes intersect with those of F. Fred Palakon's, Bobby's, his father's, and those of the directors of the films in which he is alternately the star, an extra, or a willing or unwilling spectator. As these designs overlap, intersect, obscure each other, peter out, and never resolve into a single explanatory account, *Glamorama* presents design as pattern, rather than purpose. Like the specks, machination (human or not) is purposive without purpose (in a novel very much concerned with beauty), and dislocates cause from effect (in a novel very much concerned with conspiracy).[10] The multiplicity of designs and their failure to resolve to a single purpose reflect the detachment from the real and its realization elsewhere; if *American Psycho* demonstrated that violence, while mobile, is firmly attached to the real (as the novel's "real violence" migrates from the content of the text to the context of its reception), *Glamorama* dismantles this attachment: Victor is dis- and reassembled as digital image manipulation sets him in situations and locales he does not remember or disavows. Even his account of disappearing, in the novel's originary scene, is subject to erasure. Recalling the pool party on Ocean Drive, "I might not even remember this afternoon, I was thinking. I was thinking that a part of me might destroy it. A cold voice inside my head begged me to" (545).

Glamorama's explicit engagement with cinema is an evolution of *American Psycho*'s reliance on cinematic terminology: the slow dissolves and jump zooms to which Patrick made occasional reference.[11] Sheli Ayers has suggested that the specks in *Glamorama*'s opening section, the confetti that pervades the novel, and the flies that Victor sees in some of the posh nightclubs he visits suggest digital pixelation. But given the novel's concern with pattern and randomness, the specks, confetti, and flies should be seen as static, not pixelated; the novel's quarrel with mimesis is worked out through the analog, not the digital. Specks, confetti, and flies

---

10. "Purposive without purpose" is, of course, Immanuel Kant's definition of aesthetic judgments of beauty in his 1790 *Critique of Judgment*. Redding ("'Merely Political'") and Schmid discuss *Glamorama*'s reliance on the narrative modes of conspiracy and paranoia, both very popular in the 1990s, as evidenced by the prominence of the TV series *The X-Files*. Jodi Dean's "Uncertainty, Conspiracy, Abduction" offers a fine account of *The X-Files*'s reliance on modes of paranoia and conspiracy in the 1990s. In contrast, I posit, the specks evince a concern about the relation of pattern and randomness (rather than presence and absence), a concern that situates the novel firmly within the epistemic shift that N. Katherine Hayles identifies with the posthuman (27).

11. Serpell, writing of the cinematic language in both novels, notes that its effect is "to convey a reality that is inseparable from simulacra" (60).

are stochastic: they point to the interpenetration of pattern and design. As static, a dot pattern that obscures the analog, they evoke and obstruct mimesis. They also evoke and undercut volition, pointing to the limits of design: like the specks, confetti may or may not be present on purpose (it may be the residue of a party or placed as a warning). The flies, too, reflect and undercut intentionality: they are drawn by the smell of excrement that pervades the spaces through which Victor moves, but these spaces, which are so cold Victor can see his breath, would freeze a fly, causing it to fall out of the air. In any case, *Glamorama* begins and ends with evaluations of magnitude ("specks" is its first word, "mountain" the last), and the specks, confetti, and flies are recast, in extreme close-up, as the wreckage in the wake of the bombing of a 747 airplane outside Paris. Pieces of the plane and of its passengers are scattered in the forest like specks of confetti, or flies frozen in flight. This scattering, too, is overlaid with a random dot pattern. "Since a cargo of party confetti and gold glitter—two tons of it—were being transported to America, millions of tiny dots of purple and green and pink and orange paper cascade over the carnage" (502).

As Victor's own presence is not documented but produced and reproduced, his quest for the story, for certainty, and for the distinction of reality from illusion dissolves. Like the flies, specks, and confetti that obscure and distract from the conspiracy theories, film scripts, terror plots, and carnage, purpose and coherence separate into discrete asignifying parts. In the novel's final scene Victor sees "billboards with answers on them: who, what, where, why." Violence, objectless, emerges from the static. Cause detached from effect, it serves no purpose: it simply *is*, "a flattening of the existent from which none is saved," as Perniola writes of extreme realism, "showing the existent without any theoretical mediation" (5). In an account of one of the many terror attacks in the novel, an authoritative third-person narrator states this explicitly: "The extent of the destruction is a blur and its aftermath somehow feels beside the point. The point is the bomb itself, its placement, its activation— that's the statement. [. . .] It's not the legs blown off, the skulls crushed, the people bleeding to death in minutes. The uprooted asphalt, the blackened trees, the benches splattered with gore, some of it burned—all this matters just as much. It's really about the will to accomplish this destruction and not about the outcome, because that's just decoration" (337).[12]

---

12. Patrick Walter, discussing this passage, makes a similar point: "Victor's boundless intellectual vacancy provides the perfect template for terrorism not because terrorists inscribe certain 'agendas' or 'answers' on this blank slate but instead because this ideo-

Given *Glamorama*'s explicit concern with cinema and imaging technology, Ellis's turn, in *Lunar Park,* to a more conventional literary form is, on the surface, surprising. But as Shaviro notes in an early review of the novel, Ellis asks serious questions about what it means to write, and to be a writer, in a postliterary age, the foremost of which speak to the implications, for authorship, of the dismantling of mimesis (*"Lunar Park"*). Richardson, discussing extreme narration, argues that the boundaries between homo- and heterodiegesis should be recognized as permeable: much is to be gained, he suggests, by not insisting on the difference between historical and implied authors. The blurring of this distinction is *autofiction,* a deliberate conflation of the autobiographical and the fictional that, as Durand and Mandel note, "lends crucial weight to the critical controversies that accrue to contemporary extreme authors and their works" (3).[13] Even as the distinction between the author and narrator is blurred in *Lunar Park,* characters from all of Ellis's previous novels people this text, a resolute intertextuality that extends Ellis's fictional world into our own.

Lunar Park is narrated by a Bret Easton Ellis who, after the terror attacks of September 11, 2001, retires to the suburbs with his wife Jayne and their two children (one of them his). Bret, who is the author of *Less Than Zero, The Rules of Attraction, American Psycho, Glamorama,* and, finally, *Lunar Park,* also attended Camden, the fictional version of Ellis's own alma mater. Consequently, the novel's setting is both realistic *and* surreal, documentary *and* futuristic; the explicitly paranormal elements of its ghost story are counterpoised with Bret's repeated assertions that this novel is a document of which "every word is true" (30).[14] Bret's description of cities as "mournful places, where everyday life was suddenly interrupted by jagged mounds of steel and glass and stone" and his reference to "the stained, tattered photocopies of the missing posted everywhere, which were not only a constant reminder of what had been lost but also a warning of what was coming next" (27–28) are pretty accurate accounts of New York City after the attacks on the World Trade Center, but *Lunar Park* is also set in a dystopia: Bret and Jayne flee the

---

logical blankness is the very basis of media terrorism as such. [. . .] The mayhem is the message; the fait accompli of the bomb expresses no other agenda or knowledge than its own taking place" (147).

13. Nielsen ("What's in a Name?") offers an extended discussion of *Lunar Park*'s engagement with the narrative mode of autofiction.

14. Karnicky has explored the multivalent implications of this truth-claim; see also Baker.

cities because urban areas are now plagued by snipers and suicide bombers, "morning papers ran aerial photographs of bombed-out buildings on the front page, showing piles of tangled bodies in the shadow of the crane lifting slabs of scorched concrete. More and more often there were 'no survivors'" (27).[15]

True to the themes of patrimony and authorship with which it is explicitly occupied, *Lunar Park* is characterized by replication. The narrator is worried by a copycat killer who is inspired by *American Psycho,* and stalked by one Clayton who leaves with the narrator a script titled *Minus Numbers,* an exact replica of the first draft of the novel that became *Less Than Zero,* complete with that draft's misspellings and typos (300). With replication comes error, mistakes that may prove to be permanent: *Lunar Park* is also concerned with mutation, as the interpenetration of fictions, and of fiction and reality, distorts and unsettles the contours of the recognizable. Finally, *Lunar Park*'s extremity takes the form of inversion: not merely turning the body inside-out as in *Glamorama* (though in *Lunar Park* bodies explode and are skinned and surfaces are slimed) but, through the dialogue it stages with *American Psycho,* in its pursuit of blankness. True to the irruption or trembling outward denoted by "extreme," blankness, in the form of the unrepresentable, is produced by the superimposition of one text, one design, over another, and the irruption of violence from within and through these patterns.

In *American Psycho,* Patrick, after an especially gruesome double murder, scrawls in blood the words "I AM BACK" on the wall of the apartment above "a scary drawing which looks like this" (306) but which is not included in the book. Patrick later returns to the apartment in which he wrote and drew but finds it immaculate, prowled by Mrs. Wolfe, a real estate agent; "a commercial where a stain walks off a jacket and addresses the camera" plays on the large-screen TV (368). Though this image of detachment of surface from surface "doesn't make me forget [. . .] the torrents of gore and the blood that had washed over the apartment, the stench of the dead, my own confused warning that I had drawn in—" (368), Patrick can no longer name the blood in which he wrote. Nor is he able to avow his authorship of the text, image, or carnage. He experiences a perpetual erasure that extends to his own body, his speech, and the world in which he moves: "Confused, I reach out for a moment to touch Mrs. Wolfe's arm, to steady myself, but I stop it in

---

15. See Godden ("Bret Easton Ellis") and Worthington for further discussion of *Lunar Park* as a post-9/11 text.

midair, move it to my chest instead, but I can't feel it." Though Patrick is, in fact, back, he cannot confirm this, and when Mrs. Wolfe dismisses him, he meekly assents. "I suggest you go," she says. "Don't come back." "I won't," Patrick promises. "Don't worry" (370).[16]

Lunar Park worries about whether Patrick is back. It is a ghost story in which Bret is haunted by his own writing, and *Lunar Park* is concerned with the theme of return—specifically, with the return of blankness, of what *did not* appear in *American Psycho*: scenes from the original manuscript that no one but the author had read, as well as childhood drawings that no one but the author has seen. *Lunar Park*'s concern with writing, drawing, authorship, and return comes to a head in its penultimate scene that points, as *American Psycho* pointed, beyond language and representation. Bret's son Bobby disappears, and when Bret does see him again, Bobby leaves Bret a drawing: "a landscape of the moon. [. . .] One word was written on it" (306). The same word—we never learn it—is written in the ash that lines the sides of the safe deposit box where Bret's father's ashes had burst from their own box. In is out; what is inside exits and, like a bomb, *American Psycho*'s hermetic quality (it is sealed by its final, famous, sentence, "THIS IS NOT AN EXIT" [399]) explodes in *Lunar Park*'s elegiac final pages, as the ashes and their unspeakable message are described as "exiting the text" (308). What is drawn but not shown, written but not published, traced but not spoken in *American Psycho* migrates to *Lunar Park* and, propelled outward, disappears into the extradiegetic: Bret describes the ashes as "losing themselves somewhere beyond my reach, and then vanished" (308).

THE GAME THAT MOVES

In *Less Than Zero* Clay, driving down Sunset Drive, notices a billboard. "All it says is 'Disappear Here' and even though it's probably an ad

---

16. Clark reads the absence of the "scary drawing" in *American Psycho* as evidence that "the words have been stripped of their referential and expressive functions; they offer no clue to a way out of the maze. The violence associated with these words cannot be located in the world." He suggests locating the site of violence "on the line that Patrick draws between appearance and reality [. . .] and 'reality' should be understood here precisely as what cannot be seen from or admitted to the world of appearances and empty signs that the characters inhabit" (26). But, as Patrick confesses to Jean, "the lines separating appearance—what you see—and reality—what you don't—become, well, blurred" (378); this blurring extends, I submit, from signification and vision to action and volition.

for some resort, it still freaks me out a little" (38). Invitation, exhortation, or warning, the commodification of escape or option or means (a final exit; a last resort), "Disappear Here" returns and reappears in Ellis's later novels. In *Glamorama* Victor twice sees the phrase when he returns to the house in Paris after learning that his fiancée Chloe has been impregnated by a Victor imposter—the initiation of the slow, purposeful erasure he will experience (474, 480). In *Lunar Park* Bret finds the words on the wall of his son's room after the boy has vanished (288). In both instances, each letter of the phrase is set in a different typeface, so that the words dissolve into asignifying parts, like specks, like the billboards Victor sees at the end of *Glamorama* with the answers to his questions (who, what, where, when, why). The point of this return is to elicit our recognition of Ellis's authorship of this intertextual world, even as typefaces recall an age in which an assemblage of letters from various print sources ensured anonymity. Simultaneously signature and threat, the phrase asserts Ellis's authorship and undermines it. He disappears here, into textuality, literariness, the product, it seems, of what Marc Augé calls "the new regime of fiction" in which "fiction invades everything and the author vanishes. The world is penetrated by a fiction without any author" (102).[17] This process extends to the attentive reader. In *Imperial Bedrooms* Clay, emerging from nightmares, encounters the words in red letters on a mirror (104). The perspective from which words on a mirror can be read obscures or blurs the mirror image of the reader. Visualize the scene, and you will see Clay vanish as "disappear here" comes into focus.

"Even though it's probably an ad for some resort, it still freaks me out a little." Clay has good reason to feel uneasy. His name invites us to think of someone who will be shaped and formed, impressed upon by his experience, but he is, as I've said, subtracted. *Imperial Bedrooms* encourages this perspective. It is, as Colby writes, a "non-narrative" (170), and the final lines of Ellis's last novel (specifically, the reference to "the game that moves as you play," one of *Less Than Zero*'s epigraphs, and a line from "The Have Nots," a song by the band X) evoke, reverse, and cross

---

17. Baelo-Allué suggests that Ellis represents a new kind of author: a celebrity author, one that embraces his or her identity as a commodity. Ellis, Baelo-Allué writes, "represents a new form of writing and selling fiction which does not hesitate to exploit the promotional techniques that used to be reserved for the entertainment industry alone. [. . .] Ellis's novels have been promoted through posters, trailers, fake web pages and TV appearances" (20). For more on Ellis's celebrity author status, see Annesly ("Brand Ellis").

out his first.[18] *Imperial Bedrooms* is signed with the date range 1985–2010, which led some readers to surmise that Ellis is, with this novel, signaling the end of his literary career (an interpretation that Ellis has not disavowed).[19]

Of course, whether Clay was there to begin with is an open question. In the final pages of *Less Than Zero,* sitting literally in the shadow of the billboard, Blair tells Clay, "You were never there." "I don't know if any other person I've been with has been really there, either," she continues, "but at least they tried. [. . .] You never did" (204). Twenty-five years since the publication of *Less Than Zero,* Ellis reaffirms the subtraction the billboard promised. Reflecting on the adaptation of *Less Than Zero* to film, Clay, in *Imperial Bedrooms,* notes his unlikely role as the film's moral center in his attempts to save Julian. *Imperial Bedrooms* corrects this error: the book is "another—and very different—movie" (10) in which Clay orchestrates Julian's murder, reappropriating, as I have said, the anomic amorality of *Less Than Zero* and qualifying the logic of image and commodity appeal that dictated the adaptation. Such work does not lend Clay substance—this is no affirmation of critique. *Imperial Bedrooms,* with its "filmlike aesthetic" (Colby 172), delivers the final *coup de grace* to Ellis's vexed relation to fiction. After Julian's abduction—"he disappears so quickly it's as if he was never here at all" (*Imperial Bedrooms* 154)—Clay retreats to a house in Palm Springs for a weekend of sexual violence and abuse, "and in the house was a copy of the book that had been written about us over twenty years ago and its neon cover glared from where it rested on the glass coffee table until it was found floating in the pool [. . .]

---

18. Baelo-Allué also notes the similarities between the opening of Ellis's 1985 debut and the conclusion of *Imperial Bedrooms,* identifying the latter as "a reworking of the famous opening of *Less Than Zero*" (191). Colby describes the evaporation of Clay's textual authority in the course of *Imperial Bedrooms*'s dialogic relation with the 1985 book. "Ellis has Clay disappear," she writes (169), and traces his elimination through the course of the text, a process that culminates in *Imperial Bedrooms*'s final sentence, "I never liked anyone and I'm afraid of people." With this sentence, which both Colby and Baelo-Allué see as a reference to "people are afraid to merge," Clay, writes Colby, "disappears into his first enunciation in 1985" (186).

19. Asked this question directly, Ellis responded in both the affirmative and with typical equivocation: "I don't know if I'm ever going to write another novel again, but that's just not how it works. I might say that, but that might not be the case. I might be feeling very differently about it a month or a year from now—I don't know. I can't answer that conclusively. I don't want this to be my last novel, but I'm also thinking about the novel—what more can be done with it? I'm interested in television right now. Television seems to be, in a way, where I want to take the novel. I want to take the novel into television" (Chaplinsky).

water bloated, the sound of crickets everywhere, and then the camera tracks across the desert until we start fading out on the yellowing sky" (*Imperial Bedrooms* 158–59). As Clay, and all the other characters in Ellis's intertextual world, disappear here, *Less Than Zero* figures as just another casualty.

Clay gave Muriel his vest because he was "too tired to say no," a lethargy characteristic of Generation X; in the wake of value's exhaustion, complicity undermines critique. Violence serves no purpose, it just is; unmoored from reference or signification, it is mobilized in blank fiction, where it functions as an inarticulate resistance without promise or premise. This pursuit of intensity leaves its object exploded or collapsed, and violence migrates outward, a moving target. Ellis's novels span this trajectory; through them, we can trace this movement toward and away from causality, toward and away from signification, toward and away from the real, as the criteria for critique—judgment, value, volition—disappear. The billboard marks the spot where they vanish into blankness. The book floats in the pool, a bloated corpse. And Bret Easton Ellis, like *Imperial Bedrooms*'s Clay, now claims a screenplay as his most recent work (*The Canyons* was released in 2013) and, like his characters Patrick and Victor, both of whom have a significant presence in cyberspace, he is especially active on Twitter. Even here, though, his inclination is to disappear. "Unfollow," he exhorts his subscribers. "Unfollow."

four
· · · · · ·

Something Empty in the Sky

9/11 after X

THE PLANES

In the opening pages of Don DeLillo's *Falling Man*, Keith Neudecker, the novel's protagonist, stumbling from the ruins of the World Trade Center, sees something empty in the sky. A shirt floats in the wind. Set against the bleak descriptions of "a time and space of falling ash and near night" (3), the shirt is "outside all this, not belonging to this, aloft." It is not fallen but falling, "lifted and drifting in the scant light and then falling again" (4). Keith, too, drifts in the course of *Falling Man*. He wanders toward and away from his estranged wife, Lianne, toward and away from Florence Givens, another survivor of the North Tower, with whom he has a brief affair. At the end of the novel Keith is disappearing. He is increasingly absent from his family, fading into the perpetual poker games in Vegas, decelerating the repetitions of his physical therapy exercises, emptying out, disintegrating, "becoming the air he breathed" (230).

Falling Man traces Keith's erasure in the days and months after he appears on Lianne's doorstep "like smoke" (8). But even before he hears or feels the North Tower's fall—"That was him coming down, the north tower" (5)—Keith sees the world from the point of view of one no longer in it. "There was something critically missing from the things around him," Keith reflects. "They were unfinished, whatever that means. They were unseen, whatever that means [. . .] Maybe this is what things look like when there is no one here to see them" (5). The novel's concluding chapter, which returns Keith to the moment of impact and traces his exit from the North Tower, pursues this subtraction. "He could not find himself in the things he saw and heard. [. . .] He watched them move into the stunned distance. That's where everything was, all around him, falling away, street signs, people, things he could not name" (246).

The empty shirt seems to counter this subtraction. Though empty, it *is*. It flickers into being in the course of the novel's parallel narrative, focalized by Lianne. Lianne works with Alzheimer's patients in an attempt to stave off her fear of the "breathless moment when things fall away, streets, names" (156), a fear that echoes Keith's sense, in the wake of the towers, that the world is retreating, "falling away, street signs, people, things he could not name." But in contrast to Keith, who disappears in the course of *Falling Man*, Lianne resolutely moves toward presence. From an early, striking image of her outlined in fog on a mirror (106), Lianne feels her body come into being; for her, as for Keith, the medium of the shirt is crucial for this work. In the concluding pages of the novel, Lianne pulls on a T-shirt and smells "just her, the body through and through. It was the body and everything it carried, inside and out, identity and memory and human heat" (236). Keith's movement to absence, and Lianne's to presence, leaves them in the same space, one peopled with nameless things and marked by erosion: "it was a small moment, already passing, the kind of moment that is always only seconds from forgetting" (236).

"In its desertion of every basis for comparison, the event asserts its singularity," writes DeLillo in his essay "In the Ruins of the Future." "There is something empty in the sky. The writer tries to give memory, tenderness, and meaning to all that howling space" (39). Together with Art Spiegelman's iconic *New Yorker* cover, that figures the World Trade Center towers as black spaces in a starry night, DeLillo's phrasing has been read as a gesture toward an overwhelming absence that fragments narrative, resists closure, and demands silence. Writing of "In the Ruins," Linda Kauffman describes DeLillo as trying "'desperately' to imagine the unspeakable"; the essay, she continues, traces "absence, emptiness, the howling space of the void: the rest is silence" (357).[1] The

---

1. Critical responses to DeLillo's essay have lingered on this phrase. The majority of them have reinforced the vein of Kauffman's lament. Conte writes: "After 9/11 the towers [. . .] must also be regarded in 'all that howling space'"; he describes the towers'

register of Kauffman's essay eloquently evokes the shock and horror that many felt in the aftermath of the terror attacks, an affect amply served by the discourse of trauma or tremendum defined by the violences of the twentieth century. But *Falling Man*'s spare prose and flat affect fit uneasily with this register, and the novel's designation of the events of September 11, 2001 as "the planes" signals a departure from this discourse. Multiple, mobile, flat surfaces, infinitely large, with zero thickness, "the planes" image 9/11 not as the limit case of perception but as a refusal of depth. What are the implications of this refusal for the reality of events that are, as many commentators have noted, strikingly similar to fiction? What does representation look like, when its object is something empty in the sky?

This chapter answers these questions by reading 9/11 after—both subsequent to and according to—Generation X. The 15-to-25-year-olds for whom, in 1985, *Less Than Zero* struck a chord are, in 2001, in their 30s and 40s, with jobs, mortgages, marriages (sometimes more than one). Of course, in the initial aftermath of the attacks, the "whatever generation" participated in the rest of the country's shock and horror. Ulrich writes that 9/11 was accompanied by proclamations of "the end of Generation X's cynical, self-indulgent, quietistic attitude" and that 9/11 was considered "the defining historical moment that would shake [Generation X] out of its cynicism and apathy, and confer upon it some sort of concrete identity and coherent, meaningful purpose" (29–30). But he notes that such proclamations did not retain their credibility and Generation X remains uneasily poised between the alternative and the mainstream, its allegiances in question, its definition negotiable, its identity appropriable, and its "truths" to be determined.

---

absence as "the epitome of mourning and collective trauma" (560). Walker reads De-Lillo's "howling space" as "the terror narrative that threatens to overwhelm all," and the novelist's response as "to insist upon a return to narrative as personal, partial, incomplete, to contribute to the limitless mosaic of plots that do not insist upon domination" (337). Versluys, discussing DeLillo's essay, does not reference this phrase directly, though his focus on "a communion of telling, which somehow fills the void caused by the attacks and offsets the murderous intents of the terrorists" (20) certainly echoes its sentiment. Abel's reading of "In the Ruins" departs from this trend: his interest is more on the essay's ethos of movement (its treatment of acceleration, deceleration, and speed); "In the Ruins" speaks, Abel concludes, to the response literature can posit to real-world violence (*Violent Affect* 189). In an earlier incarnation of his argument, Abel does quote DeLillo's reference to "something empty in the sky" ("'Ruins of the Future'" 1246); his focus there on the writer's response to 9/11, and he concludes that "the writer does not know if his effort will succeed." Abel's refusal of a discourse of trauma, and his reluctance to affirm terminology of moral clarity, leads Versluys to dismiss his argument as "erudite but misconceived" (196n1).

I examine three 9/11 novels by X authors: Frédéric Beigbeder's *Windows on the World*, Claire Messud's *The Emperor's Children*, and Jess Walter's *The Zero* (an additional 9/11 novel by an Xer, Jonathan Safran Foer's *Extremely Loud and Incredibly Close*, is discussed in the following chapter). Beigbeder's 9/11 novel is one of the first; Messud's has been treated harshly by critics; Walter's has been relatively neglected.[2] These novels offer me the opportunity to elicit an X attitude to the reality of 9/11, its immediacy, its presumed epochality, and its affective charge. Each contains what DeLillo calls a counternarrative, in which a character claims, falsely, to have lost someone in the attacks. In Beigbeder's *Windows on the World*, the French author (also named Frédéric Beigbeder) travels to New York City as part of his book project to write the fictional story of Carthew Yorston, a man his own age, and his two young sons who are trapped in the Windows on the World restaurant at the top of the World Trade Center. In New York, in conversation with someone who asks him why he's writing about 9/11, he gives, as an answer, that his cousin died in the restaurant with his children (the narrator/author lost no family in the attacks). In Claire Messud's *The Emperor's Children*, a young man—the character's name is Bootie Tubb—treats the attacks of 9/11 as an opportunity to vanish from his life and begin anew. He takes a bus to Miami, renames himself Ulrich New (after Robert Musil's *The Man without Qualities*), and allows his friends and family to believe he is dead. In Jess Walter's *The Zero*, the protagonist—Brian Remy, a First Responder—is called to a family meeting with his ex-wife Carla to learn that his son, Edgar, has been telling everyone in school that his father had died in the attacks. Edgar refuses

---

2. Duvall and Marzec include a brief discussion of *The Zero* (385–88) in their introduction to a special issue of *Modern Fiction Studies*, "Fiction After 9/11." They describe Walter's novel as "an undervalued text that might complicate the current discussion of 9/11 fiction" (389), stress its satiric quality, note its treatment of paranoia, and praise its political engagement with the "War On Terror" (388). Since the *MFS* issue was published in 2011, a few article-length studies of Walter's novel have appeared in print. Duvall's "Homeland Security and the State of (American) Exception(alism)" stresses the novel's "ludic postmodernism" as an assertion of irony's resilience after 9/11 (281), and Aaron DeRosa's "Alterity and the Radical Other in Post-9/11 Fiction" compares DeLillo's and Walter's representations of terroristic alterity. Both Duvall and DeRosa stress the novel's political valences: like me, they see in *The Zero* an opportunity to articulate an alternative approach to the discourse of national exceptionalism and the priority of trauma in 9/11 fiction. Kristine Miller's "Reading and Writing the Post-9/11 Cop" compares the representation of Remy, the traumatized First Responder, to firsthand oral histories to argue against the opposition of private trauma and its public representation; like me, Miller sees in the novel an opportunity to "examine the presumed boundaries between fiction and nonfiction, fantasy and reality, language and experience" (31).

to apologize: "Don't tell me I shouldn't be devastated by the death of my father just because he isn't dead!" he says (35).

Writing of the counternarrative, DeLillo posits it as a site where correction and conspiracy, accuracy and inaccuracy, witness and fiction combine. "For the next fifty years, people who were not in the area when the attacks occurred will claim to have been there. In time, some of them will believe it. Others will claim to have lost friends or relatives, although they did not" ("Ruins" 37). Tellingly, DeLillo does not follow this observation with injunctions to specificity: fiction and fact, experience and its appropriation, art and documentation join forces in his imagination of a literary response to 9/11.[3] For the novels discussed in this chapter, the counternarrative offers an opportunity to revise the relation of violence to the real at precisely this, an event heralded as the "return of the real." But, I submit, their approach to 9/11 is not an expression of youthful X 'tude. It opens up an approach to violence that refuses the affective ethos of trauma, the singularity of U.S. exceptionalism, and the presumption of fidelity that, in the informal patriotic fervor and official bellicose rhetoric, assumed such murderous manifestations in the months and years following the attacks.

Robert Capa, who coined the phrase "Generation X," described as the main problem for that generation the question of "going to war or not" (Whelen, qtd. in Ulrich 31). Recalling Capa's question, John Ulrich reflects, in 2003, that "Generation X must once again grapple with this same problem, as the Bush administration expands its war on terrorism to include military action against nations it suspects of developing weapons of mass destruction and providing assistance to the al-Qaeda terrorist network" (31). When suspicion affects patriotism, and the enemy is determined by the channel you subscribe to, the real threat is what you

---

3. In his willingness to abandon the distinction between fiction and fact, DeLillo continues Derrida's meditation on the paradox of testimony and literature in his 1998 *Demeure: Fiction and Testimony*. For Derrida, testimony, by definition, contains the possibility that it may be a fiction. "There is no testimony that does not structurally imply in itself the possibility of fiction, simulacra, dissimulation, lie, and perjury—that is to say, the possibility of literature," he writes in *Demeure* (29), and describes literature as "*the name without the thing*" (20). Just five years later Derrida's concept of literature features in his confrontation with the events of 9/11: in "Autoimmunity: Real and Symbolic Suicides," "September 11," too, is the name without the thing: "We perhaps have no concept and no meaning available to us to name in any other way this 'thing' that has just happened," he suggests (86), and locates in the repetition or reiteration of "9/11" an attempt "to conjure away, as if by magic, the 'thing' itself, the fear or the terror it inspires" and an attempt "to deny [. . .] our powerlessness to name in an appropriate fashion, to characterize, to think the thing in question" (87).

choose to believe it to be. It may even (as it is for David Simpson) be the role of belief in politics (Simpson 149). This X approach, with its attention to the variances of fidelity, also illuminates other 9/11 novels, dismissed or ignored by critics, that thoughtfully and courageously confront the attacks and their aftermath, as I demonstrate in my discussion of Jay McInerney's *The Good Life* and Ken Kalfus's *A Disorder Peculiar to the Country.* Though neither falls within the X demographic, McInerney and Kalfus, like DeLillo, employ Xers as characters through whom to focalize 9/11, and offer me an opportunity to examine what an X approach to 9/11 makes possible. Finally, I return to *Falling Man,* reading it after, or under the sign of, X: a simultaneity of presence and absence, an epistemic validity that, like something empty in the sky, disappears here. But before I do any of this: true to an event characterized by multiplicity, by twinning, by simulation and replaying, I want to pause, to rewind, and to begin this chapter again.

REALITY CHECKS

In Claire Messud's *The Emperor's Children,* Baby Boomer Murray Thwaite and Generation Xer Danielle Lipkoff awake from a night of passion in Danielle's apartment, a room with a view of downtown Manhattan, on the morning of September 11, 2001. After the shock of the initial impact,

> They lived the next hour and a half in stereo, watching through a window [. . .] and watching on the screen, as if they were simultaneously in Manhattan and anywhere on the planet [. . .] and everything they saw seemed somehow more and less real on the television because what they saw with their own eyes they couldn't quite believe. [. . .] What took place outside the window could have been credited as sorcery, some trick of the light, almost comical, so absurd, were it not for the fact that it was being filmed—the filming of it the assurance of its reality: the whole world was seeing this, and the Pentagon, too, and this was how you knew that it was really true. (411–12)

9/11 has widely been described as the inversion of the relation of fiction and reality. The real-time nature of the attacks, combined with their similarity to a disaster movie, invite reflection on the relation of reality to image and the pre-eminence of spectacle in the discursive construc-

FIGURE 5. City Workers in London Watch News of Terrorist Attacks in America. September 11, 2001. Laura Tanner writes, "For spectators around the globe, the proliferation of images rendered the 9/11 attacks spectacularly immediate yet simultaneously unreal" (59). © Reuters/Corbis.

tion of truth. This brief moment in Messud's novel parses the sense that real violence is not so much experienced as it is, like the reality of reality TV, produced.[4] Both affirmed and undercut by television, reality is registered as a matter of degree, wavering between paucity and surplus: more and less real. Authenticity, represented by experiential certainty, is similarly undercut. The twin images—the view through the window

---

4. Joseph Natoli's *This Is a Picture and Not the World* explores the extent to which cinema shapes perception of reality—especially after 9/11. In an introductory chapter framed as an interview, Kevin Nicholoff presents the formal refutation of Natoli's theory: "But the attack itself—that was real. People died. That was real. Those towers are gone. That's real." Natoli's response is worth quoting at length: "Sure. It's an historical fact. Place, date, and all. Like Pearl Harbor. Vietnam. Wait. Aren't those historical events, like all historical events, now imagined within the dimensions of a present cultural imaginary? Their existence is at once a matter of representation, which is a matter of cultural mediation. The 9/11 attack was unique in that it happened on our TV screens at the same time it happened in the world. From the very first TV images of a plane and a building the event went through the kind of mediating filtering TV gives to reality and we give to TV. At once, what we saw on TV was like a movie and we could digest it no other way" (14–15).

and the image on the screen—dislocate Danielle and Murray, who find themselves "simultaneously in Manhattan and anywhere on the planet," an undoing of "the profound disparity between the lived experiences of those 'on the ground' and the vast audience watching [that] is a dominant theme in the 'literature of Terror'" (Randall 2).

To say that 9/11 represents an inversion of the relation of fiction to reality is to return to Baudrillard's and Žižek's early responses to the attacks. Both suggest that, despite the horror, trauma, and wrenching loss of life, the violence offered some respite from the hyperreal, virtual world of globalized commodity capitalism. "We thought we had seen (perhaps with a certain relief) a resurgence of the real, and of the violence of the real, in an allegedly virtual universe," writes Baudrillard. But, he continues, such an impression belies the centrality of the image in which reality and fiction are intertwined. "Rather than the violence of the real being there first, and the frisson of the image being added after, the image is there first, and the frisson of the real is added. Something like an additional fiction, a fiction surpassing fiction" (27–29). Žižek disagrees: "*We should not mistake reality for fiction*—we should be able to discern, in what we experience as fiction, the hard kernel of the Real which we are able to sustain only if we fictionalize it" (*Welcome* 19; italics in original). In the wake of the attacks and of the subsequent war on terror to which Baudrillard and Žižek are responding, the question of whether the real has become fiction, or whether it is inextricable from its own fictionalization, is a nice point. The more salient point is that concern with the real—its availability, its attraction, and the epistemic certainty it represents—is an expression of what Alain Badiou calls the "passion for the real" characteristic of the twentieth century, for which "the real, conceived in its contingent absoluteness, is never real enough not to be suspected of semblance. [. . .] Nothing can attest that the real is the real, nothing but the system of fictions wherein it plays the role of the real" (*Century* 52). Badiou concludes that this passion for the real is the passion for the authentic, an affirmation of identity that is inextricable from destruction and purification (56). It is part and parcel of the logic that authored the atrocities and horrors that characterized the previous century.[5]

---

5. Discussing the events of 9/11, Badiou states that designating the destruction of the World Trade Center as an "attack," and the corresponding affect implied in such designation, is an expression of this passion. "It has a *fin de siècle* ring to it, but it is of another century" (*Polemics* 15). The nihilistic logic of the passion for the real, Badiou will go on to argue, is shared by the "War against Terrorism."

One may identify this logic in the reverence accorded to empirical validity in the wake of disaster, especially in early responses to the attacks. John Frow observed, in 2003, that 9/11 "figures as something like a bedrock of fact," obscuring the extent to which "brute reality" is constructed as such (76). When this "brute reality" is extended to the forms, shapes, and meanings an event may assume, injunctions of fidelity to it work to limit the kinds of sense—critical or fictional—one can make, with the effect not of imagination's abnegation but of its legislation and, by extension, a legislation of the kinds of responses, both personal and political, we can have. Speaking of U.S. public discourse in the months that followed the attacks, Judith Butler laments the alignment of grief and mourning with silence and consent, when any attempt to "understand" was considered a legitimation of the attacks and an exoneration of the perpetrators. Jacques Derrida, speaking of the same period, describes "being made to feel that it is actually forbidden, that you do not have the right, to begin speaking of anything, especially in public, without [. . .] making an always somewhat blind reference to this date" ("Autoimmunity" 87). His response is to focus on "9/11," recasting its refusal of reference as an invitation to critique. "We do not in fact know what we are saying or naming in this way [. . .] We do not recognize or even cognize, that we do not yet know how to qualify, that we do not know what we are talking about" (86).

These early evocations of 9/11's challenge to reference figure prominently in more recent studies of literary texts that take as their subject the terror attacks. "9/11 is unpossessable," writes Kristiaan Versluys, "it is a limit event that shatters the symbolic resources of the culture and defeats the normal processes of meaning making and semiosis" (1). "If there was one thing writers agreed about in response to 9/11, it was the failure of language; the terrorist attacks made the tools of their trade seem absurd," asserts Richard Gray (1). Both cite Derrida, and for both, trauma theory proves a useful tool with which to evaluate and analyze these texts. Indeed, trauma theory is the dominant paradigm through which 9/11 fiction is approached, a point reiterated by John N. Duvall and Robert P. Marzec in their introduction to a special issue of *Novel: A Forum on Fiction* devoted to 9/11 (395–96). The purview of trauma studies is the relation of history to violence: the inability of history to master violence and the crucial work of witness and attestation to history that violence demands. Trauma *happened,* and while it can be registered as presence or absence, directly or indirectly, both acting out trauma and working through it (to borrow terminology from Dominick

LaCapra) testify to its reality and to the violence of this reality. When history is trauma, its violence is real: trauma, as a discourse, checks reality's unstable, multiple, and mobile quality. For Xers, though, reality is checked not through traumatic experience but through television. Witnessing simultaneously through her window and her television set, Danielle reflects that "she had seen the people jumping, from afar, specks in the sky, and she knew that's what they were only from the TV, from the great reality check of the screen" (414).

Like Messud's *The Emperor's Children*, Frédéric Beigbeder's *Windows on the World* and Jess Walter's *The Zero* treat 9/11 as an event that is both "more and less real," and examine the nature of truth when reality (what's "really true") is confirmed by mechanical reproduction—the fact of being filmed. For all, perception, witness, memory, and mastery of 9/11 are informed by television, specifically, their acquaintance with televisuality: replaying, rewinding, repeating. Televisuality dictates, for each, their perception of causality. The sequence of events is available to be reordered, as is the inexorable quality of cause and effect: the grammatical core not only of violence itself but of the narratives constructed around it. For these X authors—as for McInerney, Kalfus, and DeLillo—infidelity, in the form of lies, affairs, and inaccurate mimesis, provides a site wherein violence's relation to the real is evaluated, negotiated, and revised. All these novels take seriously the terror attacks' quality as more and less real and, while none denies that 9/11 *happened,* each submits that the happening of an event—its brute facticity—is not sufficient to ensure its reality. If violence is real or not "really" violent, a violent event that is both more *and* less real invites questions about the kind of truth claims that surround it.

MISSION IMPOSSIBLE

The attempt to achieve a profound, "true" experience through fiction—and the inevitable failure of this attempt—dominates Frédéric Beigbeder's *Windows on the World*.[6] The novel's structural conceit posits fact and fiction in parallel. Beigbeder employs two narrators. The first is

---

6. Beigbeder's novel received mixed reviews from critics. It was termed "disgusting" and "obscene" (qtd. in Wyatt), eliciting charges of sensationalism (Brownrigg), "kitsch" (Laura Miller), and "schlock" (Lacey). More sympathetic reviews expressed admiration for Beigbeder's attempt "to imagine the unimaginable" (Douthat 50), even if the result produces what Douthat calls "a bad book" (50).

fictional: Carthew Yorston, an American from Texas, who is trapped in Windows on the World with his two young sons. The second narrator is Beigbeder himself, in an explicitly autobiographical, or autofictional, portrayal. The American Carthew Yorston and the French Frédéric Beigbeder (both parents of young children, both in their 40s, both divorced) are, like the towers, mirror images. Pursuing this logic of mimesis, Beigbeder sits in Le Ciel de Paris, the restaurant at the top of the Tour Montparnasse in Paris and the French equivalent of Windows on the World, in order to acquire some sense of what it must have been like for Yorston. The novel is thus structured as an experiment in experiential commensurability: it tests the power of literature to evoke experience, and as an experiment, it is cognizant, early on, that it will fail. As the narrator Beigbeder puts it, "For me to be able to describe what took place on the far side of the Atlantic, a plane would have to crash into this black tower beneath my feet" (8).

Of course, a plane does not hit the Tour Montparnasse, and, despite all his attempts to imagine it, the closest Beigbeder can get to his subject is an overpriced restaurant in the ugliest building in Paris (the best thing about the view from the Tour Montparnasse, he says, is that you can't see the Tour Montparnasse [7]). Even though the author brings his three-year-old daughter to the restaurant for breakfast, thinking of Yorston with his children in Windows on the World, this principle of equivalence is necessarily doomed. Beigbeder will never know what he wants to learn. Reciting a bleak list of facts—numbers, figures, estimations of quantity and force—he concludes by reiterating the novel's compelling opening sentence: "You know how it ends: everybody dies" (1). "Obviously," he later reflects, "this piece of information removes any element of suspense from this book. So much the better: this isn't a thriller; it is simply an attempt—doomed perhaps—to describe the indescribable" (55). The novel's tendency to dwell on its limits has dominated its critical reception. Alain-Philippe Durand, in his seminal 2006 account of the novel and its reception, sets the stakes of *Windows on the World* in these terms: "Can literature transcribe the unspeakable, and if so, how?" (109). Characteristically, the narrator asks himself that very question. His answer is this: "The only interesting subjects are those that are taboo. [. . .] Nowadays, books must go where television does not. Show the invisible. Speak the unspeakable. It may be impossible, but that is its *raison d'être*. Literature is a *Mission Impossible*" (295).

This affirmation of transgression seems appropriate for an early novel about 9/11 that comes so close to its topic—"the black smoke

seeping from the floor, the heat melting the walls, the exploded windows, the asphyxiation, the panic, the suicides, the headlong stampede
to stairwells already in flames, the tears and the screams, the desper-
ate phone calls" (9). Like most affirmations of transgression, it leaves
intact the distinction between representation and its object, just as dis-
obedience leaves intact the power structure from which the subject is
delinquent. But this assertion of the power of literature is interrupted by
television. *Mission Impossible* is italicized and capitalized (the French
original has it in quotation marks), referencing the iconic American television series that ran from 1966 to 1973, spawned a remake and several
films and is still immediately, viscerally recognizable by the opening bars
of its soundtrack. At the point of transgression, the gesture toward the
limits of representation, this statement about the book's *raison d'être,* its
claim for *literature,* literature, going beyond television, *is* television (that
the television program in question is an American import is appropriate—Beigbeder has affirmed his fondness for U.S. culture).

The limits of representation are thus linked to a logic of inversion.
This logic (in which each of the X authors discussed in this chapter participate, and to which we return in the discussion of *The Zero,* below) is
reinforced when Beigbeder, again, gestures toward representation's limits.
As he ruminates on the terrorists' motivations, Beigbeder recalls Jacques
Martin's TV show *Incredible but True,* and reflects on the challenge to
representation posed by 9/11: "It was an event which was unforesee-
able because it was impossible. It was, quite literally, incomprehensible,
by which I mean it passes human understanding" (264). He then offers
a list ("check box as applicable") building up to a re-enactment of the
TV show in which Martin would suggest "Incredible, but . . ." and participants would answer, "TRUE!" Like "Mission Impossible," the passage traces a closed circuit in which television is both within and beyond
the limits of representation. Television, in fact, determines and defines
representation and its limits. Beigbeder's brave gesture toward taboo,
his evocation of the unthinkable, the unspeakable, his move beyond the
limits of imagination and certainly beyond the mundanity of television,
returns him to the TV shows of his childhood. 9/11 is a repeat, a replay,
a remake.

This is not to say that *Windows on the World* fails, or that it embraces
the limits of imagination in the context of disaster. Even as it acknowledges the limits of its structural gambit (the parallels of its mimetic sym-
metries collapse), televisuality, fantasy, and fiction come to the fore as
active agents in the construction of 9/11 under the sign of simultaneous

affirmation and negation. In the course of the novel, Beigbeder abandons Le Ciel de Paris and travels to New York City on the Concorde. Because the Concorde travels so quickly—it takes off from Paris at 10 a.m. and lands in New York City two hours earlier—Beigbeder is moving through time as well as through space. Essentially, he is rewinding. Time travel is cheap, says Beigbeder, "the price of a Chanel dress" (150); sitting in the '70s-style Concorde lounge, he muses, "I think I'm writing about September 11, but actually I'm writing about the seventies: the decade that spawned the WTC, the Tour Montparnasse, and the Concorde [. . .] of which three two no longer exist" (150–51). In the final chapter, as he returns to Paris, Beigbeder addresses the reader, inviting her to imagine him lying on the floor of the airplane, "fists clenched stretched towards the cockpit. [. . .] And do you know what I thought?" he continues, "That if I just closed my eyes and took away the cabin, the engines and all the other passengers, I'd be alone in the ether, 30,000 feet up, speeding through the blue at supersonic speed. Yes, I thought I was a super-hero" (303). The reference, of course, is to Superman, who, in the 1978 film, circled the earth so many times he reversed its rotation, turned back time, and resurrected his love Lois Lane. But the reference is also to an earlier moment in the novel when Beigbeder's fictional creation Carthew, still in the inferno of the burning tower, snaps at his son: "David, I'm not Superman! I wish I was!" (191). Beigbeder's gesture, in the novel's final sentence, is a double homage: both to the films of his childhood and to the fantasies of his fictional character's kids.

Beigbeder's visit to New York City is instigated by an axial moment in the novel when his character, Carthew, addresses the narrator/author directly. Reflecting on the jumpers from the towers, Beigbeder suggests that to leap from a burning building represents "one last mani-festation of dignity: they will have chosen their end rather than waiting resignedly. Never has the expression 'freefall' made more sense" (148). Carthew, who will jump from the burning building, addresses Beigbeder (the only moment in the novel when he does so) and contradicts him. "Bullshit, my dear Beigbeder. [. . .] You don't jump 1,300 feet because you're a free man. You jump because you're a hunted animal. You don't jump to preserve your humanity, you jump because the fire has reduced you to a brute beast. The void is not a rational choice. It's simply the only place that looks good from up there, somewhere you ache for, somewhere that doesn't slash your skin with white-hot claws, doesn't put out your eyes with searing-hot pokers. The void is a way out" (149). This direct address from his fictional character propels Beigbeder to abandon his attempt to achieve experiential commensurability in Paris. "OK, Carthew, if you're going to be like that, I'll go to New York. I realize the Tour Montparnasse isn't the third World Trade Center tower" (150). He chooses, instead, affective engagement, traveling to New York City on the Concorde, seeking, through physical proximity, to traverse the experiential incommensurability on which his novel is premised.

In Manhattan Beigbeder relishes his position as a dark tourist, a voyeur of horror. "I circle the building like a vulture in search of corpses. I wander the vertical streets breathing in fresh calamity. A writer is a jackal, a coyote, a hyena. Give me my dose of desolation" (235). He seeks out a former employee of Windows on the World and engages him in conversation, introducing himself as a French writer who is writing about the restaurant. Asked why, he answers, "Because my grandmother was American—her name was Grace Carthew Yorstoun, and I didn't go to her funeral" (298). This exchange—which appears immediately after Beigbeder's reflection on why he was drawn to this topic—posits, alongside the aesthetic credo ("show the invisible, speak the unspeakable") something more personal: the missed experience propels a fictional re-enactment. For Beigbeder's interlocutor in this scene, the logic behind this explanation, or the explanation itself, remains obscure. But the reason varies between the 2003 French original and the 2004 English translation. "I'm sorry Sir," Beigbeder's interlocutor says, "but I don't understand what you're talking about. [. . .] I've got work to do. *And I don't understand french.* You're bothering me, Mister!" reads the French original (2003, 364–65; emphasis mine). In the English translation, "I don't understand french" is replaced with "I don't care about your grandmother" (2004, 298). It is understandable, of course, that the English phrases that pepper the prose of the original text would require some reworking for an American audience with no command of the French-English hybrid, *Franglais,* in which most of the novel is written. But the conversation heightens the tension between knowledge (what Beigbeder, in the Tour Montparnasse, failed to achieve) and caring (what he, as an Xer, is reputably unlikely to do).

The tension between knowledge and caring is made quite explicit in the author's note, where the occasion of the novel's translation into English identifies the tension between knowing and caring as a matter of translation of fact into fiction. The purpose of this note is ostensibly to explain why some of the graphic depictions of sex acts and some references to the Holocaust were cut from the English version. Beigbeder couches this omission in terms of fiction, fact, and tact. "A novel is a fiction; what is contained within its pages is not truth. The only way to know what took place in the restaurant [. . .] is to invent it," writes Beigbeder, and continues: "merging fiction with truth—and with tragedy—risks hurting whose who have already suffered, something of which I was intensely aware when rereading the novel in English—the language in which the tragedy *happened*" (307; emphasis mine). He concludes abruptly: "Consequently some scenes have been revised for this edition" (307). It is hard to believe that Beigbeder (who, Durand reports, did not want to endorse the cuts) is not being disingenuous here.[7] But by stating that 9/11 happened in English Beigbeder posits the original as, itself, a translation, and suggests that despite the novel's multiple gestures toward immediacy, experience is inextricable from mediation.

A *Franglais* text with an English title about an event that "happened" in English, *Windows on the World* both demands translation and resists it. As would be expected, the Tower of Babel is a recurring motif, and the image of Babel in this novel reveals a great deal about the novel's relationship to the languages in which it is written, even as the story of architectural hubris, divine punishment, and linguistic confusion seems more than apt as a metaphor for the novel's subject. Both narrators quote the Genesis text (55–56, 82, 117); Carthew, marooned in the North Tower, meditates on the appropriateness of the fable to his situation ("the Tower of Babel? I wonder if that's where I am now" [116]); Beigbeder cites a myth that there were, in fact, two (or twin) towers of Babel (231–32); and in the elegiac penultimate chapter, the absent towers seem to be resurrected as the text runs in parallel columns on the page (301–2). But the bilingual quality of *Windows on the World* powerfully counteracts the Babel metaphor: the *Franglais* in which much of the novel is written is characterized as "a global language, one that defies God: the single language of Babel. Les words du world" (135) [La langue mondiale, celle qui désobéit à Dieu: la langue unique de Babel. Les words du world (2003, 175)].[8] Given the prominence of the Babel motif, translation (both between languages and from fact into fiction) is the site where the demands of knowledge and of empathy collide. When "I don't understand" translates to "I don't care," the conflicting demands of affect and fact must be approached in terms other than those

---

7. "Officially, the editing was Beigbeder's decision," writes Durand. "In reality, it was one of several requests the publishers imposed upon Beigbeder" ("Beyond the Extreme" 114).

8. For a different reading of this passage, see Schehr (137).

of fidelity and infidelity, the logic of which has dominated the novel's reception.[9]

The interpenetration of fact, fiction, English, and French as a source of affective urgency is the crux of this conversation with the former Windows on the World employee, and it is here that the counternarrative makes its appearance. To Beigbeder's claim for American heritage (one that, he says, goes back to Daniel Boone), his interlocutor rejoins, in English, "So what?" Beigbeder responds, also in English, "We do not hate you." He continues, in French:

> "You scare us because you rule the world. But we're blood relations. France helped your country to be born. Later, you liberated us. And my cousin died in your restaurant on September 11, 2001, with his two sons."
> I don't know why I lied like that. I wanted to move him. Cowardice makes you a pathological liar. Carthew Yorstoun was my grandmother's family name. Take out a "u" and you have Carthew Yorston, a fictional character. (299)

In this bilingual exchange, the interrelation of French and English extends into the relation between fiction and fact: the name of the novel's fictional character is produced by removing a "u" from an existing French name. In English, "u" sounds like "you," suggesting that the production of fiction is predicated on an erasure of alterity, and implying that the original French of the novel is not the only language in which it can be read (hence, perhaps, its English title).

Mimicking the collapse of the personal and the political in Beigbeder's identification both as and with Americans, the linguistic interrelation between French and English extends to France and the United States. "We're blood relations. France helped your country to be born. Later, you liberated us"—these sentences extend Beigbeder's consanguineous affiliation with the United States (via his grandmother, Grace Carthew Yorstoun) to relations between the two nations and, even more globally, between the nation and its Other, "we" and "you." Real con-

---

9. My "Fiction et fidélité: *Windows on the World*" (2008) focused on the prominence of fidelity and infidelity in the novel's reception. Subsequent scholarship on *Windows on the World* has turned away from this paradigm to focus on the novel's explicit aestheticization of 9/11, tracing how Beigbeder elicits from the event a new representational system. See Lawrence R. Schehr ("Éffondrements") and Mihaela P. Harper ("Turning to Debris").

sanguinity, in its metaphorical form, is refracted through the prism of novelistic imagination to confer reality on to a fictional character. With "my cousin died in your restaurant," Beigbeder claims that Carthew Yorston is real although Carthew, who dies with his sons in Windows on the World, is "real" only within the pages of *Windows on the World*. Meditating on this statement, Beigbeder confesses, "I don't know why I lied like that. I wanted to move him. Cowardice makes you a pathological liar."

As the transnational context merges with the interpersonal one, a need to "move" (*attendrir*), to elicit an emphatic response, propels Beigbeder toward fiction. The author lies, distorts, alters the truth, takes leave of the facts. He does so not as a gesture of fidelity to a different order of truth (he doesn't know why he lied), and not out of bravado in face of representative taboos (he describes his act as "cowardly"), but in order to move his interlocutor, to make him care. This moment in the novel echoes an earlier meditation on the relation of fiction to reality that led Beigbeder to conclude, "since September 11, 2001, reality has not only outstripped fiction, it's destroying it. It's impossible to write about this subject, and yet impossible to write about anything else. Nothing else touches us" (8) [Depuis le 11 septembre 2001, non seulement la réalité dépasse la fiction mais elle la détruit. On ne peut pas écrire sur ce sujet mais on ne peut pas écrire sur autre chose non plus. Plus rien ne nous atteint (2003, 18)]. As being touched (*atteindre*) by reality propels Beigbeder to a fiction that moves (*attendrir*), the initial tension between caring and understanding is extended from a specific instance of translation to a much broader realm: defined not by mimesis but by movement, not by affect but by fiction, not by authenticity but by recycled images. In this realm, the role of literature is not to capture reality but to move its readers into a different relationship to it. The final image of that relationship—Beigbeder's mimicry of Superman—casts it as an homage to precisely such a wishful fantasy.

POISED IN THE VOID

For many scholars of 9/11 literature, the ethics and aesthetics of trauma demand disrupted, fragmented texts that attest to the *limits* of fiction. "The best 9/11 novels are diffident linguistically," writes Versluys, "the narratives shy away from the brute facts, the stark 'donnée' of thousands of lives lost. As an event, 9/11 is limned as a silhouette, expressible only through allegory and indirection" (14). Martin Randall, too, eschews "realist fiction" in favor of "hybrid forms" that attest to the challenge 9/11 poses to representation. Richard Gray demands of 9/11 texts "an enactment of difference: not only the capacity to recognize that some kind of alteration of imaginative structures is required to register the contemporary crisis, to offer testimony to the trauma of 9/11 and its consequences, but also the ability and willingness imaginatively to act on that recognition" (29–30).[10] Given these criteria, *The Emperor's Children* is not a "good" 9/11 novel, and critical responses to Messud's novel have been quite dismissive of its treatment of 9/11. The privileged background of some of her characters, the realism of her prose, and her reliance on the structure of the family romance—all are treated as evidence that the novel insufficiently registers the gravity of the events. For Randall, for example, *The Emperor's Children* raises "the question of how such a traumatizing event can be accommodated within a realist fiction" (67).

With its title, *The Emperor's Children* invites reading in terms of generational relations. The novel is set in 2001, and populated with members of the New York liberal elite Thwaite family and their friends. Boomers Murray Thwaite and his wife, Annabel, are associated with 1960s idealism, with great causes and social justice. Murray, who has great success in his practice of what he calls "moral journalism," is occupied with railing against injustice in the world and the state of liberalism in America. Annabel is preoccupied with her activities as a children's rights lawyer. Their daughter, Marina (born in 1970), and her college friends, Danielle Minkoff and Julius Clarke, are Xers. Marina, a child of privilege, lives with Annabel and Murray in a spacious Central Park West apartment and toys with the idea of writing a book. Danielle and Julius lead less comfortable lives in Lower Manhattan. Danielle, the daughter of an Ohio contractor, struggles as a documentary filmmaker; Julius, the biracial son of a Green Beret who met his wife while on tour in Vietnam,

---

10. Smith departs from the tenor of this approach: responding to Gray's argument, she contends that "the difficulty of channeling the traumatic force of 9/11 in a way that encourages new ways of thinking, feeling, and creating is intimately linked to the historical conditions of the post-9/11 period in the United States. [. . .] The novels that represent and articulate the attacks as world-changing while remaining formally familiar do indeed reflect the post-9/11 nexus of trauma, politics, and aesthetics with remarkable accuracy" (154–55). Heffernan and Salván also refuse the primacy of trauma in approaches to 9/11 novels, arguing instead for their situation within the literary tradition that has always been galvanized by the role of violence in constituting national community.

is a seductive, talented gay man who likes to conceal the mundanity of his childhood in Michigan; he barely makes ends meet by freelancing as an art critic. Murray's nephew Frederick (Bootie) Tubb represents Millennials or Generation Y: he has just graduated from high school and in the course of the novel he moves from the decaying Victorian house in Watertown, New York, where he lives with his widowed mother, to Manhattan, where he works as his uncle's secretary and endures a hopeless infatuation with Marina. In the course of the novel Bootie's hero-worship of Murray will turn to dismay and disgust when he learns of Murray's affair with Danielle and reads his manuscript, "How to Live." For Bootie, Murray's manuscript and his infidelity are "*evidence*"—in every sense of the world—that Murray is "someone for whom words had no fixed meaning" (269). Bootie writes an exposé of Murray and submits it to Marina and her fiancé, the Australian Ludovic Seeley, for the inaugural edition of Ludovic's new journal *The Monitor*. The journal's launch, scheduled for September 13, 2001, is indefinitely postponed.

The title also references the Hans Christian Andersen story "The Emperor's New Clothes," in which a fiction of authority is revealed by a child's truth-telling, and the book Marina ultimately writes, *The Emperor's Children Have No Clothes,* a work of pop sociology that speculates on what we can learn about a society from the way its children dress. Like Murray's, Marina's book is alternately smart and trite. Murray perceives it as "an artfully wrapped gift box, a flurry of elegant paper and ribbons that, when opened, proved to be empty. Perhaps not entirely empty: a few glittering, worthless marbles rolled around in the bottom" (319). The title thus points to the simultaneity of absence and presence, promise and premise; in this lightweight world, fidelity—marital, familial, idealistic—both demands truth and cancels it out. Bootie's exposé of his uncle is of a piece with his youthful idealism that caused him to drop out of college and embark on a process of self-education on his way to his goal, "the life of the mind." Bootie perceives truth as a violent, destructive, transformative force; the omniscient narrator, however, sets his idealism in some perspective. Thinking of his exposé—an analysis of Murray's unpublished manuscript—Bootie reflects that he "was going to tell this truth, show the world the man as he was. It was going to be devastating; [. . .] it was going to be great. Telling the truth: what could be more important? [. . .] So here he was, washed in sweat, his jockey shorts sticking to his skin, the rest of him palely bare [. . .] penning the article that would change the world. Or change his world, for sure. This was revolution for you" (243).

Bootie's body—plump, awkward, inconvenient, often undressed—is underscored in the course of the novel, and, though he flees the Thwaite clan and tries to vanish (decamping from Manhattan to Brooklyn), it is September 11 that provides him with an opportunity to erase it. As this idea comes to him, it is couched in terms of a simultaneity of presence and absence, the concretization of, and an escape from, his existential unease. "He had been given—his fate—the precious opportunity to *be* again, not to be as he had been. Because as far as anyone knew, he *wasn't*. [. . .] It would be as if he had been there, in the lee of the towers, vanished, pulverized, the loathed Bootie Tubb meeting his unspeakable fate" (438). Bootie takes a bus to Miami, adopts the name Ulrich, and thinks back on "the falling towers, his own personal cinema," reflecting: "It was all about control" (441).

In contrast to the Millennial, Bootie, whose ungainly plenitude propels him toward revolution, Danielle, the Xer, is the site of substitution, mistakes, and erasure. Her affair with Murray, whom she has known for over a decade as her friend Marina's father, is predicated on the chance fact that Murray encounters Danielle just after he chose not to pursue an affair with Roanne Levine, an undergraduate in a seminar he is guest-teaching. Flush with desire and alcohol, he engages Danielle in conversation, thinking that his daughter's friend "resembled Roanne Levine, but with a slightly smaller mouth, better breasts, and without the aggravating laugh" (45). With the return home of Annabel and Marina, Danielle is invited to stay for dinner, where she has "the peculiar sensation of having usurped her friend's role in the Thwaite family" (46). This substitution—not of Marina, as she thinks, but of Rowena—haunts Danielle, and throughout her email exchanges with Murray she feels that "there was something not right about it all, some touch of titillating betrayal in their pithy messages, whether the slightest flutter of the sexual or merely an inappropriate ascription of the father-daughter bond" (93). Their affair, founded thus on simulation and substitution, produces, in Danielle's mind, a bifurcated quality; her reality and morality appear in split screen. Reflecting on her first sexual encounter with Murray, Danielle notes that "she held in her mind two disparate realities: one was the fierce tenderness she felt for this disintegrating giant, the joy at his small kindnesses and vulnerabilities [. . .] The other was a certainty of wrong, a moral repugnance. This she experienced abstractly, with her mind; it was, consequently, the weaker of the two realities. [. . .] The disgust was an idea, something she knew she ought to conjure, the way an autistic child can learn to smile at his mother to show happiness" (231). In the course of her affair with Murray, this split-screen quality begins to dominate Danielle's perception, subtracting certainty from experience. Her apartment, for example, "no longer presaged a meditative solitude [. . .] [but] the stage set for a play, a site awaiting action. As if it weren't quite real on its own any longer" (260). This duality of realities persists; after Marina's wedding (Danielle, alone of the guests, is invited to stay at the family's home), she feels, again, "two incompatible but equally certain visions that she held simultaneously": Murray's established married life with Annabel and his connection with her (386). Caught between these two certainties, Danielle feels cancelled out. "It didn't matter which vision was true [. . .] So the desire, whether a fact or a figment—and yet, its reality, its unknowable fact-ness, was of consuming importance to her—was not ultimately even relevant" (386). Danielle's disintegrating sense of reality is characteristic of all the Xers in the novel. Marina is early imaged as "standing on nothing, poised in the void" (49) and Julius is a pathological fabulist.

Murray, the Boomer, is the site of the novel's most direct reflections on truth, faith, and betrayal. His relation with Annabel is predicated on a version of trust that is decidedly fraying. She is consumed with her activities as a children's rights lawyer; he is something of a womanizer (Danielle is hardly his first extramarital dalliance). But Murray's policy is to return each night to Annabel, and he makes an exception for Danielle on the night of Monday, September 10. Arranging his alibi, Murray reflects that "he wasn't, in some regard, a liar. An actor, yes; and a good one. Guilty, upon innumerable occasions, of sins of omission, a great believer that what you didn't know couldn't hurt you [. . .] a smoother of waters whose techniques had been known to include a gentle reshaping of the facts" (406). He defines his relationship with Annabel in terms of trust, though he admits that each might define that term differently. "His definition of trust, on his wife's behalf, being that she could always know herself supremely loved, and always—ah, until now!—know that at day's end he came home faithfully to rest his head beside hers" (406–7). 9/11 blows Murray's alibi; he leaves Danielle in her apartment and returns home to Annabel, confirming Danielle's earlier sense that the fact-ness of her reality is irrelevant. For Danielle, on 9/11, Murray's reassertion of the fiction of fidelity that cements his marriage to Annabel combines with the images outside her window to cancel her out. Abandoned, she feels nothing. "She was as if anesthetized, she felt nothing, nothing at all, you could have amputated a limb and it wouldn't have mattered. She had seen the second plane, like a gleaming arrow, and the burst of it, oddly beautiful against the blue, and the smoke, everywhere, and she had seen the people jumping, from afar, specks in the sky, and she knew that's what they were only from the TV, from the great reality check of the screen, and she had seen the buildings crumble to dust; [. . .] she had seen these things and been left, forever, because in light of these things she did not matter [. . .] there was no call to feel anything, there was nothing to feel" (414–15). This affectlessness is the direct result of the process of subtraction initiated by the parallel realities established by her affair, and it continues, as life does, in Manhattan after the eleventh. "And the world, in spite of the bigger disasters, or perhaps because of them, stoically kept on, you could see the bustling citizens from the window, and when you were out in the street (only when you had to be), they jostled and butted against you as if not just your wound but you were invisible, as if it would be better all around if you just weren't there. With which, if anyone had asked, you would heartily have agreed" (267–68).

Both Bootie and Danielle, then, experience 9/11 as an opportunity to disappear. They are united in this, and in their experience of the events of that day as "cinema." They are united, too, in their thwarted love for Murray, the 1960s titan. In the novel's penultimate chapter they meet: Danielle, vacationing in Miami with her mother to recover from her depression, recognizes and confronts Bootie, who is working as a waiter and who pretends not to know her. He articulates and con-cretizes Danielle's sense of fraying presence. "It's Ulrich," he tells her, "Frederick doesn't exist; and for me, for Ulrich, you don't exist." When Danielle persists, Bootie both confesses to his masquerade and denies it. "I needed to go," he tells her, "I would be dead, otherwise. [. . .] If I would've killed myself otherwise, then I'd be dead, really dead" (476–77). Reminding her that he is not her friend Bootie but a stranger, he concludes, formally: "I'm sorry for the confusion. And sorry about your friend." Danielle assents to the masquerade. "Me too," she says, affirm-ing both the confusion and the loss of her friend, though he's standing right in front of her (477). Later, she describes Bootie as "just someone I thought I knew" (478).

Bootie's assumption of the name Ulrich is an homage to the book he is reading at the time, Robert Musil's *The Man without Qualities*. In *Virtual History: Alternatives and Counterfactuals*, Niall Ferguson argues compellingly that historical thinking is informed by determinism—the idea that what happened had to have happened because it did—and limited by adherence to thinking about the past "as it actually was."

Ferguson argues that such thinking is the residue of master narratives and linear, deterministic assumptions about causality, and suggests, instead, treating the past as stochastic—he proposes "chaostory." Ferguson references a number of literary texts, including Martin Amis's *Time's Arrow,* Robert Harris's *Fatherland,* and stories by Jorge Luis Borges. The most notable intertext, though—one that opens and closes Ferguson's long chapter—is *The Man without Qualities,* a text that Ferguson finds striking both for its attention to mobility and for how it traces a detachment of reality from truth. In a passage on which Ferguson lingers, Musil writes: "A possible experience or possible truth does not equate to real experience or real truth minus the value 'real'; [. . .] in the opinion of its devotees, it has in it something out and out divine, a fiery, soaring quality, a constructive will, a conscious utopianism that does not shrink from reality but treats it, on the contrary, as [. . .] an invention" (Musil 12, qtd. in Ferguson 3–4).[11]

Like Messud's, Musil's book is poised on the brink of apocalypse. *The Man without Qualities* is set in an Austrian society that is about to celebrate the Archduke Ferdinand whose assassination in Sarajevo precipitated the First World War and the onset of modernity. It was penned in the wake of World War I and in the looming menace of World War II. As a Jewish writer whose works were banned by the Nazis, who died in obscurity and exile in 1942, Musil witnessed firsthand how history can be erased, causes can be revised, human beings can be made to disappear, and belief can assume the form of fact.

The Man without Qualities is an important intertext for *The Emperor's Children,* and its role as an intertext helps to underscore Messud's point: 9/11's epochality, like that of World War II, is, in fact, a repetition: the intertext situates the characters *within* history even as it detaches them *from* it. The present is already a remake, an homage, like a Tarantino film. Frederick/Bootie/Ulrich is Messud's equivalent of the man without qualities (who, in Musil's novel, is also named Ulrich). Bootie wanders through Manhattan in the chaotic days after the 11th, clutching a copy of Musil's book. Thinking of the terrorists, and of what they

---

11. Sophie Wilkens's translation of Musil's original German text is slightly, but significantly, different from the translation quoted by Ferguson: "A possible experience or truth is not the same as an actual experience or truth minus its 'reality value' but has—according to its partisans, at least—something quite divine about it, a fire, a soaring, a readiness to build and a conscious utopianism that does not shrink from reality but sees it as a project, something *yet to be* invented" (11; my emphasis). This incipient quality is significant, as Messud's novel ends on a note of a menace, or promise, of revolutionary violence.

have wrought, Bootie is struck by how "you could make something inside your head, as huge and devastating as this, and spill it out into reality, make it really happen. You could, for evil—but if for evil, why not for good, too?—change the world" (439). Inspired by this, and by his own experience of 9/11 as "cinema," he promises: "Ulrich would fashion the reality inside his head and then, when the time was right, would give birth to it, would make them all at last understand, would take them by surprise" (441). The novel ends on this note of menace. The new Ulrich, who has replaced his surname "Tubb" with the more appealing "New," packs, lightly, ready to depart. There is a sense that he will die young, and spectacularly. "This time, he was ready. This person in motion was who he was becoming; it was something, too; a man, someday, with qualities. Ulrich New. Great geniuses have the shortest biographies, he told himself; and take them by surprise. Yes. He would" (478). As the sentences fragment, temporal progression is dislocated: the new Ulrich is Ulrich New. Repetition ("take them by surprise") produces, as effect, affirmation: "Yes. He would." In these, Messud's novel's concluding lines, incipience, menace, the promise of revolution, like the ceaseless cyclicality of all violent transformation, is inspired in equal parts by terror, reality, and fiction.

THE WORLD INSIDE OUT

Beigbeder attempted to imagine dying in the North Tower, realized the limitations of his novelistic gesture, traveled to the World Trade Center site, and underscored the interpenetration of all these gestures with media: television, translation. Messud moves along different vectors: her realistic narrative and multigenerational cast of amusing, sympathetic characters enable her to present and toy with themes of fidelity, betrayal, complicity, and truth. For both, though, 9/11 is presented as an event that impacts (in Beigbeder's case, graphically) the lives of the characters, and its temporal specificity (8:46 a.m. and 9:03 a.m. of Tuesday, September 11, 2001) dominates the progress and structure of both novels. Jess Walter's *The Zero* departs from this tendency. The novel is narrated in short fragments, it moves backward and forward in time, disconnected from narrative and from temporal progression. 9/11 is imaged through three paradigms that operate simultaneously: it is paper (scraps of text; numbers, records, communications), organic matter (living and not), and media (the looping television footage and the crackling and spots of deteriorating film). Walter's striking opening gesture evokes all three:

> They burst into the sky, every bird in creation, angry and agitated, awakened by the same primary thought, erupting in a white feathered cloudburst, anxious and graceful, angling in ever-tightening circles toward the ground, drifting close enough to touch, and then close enough to see that it wasn't a flock of birds at all—it was paper. Burning scraps of paper. All the little birds were paper. Fluttering and circling and growing bigger, falling bits and frantic sheets, some smoking, corners scorched, flaring in the open air until there was nothing left but a fine black edge . . . and then gone, a hole and nothing but the faint memory of smoke. Behind the burning flock came a great wail and a moan as seething black unfurled, the world inside out, birds beating against a roiling sky and in that moment everything that wasn't smoke was paper. And it was beautiful. (3)

The novel opens by confusing organic with inorganic: what appear to be birds are, in fact, sheets of paper. Vision and proximity (being "close enough to see") promise to correct this confusion. But they do not suffice. From the black hole that, like a living being, wails and moans, emerges an inversion that will dictate the narrative: "the world inside out." The paper resumes its living quality: it is, again, birds, "birds beating against a roiling sky." It is, in fact, "everything that wasn't smoke," which the narrative names "beautiful."[12] From this striking opening gesture the novel focuses on the point of view of its protagonist, Brian Remy, an Xer, a police officer and a First Responder, who awakens from this flashback/dream to find himself on the floor of his apartment. Remy's vision is imaged in cinematic terms: "He was lying on his side, panning across a fuzzy tree line of carpet fiber. [. . .] The world focused into being one piece at a time." This point of view, again, combines the organic and inorganic: Remy identifies himself with an empty whiskey bottle. "They were both tipped over on their right sides on the rug, parallel to one another, the whiskey fifth and him. In this together, apparently" (3).

This conflation, or interpenetration, of the organic and the inorganic haunts the novel. Ground Zero—The Zero, in the terms of the first responders and cleanup crew—is imaged as a living thing: "hum-

---

12. See Kristine Miller (34) for an alternative close reading of this passage.

ming" (15), fanged (38), lit at night "like a stage. Or a surgery" (36). It is a "massive smoldering jungle [. . .] fire raged in its roots and hot shoots jutted from the pile" (18). Its smell, too, is a powerful presence in this novel, almost a character in its own right. "The smell never left him now," Remy reflects. "It lived in the lining of his nose and the fibers of his lungs—his whole body seemed to smell, as if the odor were working through his pores, the fine gray dust: pungent, flour of the dead" (14). The smell, both living and not, unlocatable and omnipresent, threatens to redefine the very nature of existence in terms of something empty. "The dust rose, and the smell found you, and Remy could imagine that one day everything in the world would be reduced to such a fine dust— replacing even the air, so that you not only smelled it but tasted it, and felt it too, on your skin, in your mouth, deep to your bones like a chill, that the whole world would swim in dust—finer and finer until there was nothing but an absence of substance and meaning" (44).

This interpenetration of organic and inorganic, the image of the drifting sheets of paper, and the conceit that paper—or text—is "everything," dictates the novel's plot. Remy works for a (fictitious) agency, "the Office of Liberty and Recovery," which oversees two feuding bureaus: the Remains Recovery Department and the Documentation Department. The role of the latter is to reconstruct the paper record of the world. The analogy of paper with people is made explicitly: "the people and the paper burned up or flew away or ran off, and after it happened, they were considerably less than they had been in the beginning" (19). The role of the Documentation Department is predicated on the absurdity of this analogy: "*If we do not make a fundamental accounting of what was lost, if we do not gather up the paper and put it all back, then the forces aligned against us have already won. They've. Already. Won*" (19).

Remy has vision problems: macular degeneration (which manifests as a blind spot at the center of the visual field, and interferes with the processing of information) and vitreous detachment, which causes "floaters" or specks that interfere with vision. These symptoms are repeatedly aligned with the interpenetration of paper and birds, and they attach this imagery to the motif of television—a source, throughout *The Zero*, of fascination, disgust, and a privileged kind of witness. "I haven't turned off my TV since it happened," reports one character. "I was glued to the news coverage for the first few days. [. . .] I ordered out every meal and just went from channel to channel, watching it from different angles, listening to the newscasters and the public officials" (65–66). "I watched

TV and I was sick," confesses another (83). Remy's friend Paul Guterak, a fellow First Responder, reflects: "Sometimes I wish we'd just gone to a bar that morning and watched the whole thing on CNN. [. . .] I envy people who watched it on TV. They got to see the whole thing. [. . .] I think the people who watched it on TV saw more than we did" (85).

For Remy, the television coverage is indistinguishable from his memories, and his memories are defined by his deteriorating vision. Watching cable news replays of 9/11 coverage, Remy reflects that "the news had become the wallpaper in his mind now, the endless loop playing in his head—banking wings, blooms of flame, white plumes becoming black" (8). The decrease in color density associated with macular degeneration informs, or deforms, these visual images, both in his mind and on the screen: the white plumes become black and then "gray, endless gray, geysers of gray, dust-covered gray stragglers with gray hands covering gray mouths running from gray shore-break, and the birds, white—endless breeds and flocks of memos and menus and correspondence fluttering silently and then disappearing in the ashen darkness" (8–9). The dissolution of the distinction of organic and inorganic, televised image and experienced reality, persists even when Remy closes his eyes. He sees then "what he always saw: shreds of tissue, threads of detachment and degeneration, silent fireworks, the lining of his eyes splintering and sparking and flaking into the soup behind his eyes— flashers and floaters that danced like scraps of paper blown into the world" (9).

Remy's vision problems are not a 9/11 health effect. And yet they are presented as such, as Guterak rehearses his account to a group of sightseers he ushers about Ground Zero. Guterak points out Remy's eye condition (which he calls "muscular vicious disintegration") and implies that Remy is suffering from the effects of first response. "What it is, see, is his fuggin' eyes are flaking off. From inside, is what that shit is. Creepy, huh? I mean this is some serious shit we went through here," says Guterak. Remy reflects that "he'd told Guterak ten times that his eye condition had nothing to do with the burst blood vessel in his right eye, and therefore with that day, that he'd had escalating eye problems for years. But Paul insisted on making it part of the tour" (26). This loose, and fallacious, attribution of effect to cause itself attests to the novel's concern with causality, "the loose string between cause and effect" (3) which, early in the novel, Remy identifies as "the problem. These gaps in his memory, or perhaps his life, a series of skips—long shredded tears, empty spaces where the explanations for the most basic things used to be" (5). "These were the most common gaps that Remy had been suffering, holes not so much in his memory but in the string of events, the causes of certain effects" (43). For Remy, the eye problems (to which 9/11 is falsely attributed as a cause), and the memory gaps (which do seem to be an effect of his Ground Zero experience) combine in the novel's narrative style of detached fragments and sections. Lacking background and context, these fragments trace a world in which, as Remy reflects, "the moment could slip the way so many moments slipped now—loosed of their context and meaning and floating gently to the ground" (78). With this narrative style, Walter extends Remy's symptoms to an existential malaise, undermining the privileged experience that First Responders are assumed to possess. Formed, as many Xers were, by the mediation of experience, the collapse of great ideologies, and entrenched paranoia, Remy reflects: "Maybe this was not some condition he had, but a life, and maybe every life is lived moment to moment. [. . .] What do you trust? Memory? History? No, these are just stories, and whichever ones we choose to tell ourselves—the one about our marriage, the one about the Berlin Wall—there are always gaps" (160).

The effect of these gaps is articulated by Remy's son Edgar. Like Beigbeder, Danielle, and Bootie, Edgar falsely claims to have lost someone in the attacks. Early in the novel, Remy's ex-wife Carla calls him to a meeting with the teenage Edgar, who has been telling everyone in school that his father had died. Edgar emerges from a computer game called Empire that he describes as "a communal computer experience . . . like an alternate world. It's character-driven and action-reaction oriented. Just like the real world" (30). "You do realize," says Carla, with Remy present, "your father isn't dead. He's right here" (31). Edgar refuses to apologize. He stresses that he is not delusional, he knows Remy isn't dead, and he doesn't wish Remy was dead—this is not a wish-fulfillment fantasy or an unacknowledged psychic truth (32–33). He also stresses that he is not using the claim his father is dead to articulate other emotions, like anger over his parents' divorce or, Carla is quick to suggest, Remy's commitment issues. Edgar stresses that his grief is real, and personal. He dismisses a sense of generalized grief after 9/11. Unlike "general grief," which Edgar describes as "a lie, [. . .] a trend, just some weak shared moment in the culture," Edgar's counter-narrative enables him to feel "*real* grief." "The death of a father . . . is the most profound thing I've ever experienced. [. . .] There are times when I can barely breathe. I can't . . . get over it. And I don't want to.

The only way to comprehend something like this is to go through it. Otherwise, it's just a number. Three thousand? Four thousand? How do you grieve a number? [. . .] I have chosen to focus my grief on one individual. On the death of my father. [. . .] And you know, frankly, I guess I expected a little more support from you" (34).

Not least because it is quite funny, this passage has drawn quite a bit of attention. Reviewers and critics are quick to underscore the disparity between what Edgar says (his father is dead) and what is the case (Remy is, in fact, alive), reflecting on the implications of this disparity. In these discussions, authentic experience, the inviolability of trauma, and national mourning are privileged.[13] But the counternarrative challenges us to a more risky, because affirmative, enterprise, one attuned to the power of fiction, and to the changing nature of the real (which Edgar learns about from Empire, his computer game). Like Danielle, who, with "me too," acknowledged and mourned Bootie's sorrow and her own, Carla accedes to and recognizes Edgar's grief. "I'm sorry, honey," she says, "I'm sorry we got divorced and I'm sorry about your father." She and Edgar embrace and weep, excluding Remy (35). Carla and Danielle know that the claims for loss are false. But they acknowledge the emotion, validating the grief not in its incomparable singularity but as an equivalent, affirming affect through a logic of exchange. "Sorry about your father," like "sorry about your friend," situates the object of grief as evacuated, the empty space between two equipoised alternatives, each equally valid, each revealed, in its mirror image, to be fragile, contingent, erected on shifting ground.

Just like the World Trade Center site. In the concluding pages of *The Zero*, Remy returns to Ground Zero and is struck by the extent of the

---

13. For Duvall and Marzec, the question raised by this passage is whether 9/11 can "produce a trauma that is constitutive of a new collective American identity" (386). Duvall ("Homeland") elaborates: the scene, he concludes, "satirizes the urge to find a collective traumatic identity in the post-9/11 moment. While Edgar's insistence on working through the death of his father as the only appropriate way of understanding the trauma of 9/11 (even as Edgar fully acknowledges that his father is, somewhat irrelevantly, actually alive) becomes a running source of humor in the novel, it is a humor that ultimately serves to ironize the personal form of grieving that Edgar argues to be more authentic" (288). DeRosa underscores "the absurdity of Edgar's 'authentic' mourning for his father who sits next to him on the couch," which "represents Walter's not-so-subtle attack on post-9/11 rhetoric" according to which "'9/11' has become usurped and hidden" (177). Kristine Miller disagrees: "Edgar's manufactured trauma is undeniably real and crippling, even if his grief is over an imagined death. [. . .] Edgar's story makes readers aware of the need both to make trauma meaningful through narrative and to consume such narratives cautiously, since fictions have the power to determine the course of real lives" (44).

cleanup: "Remy turned from side to side, taking the whole thing in, feeling incomplete, cheated in some way, as if they'd taken away his memory along with the dirt and debris" (307). This conflation of organic and inorganic extends, for Remy, to an interpenetration, and evacuation, of psyche and place. "Maybe his mind was a hole like this," he reflects, "the evidence and reason scraped away. If you can't trust the ground beneath your feet, what can you trust? If you take away the very ground, what could possibly be left? And yet that's what they had done" (307). Confirming his epistemic insecurity, the absence of a cause, of something to trust or believe in, the cleanup of Ground Zero casts new light on Remy's X apathy. "He had expected to feel something. But what can you feel about a place when that place has been scraped away?" (308).

THIS WAS JIHAD

For Beigbeder, Messud, and Walter, the counternarrative offers the characters an opportunity to suture themselves into the reality of 9/11. Precisely because of 9/11's virtual, mediated quality—of which these X authors are all keenly aware—fiction is crucial for ascertaining its relevance and impact. And yet, fiction means betrayal—in each of these novels, characters engage in at least one extramarital affair—and contributes to a sense of unreality, proffering layers of mediation, and underscoring art's inadequacy in the wake of so raw a disaster. Nonetheless (I submit), infidelity is a productive paradigm through which to approach 9/11 after X, because it underscores the extent to which violence, though real, is also mediated, multiple, and available to be employed to bring about other realities, personal and political. In this section I discuss two 9/11 novels: Jay McInerney's *The Good Life* and Ken Kalfus's *A Disorder Peculiar to the Country*. Though McInerney and Kalfus were born in the mid-1950s and are not, technically, Xers, like DeLillo they employ members of Generation X as characters through which to figure the events of 9/11. Both novels are preoccupied with marital infidelity, and both reflect on the use to which 9/11 can be put in forming, or fashioning, reality anew.

McInerney's *The Good Life* revisits Corrine and Russell, the protagonists of his 1992 novel *Brightness Falls*. *Brightness Falls* revolved around the market crash of 1987, chillingly described as *"paper airplanes crashing to the pavement of Manhattan"* (3; italics in original) and a crisis in Corrine and Russell's marriage. In *The Good Life,* real airplanes crash to the pavement of Manhattan, and Corrine and Russell—now the parents of twins, conceived in vitro with the help of Corrine's sister Hilary, who acted as a surrogate—are again in marital crisis. McInerney's characters make this analogy explicit. Speaking to Corrine of his friend Jim, who died in the World Trade Center, Russell recalls their friend Jeff, whose death from AIDS was recounted in *Brightness Falls*: "Jeff was my best friend, and Jim kind of took his place. And they both got taken away in a kind of mass catastrophe" (*Good Life* 189). Referring to the bull market of the 1980s, Corrine, speaking to her lover Luke, reflects, "It all came crashing down. Not like this of course, but the crash of '87 seemed, I don't know, cataclysmic at the time. [. . .] Personally, it was a real disaster" to which Luke, a First Responder, responds: "Personally is maybe the only perspective we have" (*Good Life* 157).

When Corrine and Luke meet, both experience, as Danielle did, a multiplication of realities and an underlying epistemic uncertainty. On Tuesday morning Luke had arrived late to a meeting at Windows on the World, worked at the site without gloves or a mask until blacking out, and stumbles out of Ground Zero, covered with dust, the following morning. Corrine hands him a bottle of water. Each suspects the other is a fantasy. Luke's presence is untimely; Corrine's first impression is that he is "at least a day late"; he seems to her "like a statue commemorating some ancient victory, or, more likely, some noble defeat" (*Good Life* 73), and, as she puts it, "it's hard to tell [. . .] what's real" (74). For Luke, who wonders "Is this really happening?" ("'I think so,' she replies"), Corrine's beauty has a cinematic quality that contributes to his insecurity: he's not sure she's real because, he realizes, she looks so much like an old-timey movie star (76). In the course of the novel, Corrine and Luke come to represent, each to the other, an alternative to their unsatisfactory existence. Corrine shares with Luke her fantasy of "Disappearing. I keep imagining that there must be somebody who walked away from those towers and just decided to keep walking. Start a new life. Sometimes I wish it were me. [. . .] I think about it. Keep trying to figure out a way that it would be possible" (248). For Luke, haunted by nightmares of a faceless body he saw at the World Trade Center site ("Our Lady of Ground Zero"; 184), Corrine grounds his post-9/11 reality. "Whenever I'd closed my eyes, I'd see that woman without a face," he confesses. "But there you were, giving the world a new face. [. . .] Sometimes I still wonder if it was all just an after-image, because nothing feels very real to me anymore, except being with you" (262).

After Corrine is raped by a drunken Russell and decides to end her marriage, Luke rents an apartment on Tenth Street. Together, they imagine the life they could have if they made their fantasy real. Leaving the apartment together, they are confronted by this surreal image: a "herd of Santas." "A flash of red and then another—two Santas marching up Tenth Street, one fat and the other skinny. Approaching the street, she spied two more and two more behind them, one showing what she supposed was Desert Storm camo beneath his red coat and talking on a cell phone, one carrying his red-and-white hat in his hand. A cavalcade of Santas, ten, fifteen, more than twenty in all" (353). To this vision of fantasy run amok, they respond by retreating to "Famous Ray's," which, Luke assures Corrine, is "the *real* Ray's. Forget about all those Original Ray's" (354). From this copy of a copy they retreat, again, into their original worlds, revealed now as simulacra: the "dramas of daily life." These dramas, and the "satori flash of acute wakefulness and connectedness that had followed the initial confrontation with mortality in September" (363), are counterpoised, mirror reflections. Fantasy and reality are equal, equivalent, each the other's viable alternative, as Luke thinks of Corrine: "she was his lost twin, his sundered other half, and after half a lifetime he had found her, and now he would let her go" (363). McInerney's treatment of 9/11 is thus attuned to the mediated, multiple, quality of reality. The attacks—undeniably real—unveil reality's multiplicity, its perpetual twinning, that menaces the original or authentic. Most radically imaged by the Santacon into which Luke and Corrine stumble on their way out of the apartment on Tenth Street,[14] multiplicity reconfigures all realities: lived and desired, the mundane "dramas of daily life," and the vivid "satori flash," are fragile, substitutable, interchangeable. Corrine and Russell's twin children, with which the novel opens and ends, concretize this point. Predicated on surrogacy, untimely (premature) and fragile, they are menaced by the return of Hilary, who threatens to usurp Corrine's role as the twins' "real" mother. Their precariousness is the city's: this is Corrine's bleak epiphany. Thinking of her twins, she realizes that "she would always be hovering near the surface of consciousness in the perpetual light of the restless city, alert to the sound of a cough, the thump of a falling body, the drone of a plane overhead" (355).

---

14. Santacon originated in 1994 as a part of a night of Kringle Kaos organized by the Cacophony Society. It is now a global phenomenon in which people dressed as Santa Claus gather, primarily to drink (see http://santarchy.com/). McInerney's novel may well be referencing the Santacon held in New York City on December 8, 2001.

A *Disorder Peculiar to the Country* proceeds along different lines. If McInerney's novel was predicated on analogy, Kalfus's frontally mobilizes analogy to reflect on what it means to see one event through the lens of another. Like McInerney's, Kalfus's novel also revolves around marital crisis: an acrimonious divorce becomes the grounds from which to extrapolate not only to the terror attacks but their aftermath, the anthrax scare, the war on terror, the War in Iraq, and the tortures at Abu Ghraib.

The divorce is figured as a territorial dispute. Marshall, the husband, and Joyce, his soon to be ex-wife, still share an apartment in New York City with their small children; neither is willing to move out. Even before the attacks, their relationship has "acquired the intensity of something historic, tribal, and ethnic, and when they watched news of wars on TV, reports from the Balkans or the West Bank, they would think, yes, yes, yes, that's how I feel about *you*" (7). This affirmation of difference and its incorporation into the personal domesticates the terror attacks—a move that most critics see as a fatal flaw, an undue taming of 9/11's traumatic impact.[15] But by domesticating terror, Kalfus does not tame its trauma—he brings it home. Joyce and Marshall are saboteurs. The novel begins with them witnessing the attacks on the World Trade Center. Each assumes the other is killed, and, like Al Qaeda warriors, each exults. So Joyce, as she watches the building collapse, feels "something erupt inside her, something warm, very much like, yes it was, a pang of pleasure [. . .] The building turned into a rising mushroom-shaped column of smoke, dust, and perished life, and she felt a great gladness" (3).

The chapters set in the wake of the attacks offer critical meditations on the bald analogy on which the novel is structured. Each posits a paradigm through which to view the war on terror. Joyce, plotting revenge against Marshall, sleeps with his friend Roger, according to the logic—borrowed from popularizations of images of Afghan culture—that "'the enemy of my enemy is my friend,' 'the friend of my enemy is my

---

15. Critical response to Kalfus's novel has dismissed it as unduly focused on the domestic and, consequentially, insufficiently or inefficiently political. Duvall concludes that A *Disorder Peculiar to the Country* is unable "to articulate a clear political or ethical vision" (281). Gray, too, dismisses Kalfus's novel as insufficiently registering the trauma of 9/11, though his reference to Joyce engaging in "terror sex" (she does not) would indicate that he had not read it carefully (Gray 25, see Kalfus 22–23). In an exception to this trend, Irom reads Kalfus's turn to the domestic as unsettling the cultural dominant, identifying a "process of inversion" that "[turns] the domestic idyll inside out" (527).

enemy'" and that, for Afghan women, "sex wasn't 'fun' or an expression of 'love,' it was a weapon" (63). The tortures at Abu Ghraib are figured as, at a drug-fuelled party, Marshall witnesses a scene in which a young African American man, with his head in a sack, is molested by a white woman who flashes the thumbs-up sign—the scene, with the woman's consent, is captured on film (213–18). The September 11, 2001 attack on the World Trade Center occurs literally within the domestic space: in a chapter narrated by Viola, Joyce and Marshall's daughter, an ugly argument over an antique vase is settled by Viola's younger brother, who shoots a toy plane across the room with a rubber band. "The plane swiftly gained altitude as it crossed the living room. It flew steadily, without tumbling. [. . .] When the toy piece struck, the glass changed color top to bottom, from purple to a bright, pinkish white, and the vase iridesced before it crashed and returned to its original elements so that not a single piece of it could be recognized" (141).

Analogies make sense—a point that the novel raises and, again, inverts. Marshall, walking in Manhattan, hears an enormous crash and immediately registers it in terms of the suicide bombs in Tel Aviv and Jerusalem. Just before he hears the crash, analogies are spinning out of control. The sky, Marshall reflects, "seemed unnaturally close, at the scraping edges of the city's towers, a transparent glass bowl." Then the analogies multiply: "Or it was like a teardrop swelling before its fall. Or like a child's spinning top in its terminal wobble. Or like a blow before its pain was registered" (177). What brings this accelerated burgeoning to a halt is the crash that unites victim and perpetrator, the populations of the Middle East and New York City: "within this moment they lived the terror as it had been experienced within the [Tel Aviv] pizzeria, by the bomber and his victims together" (179). Reflecting on this interpenetration—Manhattan and Tel Aviv, Al Qaeda and Palestinian terror, suicide bomber and victim, global terror and domestic discord—the narrative voice identifies the process as both justice and jihad: "In a single lightning flash the unconnected parts of the world had been brought together and made into sense. No, *sense* was not made. This was a world of heedless materialism, impiety, baseness, and divorce. Sense was not made, this was jihad: the unconnected parts of the world had been brought together and made *just*" (179).

The alliance of jihad with a justice, and the distinction of justice from sense, returns in the novel's culminating scene. Here, the novel reflects critically on its adoption of analogy and its own attempt to make sense. Marshall, losing his battle for the property and for custody, moving out of the cherished apartment, sees Joyce and the children watching the statue of Saddam Hussein being toppled on TV, and bursts out with this:

> I'm not Saddam Hussein, if that's what you think [. . .] That's what you think! [. . .] You think it's symbolic, don't you? "Another evil person removed!" Am I right? Tell me, am I right? [. . .] There's no analogy here! [. . .] I haven't gassed any Kurds, I'm not threatening anyone with weapons of mass destruction. I'm a nice guy. In fact, I think a case can be made that I'm a *great* guy—okay? Maybe not a great husband or a great father, but I did my best. [. . .] I gave up more of my basic human rights than you did! *I* was the one who was oppressed! To compare me with Saddam is totally unjust. (225–26)

"To compare me with Saddam is totally unjust"—this statement catapults representation into the context of justice. It is the analogy that is unjust—the comparison—because it is the *collapse* of analogies in the immediacy of experience that performs justice, aligns it with jihad, and distinguishes it from sense. Marshall and Joyce, like Corrine, Russell, and Luke, are Xers, for whom, as Clay learns, there is no "right," just power. Marshall's complaint speaks not to his fleecing by Joyce's cutthroat attorney or even to his political situation as an American, complicit in U.S. imperialism and human rights abuses, but to *A Disorder Peculiar to the Country*: specifically, to the analogy that had dictated the novel's subject and form thus far—for from this moment the narrative reverses course. Rather than paralleling the events of 9/11 and the war on terror, it becomes a counterhistory. So the Iraq War is won quickly and easily (229), peaceful demonstrations in Syria topple the government of Bashar al-Assad (232), WMDs are discovered and safely dismantled (230), Israelis and Palestinians magically agree on the settlements and on shared sovereignty of Jerusalem (234), Osama Bin Laden is captured (234; this novel was, remember, published in 2006) and carefully, legally, civilly brought to justice (230).

The novel's final scene invites us to imagine footage of Ground Zero on September 11, screened in reverse. Rather than the familiar images of thousands fleeing the World Trade Center site amidst a blizzard of falling debris, *A Disorder Peculiar to the Country* ends with crowds surging back in triumph, singing patriotic anthems. "This time they headed downtown, this time with their shoes on their feet. [. . .] Just-shredded confetti fell in a multicolored blizzard. The mob kicked it up again" (235). Returning to the moment before the first plane hit, Marshall,

Joyce, and the children meet. True to the perception of the United States as a global bully, a murderer, a state whose disregard of human rights is matched only by its moral certitude—a perception that the wars in Iraq and Afghanistan, and events in Guantanamo and Abu Ghraib have, for a significant part of the world, confirmed—the children are wearing "Death to Terrorists!" shirts. The united American family, victorious in the war against terror, produced by analogy, counterhistory, and fiction: simulated, contingent, nothing but a lie. This concluding image of domestic harmony, predicated on multiple infidelities, is, in every sense, untrue. It is, in the terms set forth by the novel itself, jihad: the unconnected parts of the world brought together, made just. And it is poised on the brink of implosion. Standing with his family, Marshall sees that "the vastness of the emptiness of the hole in the city [is] inflamed with human noise and aspiration. [. . .] The moment would last forever, or until everything contained within it was completely destroyed" (237).

HABEAS CORPUS

"What was beneath all those piles? Nothing? No one?" wonders Remy as he gazes as the World Trade Center site (307). The prominence of counternarratives in 9/11 novels may speak to the implications of the absence of bodies in the wake of these events. With 9/11, the image of the torn or broken human body that has historically functioned as a guarantor of violence's reality was not readily available. Achingly absent, its loss marked by images of the missing or portraits of grief, and overwhelmingly present—as smell, as dust, as scraps salvaged by workers or seagulls at the Fresh Kills landfill, the body—the confirmation of violence—is both present *and* absent, available *and* unavailable as an object of knowledge.[16] It flickers—like an image on a TV screen—illuminates us briefly, and vanishes.

What it shows is hardly flattering, and the texts discussed in this chapter navigate this uneasy terrain in a variety of ways. Beigbeder

---

16. Laura E. Tanner offers an extended reflection on the embodied apprehension of 9/11: "At the most basic level, the physical dynamics of the terrorist attacks frustrated the public's quest to reach past representation into the realm of bodily contact. The blasts obliterated not just victims' bodies but also their possessions, leaving behind materials that failed to assume the recognizable form of objects and that defied tactile embrace [. . .] The stuff of Ground Zero resisted stabilization and differentiation at every level, from the mammoth building supports that threatened constantly to collapse to the particles of dust that New Yorkers breathed into their bodies for months" (64–65).

focuses on media, and stresses mediation: in contrast to the scenes in the World Trade Center that are explicitly—even graphically—imagined, he refers to "the thunderous noise of the falls in the documentary by the Naudet brothers" (261; Beigbeder is referring to 9/11, the 2002 documentary by James Hanlon and Jules and Gédéon Naudet), and adopts an ironic and acerbic tone to reflect on the paucity of images of the dead: "When a building collapses, feel free to repeat the footage endlessly. But whatever you do, don't show what was inside: our bodies" (262). McInerney makes brief but vivid reference to bodies "falling slowly and then suddenly exploding like rotten fruit on the concrete" (75), while Walter lingers on their uncanny quality: "Here's what you didn't get on TV, it was so far up there, it didn't seem real, not until someone jumped, arms flapping crazy like they could change their minds, but of course, they couldn't . . . and you'd watch 'em grow as they came down . . . hitting like fuggin' water balloons, but deeper, you know—thumping and . . . and . . . bursting" (25). In *A Disorder Peculiar to the Country,* the bursting body is posited as eminently seeable *and* as an injunction against seeing. Marshall, trying to help a fellow victim from the site, watches as "an object that was recognizably a woman in a navy business suit, possibly a suit that could be described in regard to its cut and weave, and possibly even its likely provenance if you knew about such things, thumped hard less than twenty feet away, and bounced and burst. Her shoes had come off in mid-fall and clattered emptily against the pavement a moment later. 'Don't look,' Marshall said. 'For God's sake don't look'" (16). The specificity of seeing that Kalfus imagines, and the injunction against seeing that immediately follows it, speak to a fascination with the macabre that the X authors all refuse to disavow; tellingly, they add to vision other senses—smell, sound—that, unlike sight, penetrate orifices, underscoring the body's openness. In *The Emperor's Children,* Bootie's mother Judy calls her estranged brother Murray after 9/11. "'Tell me something, Murray: Can you smell it? What does it smell like, for God's sake?'" Murray shares some of her distance and all of her fascination. "We're too far away, up here," he tells her, promising, "I'm going tomorrow. [. . .] Marina's already been" (425). In *The Zero,* Guterak, ever the truth-teller, reports his response to tourists who inquire about the sound bodies made when they hit the sidewalk outside the World Trade Center. "I say to clap their hands as hard as they can, so hard that it really hurts. Then they clap, and I say: No. Harder than that. And they clap again, and I say, No, really fuggin' hard. And then they clap so hard their faces get all twisted up, and I say, No, really hard! And then, when their hands are red and sore, they say, 'So that's what it sounded like?' and I say, 'No. It didn't sound like that at all'" (85).

These smells and sounds are nowhere in *Falling Man*. Indeed, what DeLillo calls the event's "singularity" may be read not just as that which is distinctive but as a gravitational singularity. Like a black hole, something empty in the sky consumes world and words: both fall away from Keith, whose name means "wind"—a perpetual displacement and movement—and who is described as "a man scaled in ash" (6). Ash could be present on Keith's skin like a scaly layer, protecting it; or Keith has been "scaled," his protective layer peeled away, his skin smoothed, or removed, his body vulnerable, open. Like scales, the shirt—with which this chapter opened—reveals and conceals. Image of the presence *and* absence of the body, it is also a literal image, a flicker, the photographic residue of a jumper Keith did not quite glimpse when he was still in the North Tower.[17] In the confusion after the plane hits, "Something went past the window, then he saw it. First it went and was gone and then he saw it [. . .] white shirt, hand up, falling before he saw it" (242). In the hot windowless dark of the North Tower's stairwell, Keith sees, an after-image, the figure again: "going past the window [. . .] the man falling sideways, arm out and up, like pointed up, like why am I here instead of there" (244).

Keith's missed vision leaves him "staring out at nothing" (242), an emptiness from which the image of the shirt is formed or fashioned. Point of view is elicited from this nothingness, and shifts from Keith (who, seeing the arm, likens its posture to pointing) to a falling man's ("why am I here instead of there"), as the string of similes ("out and up, like pointed up, like why") propels reference away from referent, a process initiated (or continued) by Keith's nameless son who, with his friends, persists in calling Bin Laden Bill Lawton. Abandoned by reference, the falling man flickers: simultaneously a literary image and the

---

17. Conte links DeLillo's image of the shirt to Richard Drew's famous photograph. "The white shirt that appears to defy gravity serves as an icon of all those who stepped out into airy nothingness while yearning for an impossible rescue. [. . .] It functions as a synecdoche for all those who leapt to their death. [. . .] The image of the shirt adrift is nearly all the traumatized viewer can bear to register" (577). Carroll offers a different reading of the shirt and of this scene: he names the shirt as symbol (of trauma; the limits of representation; the unaccountable) and synecdoche: representing the falling body while remaining separate from it. Carroll concludes that the image of the shirt concretizes the denial of knowledge, reference, and certainty that characterize 9/11's purported challenge to representation.

aftermath of an imprint, it manifests through repeated viewings, like the images of David Janiak, the Falling Man performance artist, that Lianne clicks through on her computer. The repetition confirms the disappearing: "the fact that there were two of them signifies the end of any origi nal reference. If there had been only one, monopoly would not have been perfectly embodied. Only the doubling of the sign truly puts an end to what it designates" (Baudrillard 39). In the wake or in the ruins of this annihilation of reference, the body is evoked and—though not entirely—disavowed. It disappears here.

"In the absence of all basis for comparison, the event asserts its singularity," writes DeLillo in "In The Ruins of the Future" (39). True to the definition of a singularity as the place where parallel lines meet, the shirt is where the pillars of the narrative combine. Presence and absence: submersion and survival. Keith disappears: Lianne is here. "The towers, for their part, have disappeared. But they have left us the symbol of their disappearance, their disappearance as symbol," writes Baudrillard (47). But reading the shirt as a symbol is, ultimately, too easy. In the novel's final sentence Keith again sees the shirt fall, "arms waving like nothing in this life" (246). The attribution of arms (rather than sleeves) to the shirt figures it not as symbol but catachresis: a refusal of reference. Confirming the interpenetration of the nonsensible and the somatic ("arms waving"), the novel's final simile seals the equation of absence (like nothing) with presence (in this life): something empty in the sky. With the shirt, the singularity, the narrative black hole, the site where the parallel lines—or planes—intersect, the body is affirmed and relinquished, demanded and abandoned, commemorated and crossed out: a bleak and futile habeas corpus.

Not Yes or No

Fact, Fiction, Fidelity in Jonathan Safran Foer

FICTION, FACT

We have seen that a generation accustomed to pause, rewind, and remotely control the image is likely to refuse the temporal inevitability of cause and effect. In the final pages of Jonathan Safran Foer's *Extremely Loud and Incredibly Close,* Oskar, the child narrator, does just that. He arranges a series of images that he has downloaded from the internet. The images are of a falling figure that Oskar suspects may be his father, who died in the World Trade Center on September 11, 2001. "I reversed the order, so the last one was first, and the first was last," recounts Oskar. "When I flipped through them, it looked like the man was floating up through the sky" (325). *Extremely Loud and Incredibly Close* concludes with these images; the reader is expected to flip through them—to rewind. This brief moment in the novel has elicited a wide range of critical responses, from "moving and cathartic" (Bird 564) and "one of the most curious happy endings ever contrived" (Updike 140), to "poor taste" (Myers 119) and "truly horrific" (Gessen 72).

Turning away from aesthetic judgments about the flip-book to reviewers' descriptions of it, we see, again, a wide range of assertions. Gessen sees "a man falling out of one of the towers" (72), while Gornick describes "an object in the sky that *resembles* a falling body" (32; emphasis mine). Gornick has no doubt that the photographs are of "the side of the World Trade Center" (32), but B. R. Myers is less sure—the man is falling from "what *appears to be* one of the World Trade Center's towers" (119; emphasis mine). The technical nature of the medium is also debatable—the images are described as video stills (Kirn), doctored photos (Munson), and a digital simulation (Solomon). Nor is it clear how many images are being discussed: Myers counts eleven, Gornick fifteen. One point on which there is no debate, though, is this: regardless of what these images contain, what type of images they are, and how many of them there may be, what they represent is not the truth. The truth, as Kirn baldly puts it, is that "the flesh-and-blood person on the film was—in undoctored, forward-rushing fact—jumping or falling to his death" (1).

The extent of disagreement about the images—how many there are, what they depict, whether they are photos, video stills, or digital simulations—and the unilateral agreement that what they depict is not, in fact, what happened at the World Trade Center site on September 11, 2001, demonstrate more than the truism that, as W. J. T. Mitchell puts it, "words can 'cite,' but never 'sight' their objects" (152). It attests to something more fundamental: the fragility of reality as such, a fragility that the image simultaneously affirms and denies.[1] Even "in this era of political spin, agitprop, Photoshop, and made-for-TV reality, we still regard photographs—even those suspected of having been manipulated—as conveying a kernel of truth," writes David Friend (xiv). Turning to the photographic record of 9/11, he continues: "For much of the world it is pictures that have served as the only reliable vessels of the experience of that day" (xvi).

Vessels of the experience: this documentary aura ensures and refuses witness, captures reality and crosses it out. Like the bodies of those who jumped to their deaths from the World Trade Center towers, both an unarguable fact and the object of perpetual disavowal, reality flickers, exposed belatedly to the traumatized mind's eye. Writing of Richard Drew's famous image of a falling man, Mauro notes that "the scene [. . .] was not witnessed directly by the photographer. [. . .] Due to the motion

---

1. Photographs document and assert the factual quality of an event, providing, as Susan Gubar puts it in her discussion of Holocaust photographs, "indispensable evidence that the inconceivable did in fact occur" (99). Note that in Gubar's formulation, it is the inconceivable, and not the Holocaust, that the image verifies. For a discussion of the relation of Holocaust photography and photographs of 9/11, see Zelizer.

blur of the towers, the artificial proximity attributed to the 200mm zoom lens, and the closure of the shutter that obfuscates the image at the very moment of exposure, Drew could not see the moment as it flit past" (588). Precisely because of the fragility of perception to which it attests, the documentary aura persists. "Photographed images do not seem to be statements about the world so much as pieces of it, miniatures of reality that anyone can make or acquire," writes Susan Sontag (*On Photography* 4); "A fake photograph," Sontag continues, "falsifies reality" (86).

A reader who turns to the book's copyright page will see the image described as a "photo illustration based on a photograph by Lyle Owerko."[2] Photo illustration is an imaging technique according to which a digitized photograph is transformed, making its subject vulnerable to illustration, enhancement, distortion, and denial: in short, to fiction. Precisely because 9/11 represents an inversion of the relation of fiction and reality (the collapse of the towers resembled countless disaster movies), factual specificity plays a crucial role in discussions of it. Scholars seem compelled to cite facts even as they gesture to the inextricability of these facts from their discursive manifestation and ideological manipulation. For Kristiaan Versluys, for example, 9/11 "demonstrates, if not the primacy, then at least the inevitability of discourse"; at the same time (in fact, in the same sentence), 9/11 is also the "most real of all real events—220 stories crashing down, thousands of tons of steel collapsing" (3).

At work in descriptions such as these is a paradoxical affirmation and disavowal of fiction's incursion into the real. In the context of traumatic violent events, the implications of this incursion come starkly to view. The vehement iterations that the images in the last few pages of *Extremely Loud and Incredibly Close* represent everything *but* the truth attest to a venerable tradition of countering violence with the empirical and the factual; if the distinction between fact and fiction seems inaccessible, the distinction as such is valorized. In responses to the flip-book, for example, critics tend to contrast the images with some extratextual quality, stress the incongruity of the two, and urge the primacy of one over the other. Beck's major concern about the flip-book has to do less with the fact that 9/11 "did happen," and more with the extent to which "Foer's book does nothing to address why or why not" (n. pag.)—rather

---

2. Ingersoll identifies the Owerko reference but neglects to note that the image is not a photograph but a *photo illustration based on* the Owerko photograph (64); Dawes, referring to the image, describes it as a photograph that "both exemplifies and rewrites the role of visual images in the collective memory of 9/11" (534).

a tall order for any novel, let alone one narrated by a nine-year-old, but one that renders a work of fiction answerable to history, to the geopolitical causes of which 9/11 is an effect. Gornick describes "staring at the final photograph of the World Trade Center with a clean and empty sky beside it, thinking, That's it? Is this the literary use to which 'the worst day' is to be put?" (32)—a response that seems to set the novel up to fail (presumably, putting "the worst day" to *any* literary use would be ethically and aesthetically suspect) but points to the special responsibilities that fiction about real violence is assumed to bear. Robert Eaglestone castigates Foer for neglecting to "address [. . .] the issues" (19) and emphasizes the novel's general failure to comprehend "the current crisis" (22) but neglects to name the issues or define the crisis in question. What issues should the novel have addressed? Just what literary use is Gornick thinking of, just what answers to "why or why not" does Beck expect? In each case, the truth of historical violence is assumed, the value of fidelity is reiterated, but the object of fidelity remains as blurry as the images themselves.

I linger on the flip-book that closes *Extremely Loud and Incredibly Close* in order to articulate the stakes of this book's claims for the possibilities offered by fiction even, or even especially, in the context of vast and violent historical events. Foer deliberately blurs the distinction between fiction and fact, but responses to the flip-book that simultaneously assume and disavow its fictional quality foreclose investigations of this gesture. I attempt here a different approach: one that responds to evocations of the fact/fiction distinction with "Nevermind," focusing, instead, on the novels' ethics of complicity and the trajectories of fidelity they trace. My goal is to examine Foer's novels' engagement with real, historical violence, but without disavowing the fact that these are *novels*; they are *fiction*. The peril of such an approach, of course, is the radical relativism it courts. It flies directly in the face of a general sentiment that, especially in the case of historical violent events, fiction must be true to the facts in order to safeguard the reality of violence from representation and protect history from denial. But there are attractions to this approach as well. It creates the conditions of possibility for exiting cycles of violence. It attests to the role of fiction in particular, and art in general, in creating conditions for change.

Jonathan Safran Foer was born in 1977. He is the youngest author in this study, both the product of the X culture my previous chapters described *and* a register of its impact today. Violence occupies his work: his debut novel *Everything Is Illuminated* is set in the wake of the Holocaust; *Extremely Loud and Incredibly Close* takes 9/11 as its subject but the firebombing of Dresden in World War II figures prominently as well. Foer has said that "both the Holocaust and 9/11 were events that demanded retellings" (Solomon 42). With this deceptively simple statement, Foer gestures toward the alliance of historical events with narrative, testimony, and witness that such events, as he puts it, "demand"—an attribution of agency to a violent past that has, traditionally, elicited an ethos of verity and an aesthetics of disrupted, fragmented texts that attest to the *limits* of fiction. But for Foer, the demand in question is not for silence but for speech: plenitude, multiple, revisionary narratives: not telling but retelling. "*Retelling*" implies that reality, for Foer (as it is for many Xers) is always already a discursive production, and that historical events demand not the facts, but multiple versions or accounts.

X silences (it crosses out) and erupts (it multiplies); after X, both speech and silence are urgent and vexed, a paradox that is familiar in discussions of violent historical events like 9/11 and the Holocaust. Here, though, we should pause and consider the implications of putting these two together. 9/11 has often been compared to the Holocaust in its traumatic impact, its epochal situation, and its cultural reverberations. This analogy is faulty at best. But to dismiss it would be too easy. Like most analogies, analogies of 9/11 and the Holocaust have little to say about the events themselves and much to tell about the function of analogy—here, as a call to witness an epoch-making event. Regardless of whether 9/11 is, in fact, epochal (the novels discussed in the previous chapter insist that it is not), this call to witness is striking: it presupposes both historical verity *and* the necessity of this verity's verification. There is both too much knowledge *and* too little, so the *limits* of knowledge come starkly into view. The discourse of unspeakability established around the Holocaust and American slavery in the 1980s and 1990s (when Xers were teenagers and young adults) resurfaced after 9/11 in early responses to the attacks and persists in the dominance of trauma as the primary critical paradigm with they are approached. But Xers, who were admonished, as young people, to "Remember" even as what they could remember was described as unspeakable and available for witness only through television and film, had, by adulthood, an opportunity to articulate an alternative approach to historical violence, an approach defined not by history but by fiction, not by nation but by affiliation, not by conviction but by ambivalence: not yes or no.

FIDELITY, HISTORY

Everything Is Illuminated and *Extremely Loud and Incredibly Close* are strikingly similar in form and theme. Each novel tells essentially the same story: the coming-to-knowledge of a young male protagonist propelled toward an engagement with the past. In *Everything Is Illuminated,* the young (American, Jewish) Jonathan and his (Ukrainian) guide Alex (both Xers) travel to the ruins of the Jewish shtetl Trachimbrod in search of a woman named Augustine who saved Jonathan's grandfather from the Nazis. In the course of this journey the figure of Alex's grandfather increases in significance and, in the novel's climactic scene, recounts betraying his best friend to the *Einsatzgruppen* by pointing at him and saying "he is a Jew." In *Extremely Loud and Incredibly Close,* the young Oskar is obsessed with determining whether or not an image of a falling figure is his father who died in the World Trade Center, and traverses New York City in the search of a lock to fit a key he finds in his father's closet. In the course of this journey Oskar encounters his own grandfather, who survived the firebombing of Dresden by Allied forces in World War II. As the above descriptions show, Foer is no Holocaust denier or 9/11 conspiracy theorist. At the same time, the novels engage critically the tradition (specifically, what I will call a tradition of fidelity) through which they are commonly read: his characters begin from a position of moral certainty—specifically, a world in which there are clear distinctions between good and evil, victims and perpetrators—and their journey into the past is a journey into moral ambiguity in which these distinctions are no longer so clear-cut. Finally, each novel has, as its traumatic kernel, a moment that redirects our sympathies from the conventional allegiances its subject matter implies: a sympathetic portrayal of a collaborator (possibly a perpetrator) in the novel about the Holocaust; the bombing of a city by U.S. and British forces in the novel about 9/11.

Foer's novels emerge directly from a cultural conversation about history and memory that was prominent in the 1990s. In the United States, the airing of *Schindler's List,* the opening of the United States Holocaust Memorial Museum, and the declaration that 1993 was the "Year of the Holocaust" were all accompanied by much discussion about the availability of history, and of competing histories, to public memory.[3] The

---

3. Loshitzky, describing the "Holocaust Boom" of 1993–94, includes, with the opening of the USHMM, the signing of a New Jersey bill requiring Holocaust education, the rebroadcasting of NBC's miniseries *Holocaust,* and the reception of Elio Toaff,

"recovered memory debate," the development of trauma theory, the prominence of what Mark Seltzer has described as "wound culture," and highly publicized controversies (such as Nobel Prize winner Rigoberta Menchú's autobiography, attacked in 1999 by anthropologist David Stoll, and faux Holocaust survivor Binjamin Wilkomirski, exposed, also in 1999, as Swiss-born Bruno Dösseker) lent urgency, even a tinge of peril, to these debates. Dominick LaCapra and Berel Lang, both of whom published important work in Holocaust studies in the 1990s, addressed these issues directly. Each underscores that it is crucial to assert and reinforce the facts of history in the face of fiction's menacing encroach. In a comparative examination of truth claims in history and fiction, Dominick LaCapra notes that in the case of violent or "extreme" events it is appropriate to employ the truth claims of historiography to critique those of art. Taking the Holocaust as his example, he writes: "one might justifiably criticize a work of art on historical as well as aesthetic and normative grounds if it treated the Third Reich in a manner that excluded or marginalized the Nazi genocide" (*Writing History* 14). For Berel Lang this valorization of historical fact authorizes some accounts but prohibits others. "Although there are two sides to many stories," writes Lang, "for some stories there are not two sides but one. At times, in other words, the facts do speak for themselves" (*Post-Holocaust* 106). Statements such as these privilege not only history and its facts (which are presumed to be distinct from, and to pre-exist, their representation in fiction) but fidelity to them. Fidelity to the facts takes precedence— epistemically and morally—over fiction. "If there is no crucial difference between imaginative and historical writing," writes Lang, "than there can be no crucial difference between denials that [a violent event like] the Holocaust occurred and the discourse that affirms this occurrence" (*Holocaust Representation* 13).

LaCapra's work and Lang's represent this tradition of fidelity that enjoins being true to the facts, to the fundamental features of a violent event. There are, of course, significant differences between the two. Lang stresses the centrality of the chronicle as the necessary basis for responsible representation; LaCapra warns against fidelity to trauma. But both Lang and LaCapra assume a fundamental temporal progression by which the truth *precedes* fidelity to it. The subject is situated *after* history, *in the wake* of events, the facts of which she must know in order

---

Rome's chief rabbi, at the Vatican. "*Schindler's List* was the 'Jewel in the Crown' of the 'Year of the Holocaust,' confirming once again the power of popular cinema to shape collective memory and to generate topics for popular conversation" (6).

to be true to them. By doing so, they conclude, she acts ethically; ethics, in this case, takes the form of cementing violence to its reality and, by doing so, foreclosing denial of either violence or the real. Generation Xers, as we have seen, are accustomed to rewind, to replay, and to reverse causal progression. Further, the generation with no cause to fight for and with nothing to believe in, witness to the attachment to traumatic histories that dictated the form and tenor of identity politics in the 1980s and 1990s, are disinclined to participate in the problematic valorization of trauma that LaCapra terms "fidelity." (Though LaCapra warns against fidelity to trauma, he does so because such fidelity ties the subject to history in a problematic way, condemning her to a type of "acting out" that mimics traumatic repetition and prohibits the more desirable process of "working through.") My point is that both acting out trauma and working through it retain the epistemic validity of trauma's violence and privilege the historical record of it. The object of fidelity is bound up in knowledge: stating and maintaining the facts. According to this logic, fidelity to fiction not only *is* wrong, it *does* wrong.

This discourse of fidelity has a juridical valence. It organizes the facts to which the ethical subject is to be true into categories in which the moral and the legal are combined. Thus a perpetrator is guilty, a victim innocent, a bystander complicit—in the juridical and the moral sense, if not the psychological one.[4] Fictional depictions of the facts are expected to assert and maintain this moral/legal dyad, and the reader is expected to reassert and enforce this dyad by evincing fidelity to historical accuracy. This (so the logic goes) grants her work legal validity (LaCapra's wording, "one might *justifiably* criticize a work of art," is quite telling). This tradition of fidelity accords a significant responsibility to the reader or the critic of fiction who, in the quest of an ethical reading, will evaluate aesthetic productions on the basis of fidelity not only to fact but to justice. As Lang writes, "The rudimentary details of the answers to the questions of who, what, and when [are] a test of whatever else is constructed on them. *Both as a matter of fact and as a matter of justice"* (*Holocaust Representation* 13; emphasis mine). Put briefly: according to the venerable tradition of countering violence with the empirical and the factual, from which LaCapra and Lang write, "being true" means being right as well as being ethical, and "being right" means being just as well

---

4. LaCapra defines "victim" in social, political, and ethical terms, not psychological terms (*Writing History* 79). The distinction between these categories allows for the alignment of victim with innocent in a way that the psychological category of victim does not. See Mandel (*Against the Unspeakable* 56–57).

as being correct. But Xers do not so easily subscribe to this binding of the real (matters of fact) to judgment (matters of justice). As Video Backpacker puts it in Richard Linklater's iconic X film *Slacker*, "I was seeing it for real but it just wasn't right."

TRAUMA, JUSTICE

Of course, violent historical events like those dealt with in Foer's fiction are commonly approached in terms of trauma and, in the context of trauma, the epistemic stability of fidelity's object may not be a given. Both as a psychic experience (in psychoanalytic terms; Freud is the prime example) *and* as an epistemological model (in literary critical terms) for an engagement with history in the work of trauma theorists such as LaCapra, trauma is a break with established orders of knowledge. As an event that eludes psychic mastery, its reality can only be established through—to return to Foer's term—retelling. Given the prominence of this discourse in discussion of Foer's novels, it is worth investigating whether trauma offers a different approach to fidelity, one not limited to the facts.

On the face of matters, trauma is an inviting paradigm through which to approach Foer's work. The Holocaust and 9/11 are generally described in terms of their traumatic impact. In a much-cited interview with Deborah Solomon, Foer has referred to an event in his childhood that he calls "the Explosion": a classroom chemistry project gone awry that left many children injured, including Foer's best friend. Solomon's conjecture is that "in writing his novel, Foer [. . .] combined a personal trauma that occurred in 1985 with the national trauma that befell the country on Sept. 11, 2001" (44). Scholars of Foer's work have followed Solomon's hypothesis and read both of Foer's novels through the structure and theme of trauma. Philippe Codde, for example, suggests that the Explosion is the source of Foer's "intimate knowledge and understanding of traumatic events as instanced by his novels" ("Philomela Revisited" 242). For Foer, he writes, "the aporia at the heart of the traumatic experience can, indeed, only be filled with words to ease the pain [. . .] but the words can never really capture or represent the traumatic past" ("Philomela Revisited" 245–46). Writing of *Extremely Loud and Incredibly Close*, Sien Uytterschout and Kristiaan Versluys diagnose Thomas Schell (the grandfather) as melancholic, the (nameless) grandmother Schell as a victim of survivor guilt, and, drawing on LaCapra's terms, they describe Oskar as both "acting out" his trauma and "working through" it.

Though Uytterschout and Versluys do not consider the novel's status as fiction, their emphasis on the accuracy of its depiction of trauma reflects the dictate that fiction, in the context of violence, must be "true"—if not to the facts, than to the manifestations of their psychic impact. Versluys's reading of the novel in *Out of the Blue* is also predicated on the reality of trauma and the accuracy of fiction's depiction of it. Codde, who does take the special status of fiction into account, reaches a similar conclusion: "The form of the novel, far from being playful, is actually an accurate representation of a young boy's traumatized mind" ("Philomela Revisited" 251). Such readings reflect the same investment in epistemic validity and factual accuracy that I described in the opening pages of this chapter. Though fidelity is directed not to the historical record but to the psychic reverberations of violence, the undeniability of its object remains the guiding principle. This somewhat naïve assumption that the work mirrors the world disavows the novel's status as fiction, and forecloses investigations of Foer's deliberate blurring of the distinction between fiction and fact in his novels about traumatic historical events.

To take the blurring of this distinction seriously—to examine fiction's engagement with historical trauma without disavowing fiction's status as fiction—is to witness the force of this discourse's juridical dimension. When trauma is decoupled from history, the distinction between victim and perpetrator is commonly evoked to reinstate the primacy of the historical and to enforce its moral/legal valence. As an example of such a gesture, I turn to a seminal moment in 1990s trauma theory: Cathy Caruth's reading of the parable of Tancred and Clorinda that opens her important 1996 study *Unclaimed Experience*. Tancred fatally wounds his beloved Clorinda in battle; later, in an enchanted forest, he strikes at a tree that cries out in Clorinda's voice. This parable, suggests Caruth, "can be read [. . .] as a larger parable, both of the unarticulated implications of the theory of trauma in Freud's writings and, beyond that, of the crucial link between literature and theory" (3).

By reading the story as a parable of traumatic repetition, literary evidence of how "the experience of a trauma repeats itself, exactly and unremittingly, through the unknowing acts of the survivor and against his very will" (2), Caruth links literature and trauma theory and puts them in service of a vision of ethics by which the experience of traumatic violence draws diverse people together. Clorinda's voice testifies not only to Tancred's trauma but to the "the way in which trauma may lead [. . .] to the encounter with another, through the very possibility and surprise of listening to another's wound" (8). In other words: Caruth's recourse to the figure of the parable enables her to found, in *fiction*, a discussion of how trauma may float free from the historical and, in doing so, open a space for ethical engagement with traumatic experience and history.

Ruth Leys's *Trauma: A Genealogy,* a seminal 2000 overview of trauma theory, takes Caruth to task for this. In the concluding chapter, Leys turns to Caruth's book, stressing the "hazards" of her approach to trauma (292) and its "chilling implications" (297). These lie not in the link between literature and theory but in the blurring of history by fiction. "If [. . .] the murderer Tancred can become the victim of the trauma and the voice of Clorinda testimony to his wound," writes Leys, "then Caruth's logic would turn other perpetrators into victims too—for example, it would turn the executioners of the Jews into victims and the 'cries' of the Jews into testimony to the trauma suffered by the Nazis" (297). Leys's logic ("If Tancred . . . then Nazis") extends Caruth's literary-theoretical investigation to the historical-ethical realm, an extension that she, like Caruth, performs by zeroing in on the literary mechanism of the parable. "What exactly is the parable offered by Tasso's poem according to Caruth?" asks Leys, and answers: "The Oxford English Dictionary defines 'parable' as follows: *A fictitious narrative or allegory* (usually something that might occur naturally), by which moral or spiritual relations are typically figured or set forth. [. . .] On Caruth's interpretation, what the parable of Tasso's story tells us is that not only can Tancred be considered the victim of a trauma but that even the Nazis are not exempt from the same dispensation" (297; emphasis mine). In other words, referencing the parable's recourse to fiction to establish morality, Leys turns to history in order to demonstrate that Caruth's reading produces injustice.

Both Leys's argument and its vehemence (as well as the general agreement among trauma theorists that Caruth has gone too far)[5] testify to what is at stake: the danger that the distinction of perpetrator from victim may be blurred. Foer deliberately courts this danger. His reliance on the photo illustration importantly resembles Caruth's reliance on the parable: both the parable and the image blur the dis-

---

5. For a discussion of Leys's reading of Caruth and critics' responses to it, see Mandel, *Against the Unspeakable* 54–59.

tinction between fiction and truth, make claims for each, and situate fiction as the origin of possible truths. Responses to both the parable and the photo illustration mobilize trauma as a juridical instrument, wielding it to distinguish victim from nonvictim and, by extension, victim from perpetrator. The reverberations of this imperative are evident in Versluys's discussion of *Extremely Loud and Incredibly Close.* Versluys reads the book as articulating the traumatic impact of historical violent events. Struck by the fact that Foer, an American Jew whose family was affected by the Holocaust, chooses German protagonists for his novel, he makes sure to clarify in a footnote that the family "though German, is anti-Nazi" (199); describing the book as "a strong plea for tolerance, refusing to take sides," he immediately specifies that, in fact, "it takes the side of the victims, irrespective of their national origin or allegiance" (82). This is an example of how, in the context of trauma's shattering of distinctions between past and present, fiction and fact, the distinction between perpetrator and victim is maintained—not within the novel or the fiction but in critical readings and responses to it.[6] In the name of fidelity, they conflate the historical with the juridical, invest both with moral weight, and adjudicate accordingly.[7] Judgment—in the sense of evoking and applying legal categories—is both the origin and end of this kind of reading. Fiction is locked into a closed circuit, bound and circumscribed by the assumptions about violence and history that legislate and limit the kinds of responses we can have.

---

6. Additional examples are Codde's ("Keeping History at Bay") and Saal's discussions of *Extremely Loud and Incredibly Close.* Both focus on the character of Simon Goldberg. Codde argues that Goldberg haunts the narrative, and Saal underscores his "muted" presence, but for each, Goldberg—the novel's sole Jewish Holocaust victim—undercuts the radical relativism that the intersection of Dresden, Hiroshima, and 9/11 courts. Menachem Feuer, discussing *Everything Is Illuminated,* argues that Alex's grandfather is, in fact, Jewish. For all, the Jewish Holocaust victim—an image par excellence of ethnic authenticity, racial persecution, moral authority, and bare life—is evoked to counter Foer's unmooring of violence from the real.

7. LaCapra, who, as I noted earlier, privileges the truth-claims of historiography over those of fiction in the context of "extreme, traumatic" events, raises the issue of "fidelity to trauma, a feeling that one must somehow keep faith with it" (*Writing History* 22). LaCapra's distrust of fidelity to trauma responds to this conflation of the victimized with traumatized: because he insists that it is only the victim who may act out or work through trauma, "fidelity to trauma" might be more accurately described as "fidelity to *victimization* (by traumatic violence)" or fidelity to a simulacrum (as defined by Badiou; I turn to Badiou's work on fidelity later in this chapter).

FIDELITY, TRUTH

How, then, are we to approach violence after Generation X? Because fidelity determines affiliations—to be faithful is to be true—and informs representation, communication, and community even (or especially) in the absence of a god, cause, or *ism*, it cannot be abandoned. But nor can fiction simply replace fact as fidelity's object. Because fidelity produces truth claims, fidelity to fiction can deny that historical events occurred, or proffer an account of them to counteract established facts. Generation X, defined and determined by the historical events and social developments that accompanied their maturing in the 1980s and 1990s, may well find that reality "bites" and long, with McInerney's narrator in *Bright Lights, Big City,* to replace Fact with Fiction, but in *Everything Is Illuminated* and *Extremely Loud and Incredibly Close,* history is ineluctable: it *happened,* and the question of fiction's ethics in the wake of its violence remains open and urgent.[8] The question is this: When violence blurs the distinction between fiction and fact, can fiction remain fiction and be true?

To begin to answer this question, I turn to Alain Badiou's work on fidelity, truth, and ethics. For Badiou, the object of fidelity is not knowledge (which Badiou aligns with established orders of thinking) but that which breaks with knowledge. Badiou terms such a break an "event" and, for Badiou, the event need not be of momentous historical significance.[9] In *Ethics: An Essay on the Understanding of Evil,* Badiou offers four categories of an event: amorous, political, scientific, or aesthetic (the examples he gives are falling in love, the French Revolution, the Copernican revolution, Schoenberg's twelve-tone scale). Truth is not singular

---

8. Foer's novels include some significant gestures toward alternate or allohistories. Alternate history is a "what-if" exercise in imagining what might have happened had history turned out differently (examples include Xer Michael Chabon's *The Yiddish Policeman's Union*). In a discussion of allohistory in fiction, Adam Rovner describes allohistory as a philosophical genre, one that unmasks illusions we hold about historical evidence and objectivity. "Ultimately," he concludes, "these novels dispel the illusion of determinism that the historical perspective creates: this liberation enhances the freedom for thought, for reform, for change" (149–50). The multiple trajectories of fidelity in the novels I discuss do open this possibility, but their allohistoric gestures remain firmly rooted in historical actuality. The flip-book, for example, allows Oskar to imagine an alternate world, but this world is also identified as an impossible one through the grammatical form of the third conditional: "we *would have been* safe" (*Extremely* 326; my emphasis).

9. Badiou's event has, as Keith Jenkins puts it, "no particular content [. . .] its happening is not a matter of 'the facts,' of the cognitive; its significance cannot be 'proven'" (46).

but plural, and truths are not the objects but the products of fidelity: the outcome of a process of being faithful, of "being true." Thus, though an event is always situated in history (which Badiou thinks of as a reservoir of situations, each of which is a site of multiplicity), it is distinguished from history by its impact on someone who, compelled to be faithful to this impact, is propelled by fidelity into subjecthood: fidelity makes her a subject *of* an event. (In *Being and Event* Badiou defines the subject as "the process of liaison between the event [. . .] and the procedure of fidelity" [239].)

Badiou's thinking on fidelity recasts the term in three ways that are useful for thinking about violence after Generation X. First, reflecting the ethical indeterminacy that characterizes this generation's approach to violence, fidelity (according to Badiou) is not a virtue or a quality possessed by a subject. There is no faithful subject that precedes an event. Fidelity is, instead, a way of thinking or processing, of organizing. Second, reflecting the epistemic uncertainty by which presence disappears here, fidelity (according to Badiou) does not exist in and of itself; its presence or absence can't be located. Rather, fidelity can be identified only in what it produces or programs: it names as event an organization of the situation's multiplicity (*Being* 233). Finally: by organizing the situation, fidelity generates truths from within it; truth is the product, not the object of fidelity. Fidelity assembles or fashions truths, rather than mirroring or reflecting them: "*a truth groups together all the terms of the situation which are positively connected to the event.* [. . .] [It is the] result of a procedure of fidelity" (*Being* 335; emphasis in the original).

In *Ethics,* which is intended for a general audience, Badiou employs rhetoric that invites us to consider the violence with which his notion of fidelity is inflected. He stresses compulsion (an event "compels us to decide a *new* way of being" and "compels the subject to *invent* a new way of being and acting in the situation" [41, 42; emphasis in the original]) and, more importantly, force. "Truth forces knowledges," writes Badiou, adding, "The verb *to force* indicates that since the power of a truth is that of a break," it "violat[es] established and circulating knowledges" (70; emphasis in the original).[10] The subject is what emerges when someone is "riven," "punctured," and "broken" by truth (49, 46, 51). The prominence of this rhetoric in Badiou's book on ethics invites us to

---

10. "Forcing" is a mathematical technique invented by the American mathematician Paul Cohen. Hallward describes Cohen's concept of forcing and notes, "the term 'forcing' is simply Cohen's jargon for 'satisfaction in the model'" (345). The rhetoric of violence seems to be Badiou's contribution.

think about the similarity of the subject founded by the event to the subject founded by trauma, bringing Badiou's work closer to the kinds of discussions that have surrounded Foer's: Badiou's subject, though not a psychological subject, is founded by the event, and punctured and broken by truth, and is thus similar to the subject produced by the violence of trauma (specifically, trauma conceived as a literary critical term, that is, as an epistemological model for engagement with history). At the same time, Badiou offers a quite different view of the kind of subject produced by the event and of the nature of fidelity: fidelity is not, in itself, ethical; it is defined in terms not of its object but of its product; it produces truths, rather than mirroring or reflecting them.

Badiou's concept of fidelity enables us to unbind fiction about violence from the facts of history and from judgments about historical actors' innocence or guilt. If the tradition of fidelity I described in the first part of this chapter—fidelity to the facts—is defined in terms of its object (be that object historical facts or their traumatic impact), Badiou's work enables us to trouble not the object but the process by which this object presents as truth, and to see how fiction produces different, subjective, and multiple truths. Badiou does not employ fidelity as a method of literary criticism (though the encounter with a literary work may occasion an event), and, though Badiou has elsewhere written on 9/11 and on the word "Jew," his role in my discussion is to complicate the tradition of fidelity I described in the earlier part of this chapter.[11] The catch is that Badiou's thinking does not *replace* this tradition but is counterposed with it so that, with true X ambivalence, rather than choosing one over the other, we may take the two together.

Doing so enables us to revisit the relation of fidelity to history and to justice. Fidelity to the facts posits a subject who is situated *after* history, *in the wake* of events, the facts of which she must know in order *to be true* to them. Badiou's conception of the event as that which *precedes* or founds the subject invites us to consider how a subject may *create*, rather than conform to, the conditions for an ethical response. Taking the two together means the subject is situated both before *and* after ethics. Think of a palindrome—a word that can be read left-to-right and right-to-left (or a flip-book, that constructs or deconstructs causal relations, depending on the direction in which the pages are turned). Bring-

---

11. In *Handbook for Inaesthetics,* Badiou emphasizes that fidelity does not describe the relationship of work to world; its articulation remains the province of the work, which Badiou describes as "a fact of art" (12). Badiou's writings on 9/11 and "Jew" are included in *Polemics.*

ing fidelity to the facts together with Badiou's work also enables us to revisit the distinction between victim and nonvictim and the function of this distinction as arbiter of truth in fiction. In fidelity to the facts, the object of fidelity is bound up in knowledge; for scholars like LaCapra and Lang, ethics reside in being faithful not just to the facts but to their retrospective organization into right and wrong: the subject is true by being accurate, and ethical by being just. For Badiou, the object of fidelity is fidelity itself, and ethics is the outcome of a subject's maintaining the compulsion to live, and be, otherwise in relation to the event: "being faithful to a fidelity." Taking the two together is to both affirm and disavow the object of knowledge, to focus on trajectories of fidelity *within* fiction, and to consider fiction's ethics of truth without disavowing fiction's status as fiction.[12] Think of a parable: to return to Leys's definition, "A fictitious narrative or allegory (usually something that might occur naturally), by which moral or spiritual relations are typically figured or set forth."

It is time now to turn to Foer's novels and to trace the operations of fidelity that they solicit and resist.

"IT TOOK HIS SAYING SO TO MAKE IT TRUE":
Everything Is Illuminated

Everything Is Illuminated alternates between the chronicle of the fictional shtetl of Trachimbrod from its founding to its destruction by the Nazis (narrated by Jonathan), and the picaresque journey that Jonathan undertook to the site of Trachimbrod in the company of Alex, Alex's Grandfather, and their dog (narrated by Alex).[13] Jonathan and Alex (both Xers) write their stories in the course of the novel, each mailing to the other the chapters as they are completed. Alex prefaces each chapter he writes with a letter to Jonathan in which Alex comments on the

---

12. Fidelity to fiction thus defined is quite different from what Badiou describes, in *Ethics,* as fidelity to a simulacrum. For Badiou, in contrast to fidelity to fidelity (ethics), fidelity to a simulacrum is a condition of possibility not for ethics but for evil, which Badiou defines as an assertion of identity that forecloses engagement with otherness (his example, in *Ethics,* is Nazism). Though I cannot here offer an account of the role of fiction in Badiou's philosophy, Badiou generally uses "fiction" in its sense of fashioning and forming, as opposed to illusion or delusion.

13. Through capitalization I distinguish between Jonathan's grandfather and Alex's Grandfather.

story Jonathan is writing, reflects on his own story, and meditates on the nature of reading and writing. Jonathan sends Alex chapters of his chronicle, each also prefaced with a letter. Though Jonathan's letters are not included in the novel, we can surmise, from Alex's letters to Jonathan, that Jonathan comments on Alex's writing, corrects his English, and encloses some money.

The double narrative of *Everything Is Illuminated* would seem to oppose the fictional (Jonathan's magical-realist chronicle of the shtetl) with the factual (Alex's relatively realistic account of their journey to Trachimbrod in post-Soviet Ukraine).[14] But as the novel progresses, this distinction begins to blur. Writing to Jonathan, Alex expresses some reservations about Jonathan's version of Trachimbrod, specifically the explicit descriptions of sex acts that the more prudish Alex deems inappropriate (179). He also refers to Jonathan's comments on his, Alex's, written account of their journey. Jonathan had shared with Alex a personal memory and Alex has included this memory in his own account. After reading Alex's chapter, Jonathan asks Alex to revise his story to remove that anecdote, but Alex refuses. "I must tell you that this is not a possibility. I accept if because of my decision you choose not to present me any more currency, or if you command for me to post back the currency you have given me in the previous months. It would be justifying every dollar, I will inform you" (179). At this point Alex reflects, "We are being very nomadic with the truth, yes? The both of us? Do you think that this is acceptable when we are writing about things that occurred?" (179).

On one level Alex's phrasing is a version of the dictate that historical events—especially violent ones—should not be subjected to fictionalization. Ribbat, for example, reads Alex's disingenuous question as "a dictum that sums up contemporary debates on mediated memory and popular culture and links them to earlier debates on Holocaust representation" (214). But read in context, the "truth" Alex is referring to is not a stable entity, and it is not (or not merely) the Holocaust.[15] The context is this: reflecting on Jonathan's chronicle, Alex complains that it is not "high-fidelity"; Jonathan's request that Alex revise his own account

---

14. For a thoughtful discussion of the two narrative modes at work in the novel, see Francisco Collado-Rodríguez.

15. Markovits points out that *Everything Is Illuminated* "works [because] it isn't really about the Holocaust" (n. pag.). For Gessen, though, the one thing that "is treated with the utmost seriousness [in *Everything Is Illuminated*] is the Holocaust" (68). For Sicher, the Holocaust figures in Foer's novel as "a postmodern sign of loss" (174).

propels Alex to ask, "If we are to be such nomads with the truth, why do we not make the story more premium than life?" (179). Alex goes on to describe this possible, premium narrative. His account would involve Alex's Grandfather playing the role of Augustine, the woman who saved Jonathan's grandfather from the Nazis; if such an alternative is not acceptable, Alex offers to be, himself, the savior: "We could write Grandfather into the story. [. . .] He could be Augustine. August, perhaps. Or just Alex, if that is satisfactory to you" (180). The multiple possibilities Alex points to, some of which come true (the end of the novel will reveal that Grandfather's name is, in fact, Alex), permeate his prose, underscoring the nomadicity of reference: in the course of *Everything Is Illuminated,* Alex will become "just" in the adjectival, not merely the adverbial sense; not "just" in the sense of being limited, but "just" in the sense of making right.

This fundamental instability of language, the perpetual movement of the signified behind or beneath the signifier that illuminates and obscures it, is familiar to Xers schooled, as Foer was, in poststructuralism and deconstruction. But the implications of being nomadic with the truth are weighty, too. Alex wishes to depart from the facts because he has reached that point in his own chronicle where he must recount the details of his Grandfather's confession that he murdered his best friend, Herschel, betraying him to the *Einsatzgruppen* by pointing at him and saying, "he is a Jew." As Alex puts it, to write an accurate account of his journey with Jonathan is to "point a finger at Grandfather pointing to Herschel" (178). "Herschel was a Jew," Grandfather confesses, in the chapter narrated by Alex. "He was my best friend. [. . .] And I murdered him" (228). The confession identifies Grandfather as a perpetrator: Alex's reluctance to relate this part of the story stems from his conviction that a written account must be faithful to the facts. But as the account continues (and remember: Alex is its reluctant author who has already expressed his desire not to tell this story) "murder" moves, morphing into betrayal: Grandfather identifies Herschel to the soldiers who are separating the Jews from the other townspeople and shooting those who fail to cooperate. As Alex describes it, Grandfather, fearing for his life and for the lives of his wife and child (Alex's father), points at Herschel and says, "he is a Jew this man is a Jew" (251). By exonerating Grandfather of the murder and providing him with a motive, Alex's account reverses the trajectory of Grandfather's initial confession. Even while Grandfather clarifies that "I murdered Herschel" means "I betrayed Herschel," the distinction implicit in the clarification is immediately crossed out: "what I did was *as good as* murdering him. [. . .] Herschel would have been murdered with or without me but it is still *as if* I murdered him" (247; emphasis mine).

Alex is writing these chapters; by writing he is, in his own terms, also "pointing a finger." His account of Grandfather's confession flirts with the juridical injunction with which fidelity to the facts is aligned, and troubles the distinction between fact and fiction that fidelity is invoked to establish. The "good" in "as good as" invests morality with epistemic value; the "still as if" authorizes an account that is parallel to, and coextensive with, the facts: faithful to something other than history. Alex expands on this distinction between an account that is accurate and an account that is right—a right characterized as fidelity not to fact but to fiction. "I would never command you to write a story that is as it occurred in the actual," he says to Jonathan, "but I would command you to make your story *faithful*" (240; emphasis mine). "Faithful" means not only a fiction that differs from history in the poetic sense (relating, as Aristotle puts it, not what has been but what could be); in Alex's formulation, it assumes an ethical dimension—being true not to what has been but to what *should* be—and situates the object of fidelity *within* fiction. (This point is reiterated when Alex, disgusted by Jonathan's most recent chapter of the chronicle of Trachimbrod, shares the text not with Little Igor, his beloved brother, but with his dog, "who acted *faithfully* with it" [240; emphasis mine].)

Despite its ethical inflection, writing what should be does not make you a good person, and in this novel, writing, in its dual work of establishing and revising, becomes both betrayal and fidelity. Meditating on the confession to Jonathan, Alex writes:

> Jonathan where do we go from here what do we do with what we know Grandfather said that I am I but this could not be true the truth is that I also pointedatHerschel and I also said heisaJew and I will tell you that you also pointedatHerschel and you also said heisaJew and more than that Grandfather also pointedatme and said heisaJew and you also pointedathim and said heisaJew and your grandmother and Little Igor we all pointedateachother. (252)

Within this explosion of complicity, "pointing a finger" combines writing, betraying, condemning, killing, *and* being true. It defies the juridical distinction between victim and perpetrator that traditionally limits fiction about violence to the facts of history. This parabolic gesture sets forth an ethics of complicity that forgoes the distinction between perpetrator and victim. Given that the title of the book is *Everything Is Illuminated,* and the finger-pointing chapter is titled "Illumination," it is significant, I think, that the only "illumination" in this chapter refers to the light from the fire that consumes the synagogue and the Jews— including Herschel—inside. This light "illuminated those who were *not* in the synagogue those who were *not* going to die" (251; emphasis mine). Illumination obscures the victims; it is the survivors, collaborators, and perpetrators who must continue in its bleak light. When *everything* is illuminated, distinguishing between those who murdered, those who betrayed, and those who survived fades in light of Alex's urgent question, "What do we do with what we know?"

In the novel's concluding pages, Alex's wistful vision of "being nomadic with the truth," and his suggestion that he and Jonathan, in making their story "excellent," could replace Grandfather with "just Alex" (180), is realized in the final (unfinished) letter from Grandfather to Jonathan, which Alex has presumably found and translated. Speaking of Alex (whom he had, up to this point, referred to as Sasha), Grandfather relates, "I said his name, Alex, which has also been my name for forty years" (275), and the letter presents, as fact, a passage from Jonathan's diary which Alex, in the course of the journey with Jonathan to Trachimbrod, has read but which Grandfather (who speaks no English) could not have. The passage from the letter and from the diary is a fantasy of justice in which Alex expels his abusive father from the home he shares with his mother, his brother, and his Grandfather. The novel's reader first encounters this passage when Alex reads Jonathan's diary (160) and again (the passage is repeated verbatim), in the letter from Grandfather to Jonathan that has been translated by Alex (274). It is unclear whether Jonathan, Alex, or Grandfather is its author.

> He told his father that he could care for Mother and Little Igor. It took his saying so to make it true. Finally, he was ready. His father could not believe this thing. What? he asked. What? And Sasha told him again that he would take care of the family, that he would understand if his father had to leave and never return, and that it would not even make him less of a father. He told his father that he would forgive. Oh, his father became so angry, so full of wrath, and he told Sasha that he would kill him, and Sasha told his father that he would kill him, and they moved at each other with violence and his father said, Say it to my face, not to the

floor, and Sasha said, You are not my father. (160; the identical passage
is repeated on page 274)

This passage is the epistemic crux of the novel, as it marks the spot
where fact and fiction intersect. Jonathan had initially written this passage in the diary he kept on the journey to Trachimbrod after hearing
Alex's accounts of his father's abusive behavior; Alex read this passage
in Jonathan's diary. Describing his initial encounter with the passage,
Alex writes, "I understood what he was doing when he wrote like this.
At first it made me angry, but then it made me sad, and then it made me
so grateful, and then it made me angry again, and I went through these
feelings hundreds of times, stopping on each for only a moment and then
moving on to the next" (160). The passage's reappearance at the end of
the novel (it immediately precedes Grandfather's suicide) puts this affective instability to rest. It identifies the distinction between fact and fantasy as a question of fidelity, but leaves the object of fidelity undecidable.
In translating, Alex may have been faithful to the letter's literal contents,
or he may have rendered them in such a way as to replicate the passage
in Jonathan's diary he had read months earlier, or he may have fabricated the passage in his earlier account. In all these scenarios, the passage is both fiction and true. Further: like "pointing a finger," "it took
his saying so to make it true" posits truth as posterior, not anterior, to
speech and to writing, the product not of telling but of retelling, and as a
necessary break with a violent past. As this parable is written and rewrit-
ten, fiction comes to the fore: it is both the object of fidelity *and* the site
of justice.[16]

"IT HAPPENED TO ME":
Extremely Loud and Incredibly Close

Jonathan and Alex are Xers but Oskar, the narrator of *Extremely Loud
and Incredibly Close,* is not. If *Everything Is Illuminated* is structured
by dual narratives that conflict, revise each other, and intersect, all in

---

16. Hungerford ("Jonathan Safran Foer") discusses this passage as well, though she
dismisses its epistemic instability as "postmodern cleverness" (616). Reflecting on the
novel's "aesthetics of complicity," she concludes that Foer "steps back from this specific
redistribution of pain to a humanistic reflection on pain as an element of life itself"
(617). For Ardoin, in contrast, the scene represents the book's larger project, described
as "a kind of aesthetic unshackling" from "the rigid repetition of the past" (200).

the shadow of the Holocaust, *Extremely Loud and Incredibly Close* takes, as its point of departure, not one disaster but two: the firebombing of Dresden in February 1943 by U.S. and Allied forces, and the terror attacks of September 11, 2001 by Al Qaeda. By bringing these together, Foer underscores, again, the limitations that the victim/perpetrator distinction imposes, limitations that had, in the latter half of the twentieth century, been firmly marked by silence. Keith Gessen has noted how *Extremely Loud and Incredibly Close* echoes, in its passage on the destruction of Dresden, W. G. Sebald's *A Natural History of Destruction,* a literary and photographic meditation on the Allied destruction of German cities in World War II. Gessen's concern has to do with how echoes of Sebald's prose in Foer's book raise questions of influence and originality. But there is another, more important connection: In *A Natural History of Destruction,* Sebald stresses the paucity of literary works about the Allied destruction of German cities. Meditating on this silence, he situates it firmly within the victim/perpetrator distinction: precisely because they were perpetrators of horrifying violence, writes Sebald, Germans could neither imagine themselves as victims, nor could they demand that they be so imagined.[17] It falls, then, to the descendants, the inheritors of this history, to do so.

Such a one is Oskar. He is the product of both Dresden *and* 9/11. His grandfather, Thomas Schell Sr., lost his first love, Anna, in the bombing; years later in New York he is drawn to Anna's sister, Oskar's grandmother, who writes Oskar letters throughout the novel. Their child is Oskar's Dad: Thomas Schell Jr., who dies in the World Trade Center. The two lost figures—"Anna" and "Dad"—are palindromes: words that can be spelled backward and forward. The novel underscores this point: Oskar's grandfather recalls "[writing] 'Anna' in the air—backward and right to left—and when I was on the phone I'd dial the numbers—2662" (16); Oskar, thinking of his father, imagines saying "'Dad?' backward, which would have sounded the same as 'Dad' forward" (236). Writing about narrative and history in a very different context, Peter Brooks describes the palindrome as "a repetitive text without variation or point of fixity, a return which leads to an unarrested shuttling back and forth" between "human plots" and "eternal orders which render human

---

17. Sebald writes: "As far as I know, the question of whether or how [the bombing] could be strategically or morally justified was never the subject of open debate in Germany after 1945, no doubt mainly because a nation which had murdered and worked to death millions of people in its camps could hardly call on the victorious powers to explain the military and political logic that dictated the destruction of the German cities" (13–14).

attempts to plot and to interpret plot not only futile, but ethically unacceptable" (524–25). "We are condemned," Brooks continues, "to repetition, rereading, in the knowledge that what we discover will always be that there was nothing to be discovered" (525).

Extremely Loud and Incredibly Close is structured by precisely such shuttling back and forth, figured by the game of "Reconnaissance Expedition." This is a game that Oskar plays with his father in which Oskar must find and retrieve some object. Their last game took place in Central Park on the weekend before his father's death, and was never completed. After 9/11, Oskar continues to play the game, but instead of searching Central Park for buried objects, he searches the boroughs of New York City to find the lock that fits a key he finds in his father's closet. Looking at all the people he met on those wanderings (they come to see him perform as Yorick's skull in his school production of *Hamlet*) Oskar muses: "They didn't know what they had in common, which was kind of like how I didn't know what the thumbtack, the bent spoon, the square of aluminum foil, and all those other things I dug up in Central Park had to do with each other" (143). Of course, Oskar is what they have in common, a point made clear at the conclusion of his quest, when Oskar meets William Black, the owner of the key, only to discover that the object of his quest is a mirror image of himself: another bereaved son.

What he refers to as "the worst day" did not just happen *to* Oskar. He is the product *of* it, not only through the firebombing of Dresden (another "worst day") but his "heavy boots" (as he describes his depression), his hypochondria, his fear of Arabs, elevators, smoke, and tall buildings (36), and especially his compulsive inventing. From the abrupt opening sentence ("What about a teakettle?"), the prose of the novel evokes invention run amok, a crisis characterized not by imagination's limits but its excess, and centered on the image of the falling figure. "There's one body that could be him [his father's] [. . .] when I magnify it until the pixels are so big that it stops looking like a person, sometimes I can see glasses. Or I think I can. But I know I probably can't. It's just me wanting it to be him" because, Oskar continues, "*I want to stop inventing. If I could know how he died, exactly how he died, I wouldn't have to invent him dying inside an elevator that was stuck between floors* [. . .] *and I wouldn't have to imagine him trying to crawl down the outside of the building* [. . .] *or trying to use a tablecloth as a parachute* [. . .] *There were so many different ways to die, and I just need to know which was his*" (257; emphasis mine).

Because an event, for Badiou, is a break with established knowledge, it is unspeakable, external to the ordering processes of language. We may think of fidelity as a process of articulating the event or naming it ("that's what happened") that, by doing so, brings a subject into being ("it happened to *me*"). Oskar keeps the image of the falling figure in a scrapbook titled "Stuff That Happened to Me." He found the image on a Portuguese website—such images are not available in the United States—and complains: "It makes me incredibly angry that people all over the world can know things that I can't, because it happened *here*, and happened to *me*, so shouldn't it be *mine*?" (256, emphasis in original). At the end of the novel Oskar returns to the falling figure and wonders: "Was it Dad? Maybe. Whoever it was, it was somebody" (325). After relinquishing ownership, certainty, and specificity, Oskar *rips the pages out* of "Stuff That Happened to Me" and assembles them, in reverse order, to create the flip-book.

This X ethic, that crosses out and marks the spot, affirming the happening of an event and opening it up, makes possible an extension beyond the victim/perpetrator distinction that locks fiction into a closed circuit. It demands certainty but underscores its unavailability. This is the key, I think, to the novel's title. At the culmination of his quest, Oskar is not meeting William Black for the first time; he is re-encountering a figure he had just missed at the start of his search because Black had, at that moment, been "extremely loud" (293) while Oskar had been "incredibly close" (394). Between "extremely loud" and "incredibly close" is another meditation on the falling man, a meditation that attends to the potential and limits of the digitized image: "I started thinking about the pixels in the image of the falling body, and how the closer you looked, the less you could see" (293). But this indeterminacy cannot be owned, affirmed, or (in the form of traumatic capital) safeguarded. If, as Badiou puts it in *Ethics*, "to enter into the composition of a subject of truth can only be something that *happens to you*" (51), such work, for Oskar, is predicated on *abandoning* the kind of thinking that had him complain that "it happened here, and happened to me, so shouldn't it be mine?" By eschewing the logic of nation, subject, and trauma, and by ripping the pages out of "Stuff That Happened to Me" to create the flip-book, Oskar resurrects and affirms this deeper, harder truth: "It happened to everybody," as Alex's Grandfather, in *Everything Is Illuminated*, says of Herschel's death. "Just because I was not a Jew, it does not mean that it did not happen to me" (245–46).

FACT, FICTION, FIDELITY: NOT YES OR NO

I wrote above that analogies of 9/11 and the Holocaust have little to say about the events themselves and much to tell us about the function of analogy. Attending to trajectories of fidelity, rather than their objects, underscores the artifices (analogy, parable, palindrome) by which this work is accomplished. I have described Xers as schooled in looking at and through what presents as given: their resolute superficiality intersects with deep critique; they gaze at and through the veil. Like Oskar, whose quest is propelled by the word "Black" written in red pen (44–46), my approach to Foer's work is informed by this double vision. Reading these very similar novels together, after (that is, according to) Generation X, illuminates the intersection, multiplicity, and negation that violence after X enacts.

In *Everything Is Illuminated* the bifurcated narrative (there are two narrators and two plots) posits two trajectories of fidelity. These are distinguished by their objects: fidelity to the facts (Alex's realistic account of the journey through post-Soviet Ukraine) and to fiction (Jonathan's magical-realistic fable of the founding of the mythical shtetl). In the course of the novel, these trajectories intersect. Fact joins fiction as the object of fidelity, and the novel ends by positing fiction as the site not only of ethics but of justice—justice defined by departure *from* history, not fidelity *to* it. Alex denies his father; as Grandfather writes to Jonathan, his generation can live without violence only on condition of that negation. "They must cut all the strings, yes? With you [. . .] with their father [. . .] with everything they have known" (275). Writing, rewriting, affirming, denying, pointing a finger: with these parables (following Leys's definition of the term, as a fiction that figures moral or spiritual relations), fiction comes into focus as both the object of fidelity *and* the site of justice. *Extremely Loud and Incredibly Close* examines not fidelity's object but its origin, revising the assumption that fidelity's trajectory mimics that of history at its very core: the relation of cause and effect. The image of this approach is a palindrome—the literary equivalent of control over the image, of rewinding and replaying, that defined Xers' attitude toward visual culture. *Extremely Loud and Incredibly Close* relies on visual and textual palindromes to sketch trajectories of fidelity that lead away from history and toward different, subjective, and multiple truths.

The flip-book, with which this chapter began, concretizes this X quality. We know the figure falls down, but we see it float up. And, Oskar continues, "if I'd had more pictures, he would've flown through a window, back into the building, and the smoke would've poured into the hole that the plane was about to come out of" (325). His father would tell a story in reverse, from "'I love you' to 'Once upon a time . . .'" and, Oskar concludes, "I'd have said 'Dad?' backward, which would have sounded the same as 'Dad' forward. [. . .] We would have been safe" (326). "Safe" is what Oskar and his Dad were and it is what they were not; in affirming both, Oskar is being faithful both to what did happen and to what he imagines would have happened if he had enough images to make it so. Lacking these, he echoes Alex's call for fiction to join fact as the object *of* fidelity, and revises the temporal precedence of the object *to* fidelity.

This attitude is not unique to members of Generation X. In fact, Grandfather's statement "It happened to everybody," like Oskar's extraction of the image from "Stuff That Happened to Me," refuses *any* identitarian ethos, proffering, instead, intersection, multiplicity, and negation. This work comes to the fore in Oskar's grandmother's dream, described in her last letter to him. "I had been dreaming about where I came from," she writes, and proceeds to describe the bombing of Dresden in reverse. "In my dream, all the collapsed ceilings re-formed above us. The fire went back into the bombs, which rose up and into the bellies of planes whose propellers turned backward, like the second hands of the clocks across Dresden" (306–7). Like Oskar, who would have created (or decreated) the events of 9/11 if he had additional images, his grandmother extends this description to infinity: "God put together the land and the water, the sky and the water, the water and the water, evening and morning, something and nothing. He said, Let there be light. And there was darkness" (131). "There was darkness" is a denunciation of language's potential to bring a world into being, a refusal of the divine, a choice of the void over the terrible flames. But it is also faithful to the wishful conceit of painters separating green into yellow and blue, lovers dressing, and animals descending from the ark, a logical extension of this reversal of cause and effect to the expectant darkness before the first light. Oskar's grandmother refuses to choose one over the other. She is writing this letter in an airport, a liminal space, one defined both by absence and presence, by being and disappearing. "Everyone was coming or going," she reflects, but "no one was staying." This is where she chooses to remain: "Not coming or going. Not something or nothing. Not yes or no" (312).

I took as my title to this chapter "Not Yes or No" to undercut one final trajectory of fidelity: the generational identity on which this book is premised. Both Oskar and Alex are, essentially, orphans; nurtured not by their Boomer parents but by their grandparents, who were schooled not in Boomer idealism but by irredeemable disaster. "Not Yes or No" suggests that Badiou's work on fidelity joins the tradition of fidelity to the facts of disaster. Taking the two together, I suggested, is to affirm *and* disavow the object of knowledge, to focus on trajectories of fidelity *within* fiction, and to consider fiction's ethics of truth *without* disavowing fiction's status as fiction. It is not enough, of course, to rest within these paradoxes, and in the final lines of this chapter I want to address what it means to embrace and recognize fidelity without truth, to eschew the truth claims of competing, painful histories. After all, what's to keep the ethics of complicity I've described here from serving as a rationale for irresponsible, dehumanizing depictions or simulations of violence?

The answer, of course, is: nothing.

I know I tread on uneasy ground. The impetus to accuracy in the face of violence is a formidable one. It aligns fidelity with ethics and sets as its stakes the dismaying implications of blurring the distinction between perpetrator and victim. But it also prohibits investigation into why, how, and at what cost the violence of reality and the reality of violence are produced, asserted, and maintained. If violence, itself real, renders reality precarious, fiction that is untrue illuminates what infidelity makes possible in a world in which reality is created by violence (state-sponsored or not) and "fidelity to trauma" (LaCapra's term) weds identity to its fantasy of subjection. In this world, truth is nomadic; the distinction between perpetrator and victim is fragile and contingent, the effect of ever-shifting fidelity rather than a manifestation of immediate verity. In the patterns of these wanderings the dictates of fidelity fade in light of the opportunities that fiction opens up.

"With our writing, we are reminding each other of things," writes Alex to Jonathan, "We are making one story, yes?" (144). Alex is wholly aware of what "one story" can do. It can enchain its tellers to a vitriolic past, according to which "everything is the way it is because everything was the way it was" (145). Or it can break free, and set the stage for revolution; infidelity as a means of salvation. "I beseech you," Alex concludes, "to forgive us, and to make us better than we are. Make us good" (145). Oskar would say: invent.

I do not, of course, quarrel with the factual quality of violence and its very real impact on the bodies, minds, and lives of its objects. Neither does Foer. Nor do any of the Generation X authors discussed in this book. This chapter has pursued the implications of the nomadic quality of violence's reality (which I articulated in the chapter on Bret

Easton Ellis, "The Game That Moves") and the implications of the collapse of violence's object and its agent, in the context of fictionalizations of historic events—the Holocaust; the attacks of September 11, 2001—that, as I demonstrated both here and in the previous chapter, "Something Empty in the Sky"—are events that are considered more real than real, most real of all real, the arbiter of fiction's cessation. Foer's novels refuse this limited and limiting approach. They affirm fiction in its plenitude and figure truth as a matter governed by decision about what to be true to, and how. My readings of his novels in "Not Yes or No" aim to show what possibilities are opened up if we are willing to revisit the dictate that fiction in the wake of historical violence must perforce be true to facts about that violence.

We live in a world in which "the truth" is tied to the fact of its fabrication and reality is produced by visual regimes, as the manifestations of religious extremism and patriotic fervor cause us to question the value of fidelity to an idea, an ideal, a country, or a god. In this world, to affirm *and* disavow the object of knowledge, to focus on trajectories of fidelity *within* fiction, and to consider fiction's ethics of truth *without* disavowing fiction's status as fiction is to be, as Alex put it, "nomadic with the truth." Being nomadic with the truth, refusing to choose, acknowledges and claims the fictions that form and fashion what we believe to be true, how we are true to it, and why.

I Am Jack's Revolution

Fight Club, Hacking, Violence after X

EXPECT US

In early 2013, a hacker with the handle AnonGhost defaced a number of
government websites across the world.[1] AnonGhost's profile picture is a
skull in a Guy Fawkes mask, an image that signifies its association with
Anonymous, the cyber collective that rose to prominence in 2008. So
does the message, quoted below, which concludes with the slogan associated with the collective's activities: "We are anonymous. . . . We do not
forgive, we do not forget. Expect us."

> To the Governments of the world We are watching you. . We can see
> what you are doing, we control you. We are everywhere. . Remember
> this. The people you are trying to stop on, we are everyone you depend
> on. We are the people who do your laundry and cook you food and
> serve you dinner. We make bed. We guard you, while you are sleeping.
> We drive the ambulances We direct your calls. . We are cooks and taxi
> drivers. We are everyone you come into contact with on a daily bases.
> We know everything about you. We process your insurance claims and
> credit card charges. We control every part of your life . Together we

---

1. AnonGhost has also gone by the handle "The Mauritania Attacker Team." The
attacks were reported on *Cyberwar News* on January 18, 2013, on *Hackread.com* on
January 27, 2013, and on *Thehackerspost.com* on February 12, 2013.

stand against Israel. We are anonymous We are legion. . United as ONE. Divided by Zero. . We do not forgive injustice. We do not forget oppression We are coming soon to release Gaza. . Expect Us. . We are Anon-Ghost we are legion. We do not forgive, we do not forget. Expect us.[2]

AnonGhost's defacement message pays obvious homage to *Fight Club.* "The people you are trying to step on, we are everyone you depend on" is Tyler Durden's warning to the police commissioner in Chuck Palahniuk's 1996 underground classic. In the popular film adaptation by David Fincher, Tyler (played by Brad Pitt) and his followers kidnap and threaten the commissioner, who is attempting to identify and arrest the members of Tyler's anarchist group. The men are all working as waiters at the banquet where the commissioner is scheduled to speak. They abduct the commissioner, drag him to a restroom, lock the door, wrestle him to the ground, duct-tape his mouth, and a hold a knife to his testicles. Then Tyler, speaking directly into the camera, issues this warning: "Look, the people you are after are the people you depend on. We cook your meals, we haul your trash, we connect your calls, we drive your ambulances. We guard you while you sleep. Do not fuck with us" (*Fight Club* 1999).

This chapter probes the source of *Fight Club*'s attraction for cyberculture, and with it, the impact of violence after Generation X on a global, networked new millennium. *Fight Club* is, in essence, a hacker text. Its presence in cyberspace signals a coming-to-being of violence that evolves from fiction and fantasy and image that can be endlessly replayed (especially on DVD) to the Anonymous phenomenon and to this recent manifestation, in AnonGhost's warning, as a virtual call to arms in a visceral geopolitical context.

Fight Club concretizes many of the issues surrounding violence and Generation X that I have touched on in this book. In both the 1996 novel by Xer Palahniuk and the 1999 film adaptation by Xer Fincher (starring Edward Norton, Helena Bonham Carter, and Brad Pitt—all Generation Xers), men get together for bare-knuckle fistfights, an attempt, in the world of market capitalism and commodity fetishism, to connect to a primal, sensual immediacy via violence. "Tyler Durden," the manifestation of this anarchic force, emerges from the

---

2. The warning appeared on Israeli and other government websites in January 2013. Versions of the original vary slightly, but all contain misspellings and grammatical errors. Ashraf (quoted here) and Lee quote the warning and supply links to mirrors of the defacements.

unnamed narrator's GenX malaise to wreak havoc on his corporate, commoditized world, attesting to the reciprocal relation of reality and fiction, and the formative role of violence to this relation, that I underscored in this book's opening chapters. The figuration of terrorism, its complicity with media, and—in the 1999 film version—the spectacular rewriting of the urban skyline tempted critics to read *Fight Club* as a 9/11 pre-text.[3] History is targeted, eradicated, and helplessly repeated, in a movement that scores in broad strokes the same ethical issues that Jonathan Safran Foer's twenty-first-century fiction more delicately shades. Add to this *Fight Club*'s alignment with a punk or grunge aesthetic, the flurry of anxiety around violence in the media that accompanied the film's release, and the persistent reports of copycat fight clubs, real-world violence inspired by the novel and the film, and we have an X phenomenon *par excellence*.

I want to focus on one further move that *Fight Club* makes: its migration to the digital and to cyberspace, and its wielding online in the name of political causes. *Fight Club*'s musings on fantasy, violence, commodity fetishism, and revolution express the dis-ease with reality, the drive to revise and remake it, that McKenzie Wark, in his 2004 *A Hacker Manifesto,* says are fundamental to the hacker class. "To the hacker, what is represented as being real is always partial, limited, perhaps even false," writes Wark (074). In Wark's crypto-Marxist vision, hackers, by virtue of their mastery and creativity, have access to the means of production that Marx, in the industrial age, exhorted workers of the world to lay claim to. Information-age hackers hold the power to form the real, re-form, revise, and transform it. "When the powers of the false conspire to produce the real," writes Wark, "then hacking reality is a matter of using the real powers of the false to produce the false as the real power" (209).

To traverse the ground from the mid-1990s, when Palahniuk wrote the novel, to the first decades of the twenty-first century, I situate *Fight Club* in the context of 1990s hacker culture, antisecurity activism, and online communities, tracing its attraction to cyberculture from the 1990s to 2013. "*Fight Club*" in this discussion means the 1996 novel *and* the 1999 film, including its DVD release in 2000.[4] This multi-

---

3. See Thompson (61), Kavaldo ("With Us or Against Us"), and Petersen.

4. This chapter moves between three versions of *Fight Club*. I cite Palahniuk's 1996 novel as *FC 1996*, Fincher's 1999 adaptation as *FC 1999*, and items specific to the 2000 DVD release of Fincher's adaptation as *FC 2000*. Phrases that appear in both the film and the novel are cited as *FC 1996, 1999*.

plicity is deliberate: it attests to *Fight Club*'s X origins. For Generation Xers, heirs to the affirmative ethos of multiculturalism and the combative atmosphere of identity politics, identity often appears as unstable, insecure, and available to be marketed, co-opted, and commodified. Like the narrator, who is both himself and Tyler Durden, *Fight Club* is multiple and various (and in the final scene of Fincher's adaptation the characters played by Edward Norton and Helena Bonham Carter face a pair of exploding skyscrapers, their silhouettes almost identical, a hint at further replication). True to X's experience of widespread complicity with the violence of a globalized, commoditized world, *Fight Club*'s quest for self-certainty through violence (an answer to Tyler's question, "how much do you know about yourself if you've never been in a fight?" [*FC* 1999]) morphs into the menace of organized religion, corporate culture, and terror—especially after Tyler disappears.

Though X was conceived as a generational appellation, it is also, of course, a point of view. *After* X—that is, in the twenty-first century— the form and function of X culture needs to be taken into consideration in our reflections on contemporary revolutionary phenomena. The ethos of radical freedom associated with the online collective Anonymous, the cyber watchdog group WikiLeaks, the Occupy movement, and the Arab Spring have generally been read in light of the promise offered by the social networking paradigm of Web 2.0. But these movements have X culture in their DNA. In contrast to, say, the Guy Fawkes mask in *V for Vendetta* (adapted in 2005 from Alan Moore's 1988 graphic novel by Xers Lana and Andy Wachowski), a mask that plays a visible role in activities associated with Anonymous, and to which I return in the final pages of this chapter, *Fight Club*'s presence in cyberspace is programmatic, structural; it works silently, invisibly, to program the revolution. *Fight Club* is also associated with Anonymous: it dictates the first and second "Rules of the Internet," developed in discussions on /b/, the "Random" forum on 4chan (the online imageboard from which Anonymous emerged), but, again unlike *V for Vendetta,* which lost much of its moral ambiguity in the 2005 adaptation, *Fight Club* keeps its anarchic promise intact as it migrates from novel to film to cyberspace. As issues of class, consumerism, disease, and religion alternately come into view and disappear, the X premise retains its resilience. It all comes down to this: a violence that is mobile, malleable, viral, nomadic, that disregards historical precedent and dismisses distinctions of fantasy and fact.

YOU DO NOT TALK ABOUT *FIGHT CLUB*

In both the novel and the film, Tyler Durden and the anonymous narrator organize bare-knuckle fight clubs in the basement of a bar, and develop the rules, the most famous of which are the first two: "The first rule of fight club is you do not talk about fight club. The second rule of fight club is you do not talk about fight club" (*FC* 1996, 1999). Tyler coordinates the fight clubs into a militaristic operation, which he calls "Project Mayhem." The goals of Project Mayhem are variously defined, but they are, at bottom, the destruction of civilization. Project Mayhem represents a radical revolution: blast the world free of history; eliminate the debt record; save humanity by destroying it. In the course of the story the narrator realizes that he is, in fact, Tyler Durden. Here the novel and the film part ways. The novel ends with the narrator in an insane asylum, possibly hallucinating the communications he is receiving from Tyler's acolytes, who are eager to instigate his second coming. The film ends less equivocally, as the narrator witnesses the demolition of an urban cityscape orchestrated by Tyler; at the same time, the film (especially in these closing moments) identifies itself as having been hacked by Tyler, who has spliced images of pornography into the tape.

Fincher's film, released just six months after the massacre at Columbine High School that rekindled early 1990s debates about violence in the media, was considered a box-office failure. It was released on DVD soon after, in 2000, in a two-disk special collector's edition. On DVD, *Fight Club* established its cult following and earned its keep with its studio, 20th Century Fox. Fincher was actively involved in the DVD design, part of a movement by directors in this period to explore the new medium (DVDs had entered the market just a few years earlier, in 1997). In contrast to analog (the mere replication of the film on VHS), the digital medium can contain a vast amount of information. Consequently, DVDs represented an opportunity to repackage the film, correcting or controlling the real-world variables that impacted its reception in theatres. On DVD, the film proper could also be accompanied by additional material such as trailers (domestic and international), interviews, deleted scenes, behind-the-scenes spots, segments on production, and alternate video and audio tracks. This wealth of material complicates traditional notions of intentionality and authorship; the DVD, as Deborah and Mark Parker write, "becomes another text, intimately related to the film, complicating the experience of the film, but nevertheless not quite the film" (13; they mention *Fight Club* specifically). The *Fight*

Club DVD was designed simultaneously to highlight and undercut the implications of film as a commodity. The collector's edition included a faux merchandise catalog, trailers for the film that the studio had reportedly refused to air, and was designed to look like pornography, in a plain brown wrapper tied with twine. The effect was a dual deconstruction of commodity fetishism and cinematic spectatorship, a point not lost on the reviewer for *Entertainment Weekly*: "every facet of the *Fight Club* DVD aims to vivisect the film itself. [. . .] This whole endeavor is designed to subvert the idea of movie watching as benign activity" ("Fight Club" Review).

For Xers, raised on home media, accustomed to rewind, repeat, and re-view, and now firmly between the ages of eighteen and thirty-four (the most coveted marketing demographic), the home media availability of *Fight Club* was especially welcome. "The level of technical craft and artistry on display in *Fight Club* is awesome and becomes more impressively evident on repeat viewings" (Crowdus 46). The film contains a number of splices of single-frame images of Tyler. Too brief to be seen by the naked eye, these splices were created specifically for "the DVD crowd," a statement that presupposes an audience awake to what this particular medium has to offer.[5] Xers' fondness for *Fight Club* has to do less with the plot and more with those moments where, under and through Norton's cool hypnotic voice-over and Fincher's slick graphics, Tyler is there: the film, rewatched, is an exercise in re-cognition. Not readily visible in theatres, the subliminal images become available to the patient re-viewer, armed with a remote, who is inclined to look past the story and dwell on the image, its construction, and the ways it is deconstructed or interfered with. *Fight Club* fans take great pleasure in identifying these moments in the film that essentially attest to Tyler's control of it (these moments are also an extension of the conceit by which Tyler, a nighttime projectionist, splices images of pornography into the films he screens). Like the image of the penis that flickers immediately before the film's final credits, and like the FBI legal disclaimer (on the DVD) that presents as an admonishment by Tyler to the viewer, the subliminal

---

5. *Fight Club* (2000), voice-over commentary. Thompson, critiquing *Fight Club*'s punk aesthetic, notes the film's penchant for being re-viewed, but sees it as rendering the viewers complicit in the film's commoditization of punk's ethos of resistance. "Whatever desires *Fight Club* might awaken quickly become channeled into repeated viewings of the film. Rather than moving consumers to become producers, the film's material effect seems to be not just consumption but repeated consumption of the same Hollywood commodity" (61–62). I turn to *Fight Club*'s engagement with complicity and resistance in the following section.

FIGURE 6. *Fight Club* (1999). Screen grab. Brad Pitt as Tyler Durden. This is one of several images of Pitt spliced into the film stock. © Fincher/Fox.

images of Tyler all underscore how Tyler, the ghost in the machine, has hacked it, and turned the technology to his own purposes.

"DAMN KIDS. THEY'RE ALL ALIKE":
Fight Club's Hacker Logic

Palahniuk is no stranger to 1990s cyberculture. He utilized online bulletin boards and chatrooms for research for his first novel *Invisible Monsters* (the writing of which preceded *Fight Club*), posing as "Cherry" to obtain information about the possible effects of transgender hormone treatments (Kleinman). He registered chuckpalahniuk.net in 1999, shortly after the creation of the Internet Corporation for Assigned Names and Numbers (ICANN) in 1998. Of course—and unlike the narrator, who is often seen at his terminal—Tyler does not use a computer. But his attitude toward information infrastructure and technology is nonetheless quite characteristic of the hacker underground. In the 1950s and 1960s, hacking required access to hardware, source code, and mainframes. These resources were controlled by universities and corporations, a situation that encouraged a codependent relationship with institutions (though hacking has always included an anarchic strain). The development of the personal computer in the 1970s and its general availability in the 1980s freed hacking from its dependence on institutional warrant. To members of Generation X, hacking (popular-ized by the 1983 film *WarGames*) represented "a world of predomi-nantly male authority into which they [young boys] could trespass with relative ease, where they could explore and play pranks, particularly with large institutional bodies. [. . .] It was a world of excitement that allowed them to escape the home and be precisely the 'noise' in the system that they had fantasized about" (Thomas xiii). In the 1990s, high-profile hacking groups like Cult of the Dead Cow and L0pht per-petuated hackers' historical grudge against Bill Gates and attacked Microsoft (a company explicitly named in Palahniuk's novel), claiming their activities were done in the name of transparency, freedom, and human rights (Thomas 90–110).[6]

Though many of these hackers would adhere to what Steven Levy, in his seminal *Hackers: Heroes of the Computer Revolution,* describes as "the Hacker Ethic" (26–36), Levy's positive, antiauthoritarian, col-lectivist ideal, forged in the early 1950s, was losing purchase by the time his *Hackers* was published in 1984. Three studies of hacking pub-lished around the turn of the century outline the contours of 1990s hack-ing: Eric S. Raymond's *The Cathedral and the Bazaar* (2001) describes the politics and ethics of open-source software and includes a chapter titled "How to Become a Hacker"; Paul A. Taylor's *Hackers* (1999) and Thomas's *Hacking Culture* (2002) are more attuned to hacking's darker side. Tellingly, both Taylor and Thomas reference Generation X, though they differ on whether X represents a development or a depar-ture from the history of hacking. Taylor sees a connection between the "generation-x anarchist hackers" of the 1990s and their predecessors in the 1960s, 1970s, and 1980s: all distrust authority, embrace liberty, and eschew bourgeois norms and values (Hannemyr, qtd. in Taylor 24). Thomas stresses distinction, citing a source who states, "The GenXers are a 'post-punk' generation, hence the term, 'cyberpunk.' Their music has a little more edge and anger and a little less idealism. [. . .]Their world is a little more multicultural and complicated, and less black-and-white" (Mizrach, qtd. in Thomas 31–32).

Discussions about cyberpunk and hacking in the 1990s, when *Fight Club* was written and the film was released, indicate the utility of the

---

6. "The 1990s were a time when hacking moved away from individual practice toward notions of group identity and political action," writes Thomas in 2002. "In the wake of the AT&T break up, with the rise of the Internet, and with the increasing global-ization of technology, hackers have begun to engage in more concerted political action, at both local and global levels" (89).

Generation X context for thinking about *Fight Club*. Thomas, Taylor, and Raymond all discuss the term. Unlike Thomas, for whom "cyberpunk" is an appropriate designation for Generation X hackers, Taylor and Raymond dissociate "hacking" from "cyberpunk," with Taylor noting that the ethos of resistance that the cyberpunk genre borrows from punk is in some tension with hacking after the development of the personal computer, Microsoft's market dominance, and the rise of white-hat security, and Raymond dismissing the term outright (his impatience seems to accord with his vision of hacking as an aesthetic, koanlike pursuit: he directs would-be hackers to transform their attitudes, provides a number of mantras to repeat, and suggests the study of music and Zen [197–208]).[7] My point is not to assess the correctness of the term "cyberpunk" for hacking and certainly not for *Fight Club,* but rather to note the utility of Generation X as a context through which to understand these conflicting proclamations. Cyberpunk represented an attitude of resistance to the system, an attitude that was useful only to the extent that the resistance it represented had not (yet) been co-opted by the system; once its complicity or corruption had been established, cyberpunk, as an ethos of resistance, was bankrupt, and had itself to be resisted—hence Raymond, in "How to Become a Hacker," directs: "Don't call yourself a 'cyberpunk,' and don't waste your time on anybody who does" (208). In discussions about the relevance of cyberpunk to hacking, the drive to both embrace an attitude and to eschew it represents a condition that, for Xers, was all too familiar: Xers were well aware of their inextricability from a system that co-opts resistance, commodifies and recycles it, and repeats the process indefinitely. *Fight Club* describes this procedure precisely. Tyler seeds the country with fight club franchises, confirming the narrator's bleak vision in which, "when deep space exploration ramps up, it'll be the corporations that name everything, the IBM Stellar Sphere, the Micro-

---

7. Reflecting on the dubious appropriateness of "cyberpunk" for 1990s hacker culture, Taylor writes: "Cyberpunk portrays the amalgamation of the technological knowledge of hackers with the anti-establishment ethos of the punk rocker. The potential for this amalgamation to produce a source of opposition to the dominant social constituencies is aided by the fact that technology is now more readily accessible and potentially manipulable than ever before. A complicating aspect of this potential for rebellion, however, is the degree to which hackers oppose dominant social forces within computing whilst at the same time containing their very traits. For example, whilst generally opposing trends towards the increasing commodification of information and by extension the ethics of the free market, some hackers at least almost personify market values, leading to the claim that they are not an alternative culture at all" (169).

soft Galaxy, Planet Starbucks." Project Mayhem—the gritty anarchist ethos of fight club gone cultlike and corporate—transforms the narrator's world into "Planet Tyler" (*FC* 1999).

This co-presence of complicity and co-option is at the heart of *Fight Club*'s hacker logic, a logic that has more in common with "The Conscience of a Hacker," published online in 1986 by Xer Lloyd Blankenship (aka The Mentor), than with Levy's Hacker Ethic. Under the title "The Hacker's Manifesto," and accompanied with a note about The Mentor's arrest, the text was influential for 1990s hackers (it merits a guest appearance in Fincher's 2010 *The Social Network*, about the rise of Facebook).[8] A close look at "The Hacker's Manifesto" reveals similarities between hacker culture and *Fight Club*'s attitude toward institutions, power, and technology. Though much of "The Hacker's Manifesto" rehearses familiar youth themes of alienation, disgust, and the discovery of an alternate community ("This is it . . . this is where I belong . . ."), it is striking in its mastery of language, rhythm, and tone. "The Hacker's Manifesto" is structured as a response to a dismissive adult culture, a culture represented by the phrase "Damn kids. They're all alike," which is repeated, with variations, in the course of the short piece. In the same manner that a hacker will take control over a system, The Mentor appropriates this denigration, essentially "hacking" language. He transforms the dismissive adult phrase into a call for arms, turning abasement into menace: "You bet your ass we're all alike . . . [. . .] This is our world now . . . [. . .] You can't stop us all . . . after all, we're all alike."[9] Such a move is, as E. Gabriella Coleman writes, "the very nature of hacking—turning a system against itself" (*Coding Freedom* 98).[10]

---

8. The presence of this text in Fincher's film is of a piece with Fincher's depiction of Mark Zuckerberg, the founder of Facebook, as a disaffected loner. Many reviewers of the film have noted that this depiction departs from Zuckerberg's biography.

9. See Thomas 71–80 for another detailed close reading of "The Hacker's Manifesto."

10. Like Levy, Coleman repeatedly uses "hacking" to describe an attitude toward other media. Writing of free software advocate R. M. Stallman, for example, she describes him as one who "approached the law much like a hacker treats technology: as a system that by virtue of being systematic and logical, is hackable. In other words, [Stallman] relied on the hacker technical tactic of clever reuse to imaginatively hack the law" (*Coding Freedom* 69). Raymond, too, stresses that hacking is an attitude toward media. Both Raymond and Taylor cite Sherry Turkle who, in her seminal *The Second Self: Computers and the Human Spirit,* describes the hack as "a concept which exists independently of the computer and can best be presented through an example using another technology complex enough to support its own version of hacking—and hackers" (Turkle 207).

At the center of "The Hacker's Manifesto" is the encounter with the computer. What the hacker likes about the computer is the fantasy of control it promises. "I made a discovery today. I found a computer. Wait a second, this is cool. It does what I want it to. If it makes a mistake, it's because I screwed it up." This fantasy of control is *Fight Club*'s too, and "The Hacker's Manifesto" shares with *Fight Club* an intermedial quality: it is not about computing or about technology but about the promise of control that hacking represents, a promise that is, importantly, free from technological constraints. Discussing this moment in "The Manifesto," Thomas stresses that "the claim being made here is not a technological one. [. . .] In The Mentor's discussion and description of the computer, we in no way are told what it is that a computer can do; nor are we told how he will use it. What we are given is a discussion of the newfound relationship to technology itself" (76). By detaching hacking from computing, Thomas locates, in the "Manifesto," an affirmation of the definition of hacking that Taylor attributes to the computer underground for whom "hacking still refers, in the first instance, to the imaginative and unorthodox use of *any* artefact" (xi). On this point, adherents to Levy's Hacker Ethic and The Mentor's Manifesto concur: Raymond, too, locates the original sense of hacking in this attitude toward objects, stressing hacking's "true and original sense of an enthusiast, an artist, a tinkerer, a problem solver, an expert" (xii). For some software hackers, he continues, "the hacker nature is really independent of the particular medium the hacker works in" (196). Coleman, discussing hackers' relation to their computers, agrees: Hackers, she writes, are "attuned not simply to the workings of technology but also seek such an intimate understanding of technology's capabilities and constraints that they are positioned to redirect it to some new, largely unforeseen plane" (*Coding Freedom* 98). Hacking exceeds computing; its aesthetics inhere in a creative, mobile attitude toward objects in the world: objects that are alternately recalcitrant, frustrating, and alternately pacific, symbiotic, partners.

This attitude toward objects informs *Fight Club* on multiple levels, and is reflected in the book's thematic issues as well as the film's representational ethos, an ethos underscored by Fincher's stylish cinematography.[11] The narrator, who works as an automotive recall specialist, is

---

11. Crowdus notes what critics praised about the film: the "hyperkinetic camera movements, photo montages, subliminal imagery, freeze frames, terse editing rhythms, and some stunning, computer-generated visualizations of the Narrator's thought processes, including a bravura minute-and-a-half backward tracking short originating in the

keenly aware of the devaluation of human life compared with that of objects. His job is to apply this formula: "You take the population of vehicles in the field (A) and multiply it by the probable rate of failure (B), then multiply the result by the average cost of an out-of-court settlement (C). A times B times C equals X. [. . .] If X is less than the cost of a recall, then we don't recall" (FC 1996, 1999). He collects objects that blankly attest to the commodification of labor, "proof they were crafted by the honest, simple, hard-working indigenous aboriginal peoples of wherever" (FC 1996, 1999) and complains, "the things you used to own, now they own you" (FC 1996, 44).[12] In the course of his acquaintance with Tyler, the narrator relearns the utility of objects. The first three pages of the book alone (narrated from his enlightened perspective) include instructions for homemade gun silencers, nitroglycerine, plastic explosive, and napalm (such anarchic recipes proliferated online; early issues of the hacker zine *Phrack,* where The Mentor's "Manifesto" first appeared, also published directions for homemade bombs and explosives). *Fight Club* thus presents its narrator according to the traditional definition of hacking as "an attempt to make use of any technology in an original, unorthodox and inventive way" (Taylor 14–15). Furthermore: the narrator's directions for making these devices include accounts of his own frustrations and failures and reflect the collective nature of these endeavors. "A lot of folks mix their nitro with cotton and add Epsom salts as a sulfate. This works too. Some folks, they use paraffin mixed with nitro. Paraffin has never, ever worked for me" (FC 1996, 12). The "never, ever" (which attests to the frustration, grind, and glitches that characterize hackers' work), and the evocation of community ("a lot of folks," "some folks") express the unique combination of individuality and collectivity that Levy, Raymond, and Coleman all identify as fundamental to hacker culture.

The film's bravura wielding of point of view reverberated strongly with issues pertinent to computer culture in the 1990s when the book was written and published and the film was developed, marketed, and released. Linux (featured on the front cover of *Wired* in August 1997) figured, for hackers, an important challenge to the growing, and increasingly corporate, software industry (generally represented by Windows, Microsoft's operating system; Microsoft rose to prominence in the 1990s

---

protoplasmic fear cells of his brain, an IKEA catalog rendition of his trendy apartment furnishings, and a nightmarish plane crash" (46).

12. The 1999 film attributes this phrase to Tyler.

with Windows 3.1). Linux was an openly sourced version of Unix; it could replace Windows on Intel-based PCs, and for many hackers it was the epitome of Levy's Hacker Ethic: a direct rebuttal to the corporatization, privatization, and market control represented by the software industry and Microsoft. Leaked Microsoft memos that attested to the threat posed to the company by open-source software like Linux received widespread press coverage in late 1998, and 1999 saw a trend by software companies to switch to Linux for their business applications and a notable rise in Linux IPOs (Fincher's *Fight Club* was released at just this time, in October 1999).[13]

But beyond the issues of free software production, the competing operating systems (Linux and Windows) speak directly to *Fight Club*'s critique of institutional power and the potential of liberation from it. Linux represented the ability to turn any PC into a Unix machine. Much software written under Unix is portable, that is, not dependent on machine type, and is thus adaptable to a range of environments. Unix is a far more versatile operating system than Windows, and one beloved by hackers. The difference between Windows (with its graphical user interface or GUI) and Unix/Linux (with its command-line interface) is widely figured through terminology of transparency and opacity, and colored by hackers' traditional distaste for large corporations. Writing almost a decade apart, Thomas and Coleman, describing hackers' fondness for Unix/Linux, apply strikingly similar rhetoric, attributing exclusion and opacity to Windows, inclusion and transparency to Unix/Linux.[14] For viewers of *Fight Club* who were versed in these issues, the computer-generated penguin that represents the narrator's "power animal" could

---

13. Raymond describes the leaked Microsoft memos (183) and the rise of Linux to market prominence (186–87). Coleman, reflecting on this period, describes the effect of the media attention to Linux as "turning Linux and open source into household names" (*Coding Freedom* 82).

14. Thomas, writing in 2002: "For Linux, the user is an integral part of the operating system; in order to operate the machine, he or she must understand how the computer and software work. In contrast, Windows uses a graphical interface to hide the workings of the machine from the end-user and, as a result, virtually excludes the user from the operating system. While Linux renders the computer and its operating system transparent, Windows makes the computer and its operating system opaque" (85). Coleman, writing in 2012: "Unix offers a more interactive relationship between user and OS than Microsoft Windows does. Unix is architecturally transparent; every part of the system is a 'file' that can be seen, altered, and customized. It gives users the ability to 'go behind the scenes,' to individually configure the system for specific needs and operates along a similar logic to that of open source" (*Coding Freedom* 36). For an account of how the concept of transparency changed in the course of the Macintosh–Microsoft wars, see Turkle (2005) 9–10.

not but evoke Tux, Linux's official mascot (also a penguin), and the special effects in which a virtual camera, unconstrained by infrastructure, moves along the brain stem, among synapses, and between walls, passes through ceilings and building stories, and zooms in for impossible close-ups, tracking the potential for mayhem that devastates corporate culture, represented the perspective afforded by open-sourced Linux. In marked contrast to this mobile, creative, deindividualized perspective, the narrator, prior to his liberation by Tyler, moves through an IKEA marketing catalog, in which products pop up, Windows-like, to furnish his unsatisfactory, illusory environment.

Writing of Linux and GUI in 1999, Xer Neal Stephenson articulates the conflict that the narrator-Tyler duo manifests. He describes GUI interfaces like Windows as "products, contrived by engineers in the service of specific companies" (88); his image for GUI is Disneyland: "a product of seamless illusion—a magic mirror that reflects the world back better than it really is" (50). Unix, on the other hand, has "a kind of complexity and asymmetry that is organic, like the roots of a tree, or the branchings of a coronary artery" (89). Product not of corporate culture but hacker subculture, it represents a profound challenge to corporate dominance. "If you know what you are doing, you can buy a cheap PC from any computer store, throw away the Windows disks that come with it, turn it into a Linux system of mind-boggling complexity and power. You can configure it so that a hundred different people can be logged on to it at once. [. . .] You can hang half a dozen different monitors off of it and play Doom with someone in Australia while tracking communications satellites in orbit and controlling your house's lights and thermostats and streaming live video from your webcam and surfing the Net and designing circuit boards on the other screens" (128). This power, complexity, community, and slight sense of menace lures Stephenson but makes him hesitate. "Sometimes," he concludes, "I just want to go to Disneyland" (129).

The issue, not only for X hackers but for Xers in general, is the familiar trifecta: reality, media, violence. Tyler is explicitly connected to media—not despite but because of his hands-on attitude and his expertise with the inner workings of systems (as opposed to the narrator's boss, who inquires about color-coordinating a Windows icon during a presentation on the World Wide Web in what looks like Windows 3.1, asking, "Can I get that in cornflower blue?" [FC 1999]). Tyler works for a chain of movie houses splicing small reels into five-foot reels that run on a single self-threading projector. Tyler also works as a projectionist, and the relationship between Tyler and the narrator is imaged as a change-over from an earlier, two-projector system. The changeover underscores the constructed nature of perception. Reality is an illusion, the effect of technology—here, of multiple moving images—and is subject to being manipulated and disrupted. "Changeover. The movie goes on. Nobody in the audience has any idea" (FC 1996, 1999). This image of control extends from archaic, two-projector technology outwards. Relying on the logic of the changeover, Tyler splices single frames of pornography into family-friendly films. Like the changeover (when done properly), the splice is invisible: no one sees it. But the invisible image has an effect. "Tyler spliced a penis into everything. [. . .] Nobody complained. People ate and drank, but the evening wasn't the same. People feel sick or start to cry and don't know why" (FC 1996, 31).[15]

Fight Club thus participates in the logic of remediation by which, as Jay David Bolter and Richard Grusin write, each new medium promises to present a more immediate or authentic experience of reality than the previous one. Reality is alternately transparent and opaque, accessed by faith or critique as each medium presents itself, as medium, to perception (19–21). On the surface, *Fight Club* seems an unlikely candidate for discussion of new media. The narrator and Tyler choose a Luddite existence, squatting in a house without reliable electricity or amenities, and the technology on which Tyler's splicing relied was archaic even while Palahniuk was writing his book in the mid-1990s. But precisely because of its archaic quality, *Fight Club* underscores the technological revolution that Xers lived through in the 1980s and 1990s: the rise of home media, of digitization, and the personal computer. As the change-over system is being phased out (it will disappear utterly with digitization), Tyler's labor, already invisible, becomes obsolete. Fincher's DVD, the product of digitization, underscores this archaic aspect, as the chapter titles flutter audibly like reel-to-reel film in movie-house projectors. Even as Tyler expresses contemporary media's unique preoccupation with the real, "the transparent presentation of the real and the enjoyment of the opacity of media themselves" (Bolter and Grusin 21), Generation Xers, poised between analog and digital, the window and the command line, gazing at and through visual interfaces, see it disappear

---

15. "A single frame in a movie is on the screen for one-sixtieth of a second. Divide a second into sixty equal parts. That's how long the erection is. Towering four stories tall over the popcorn auditorium, slippery red and terrible, and no one sees it," reports the narrator (FC 1996, 30). In the book, Tyler is an equal-opportunity offender, splicing both penises and vaginas into the films.

here. Tyler's expulsion from the medium catapults him into reality which he then reconfigures: reality becomes virtual—a medium, as Bolter and Grusin describe virtual reality, "whose purpose is to disappear" and, consequently, "to foster in the viewer a sense of presence" (21–22).

But while Tyler emerges *from* technology, he is never confined *to* it. He represents the hacker principle that "information wants to be free" and the promise that always lurks in the virtual: that it and the real can exchange places, that the virtual can become real, that the virtual is the only real, and only the initiated know it. Like the recipes for home-made explosives that the narrator recites, the effect is to reorder an alien, alienating environment, rendering it obedient, cooperative, and—like Unix, which can be implemented on any machine—replicable. In organizing the fight clubs into Project Mayhem, Tyler essentially assembles a gigantic organic computer that does, to paraphrase The Mentor, what he wants it to (Project Mayhem's mechanistic quality is represented in its first and second rule: don't ask questions). And again like Tyler, *Fight Club* moves through media. In a manner similar to the phrase "they're all alike" in "The Hacker's Manifesto," *Fight Club* is appropriated and mobilized, its nomadic quality underscored as it wanders from book to film to DVD and outward: to copycat fight clubs in real life, to files that have been ripped, saved, and distributed on bootleg copies or posted to file-sharing websites, to calls for Projects Mayhem in 2002 and 2012, to the 4chan forum /b/, birthplace of Anonymous, and even to the Israel/Palestine conflict in 2013.

PROJ3KT M4YH3M:
Fight Club and Early Antisec

In 2002 the antisec hacking group el8 published a manifesto in which they adopt the term "project mayhem" and Tyler's warning. Parmy Olson, writing of early antisec in *We Are Anonymous: Inside the Hacker World of LulzSec, Anonymous, and the Global Cyber Insurgency,* describes el8 as an extreme incarnation of the antisecurity movement that originated in 1999 (Olson 285), part of a resistance to "full disclosure" (a policy in cybersecurity by which cybersecurity experts, known as white hats, publicize the vulnerabilities they identify in systems and sites).[16]

---

16. According to anti.security.is (published in 2001), a manifesto of the antisec movement, antisecurity aims to "encourage a new policy of anti-disclosure among the com-

The association of el8's "project mayhem" with *Fight Club*'s was noted immediately: Thor "Jumper" Larholm, a white-hat security researcher, described the group as "a copycat of the movie, only moved to the hacker scene" (qtd. in McWilliams). el8 published a number of manifestos in 2001 and 2002. These manifestos were written in an orthography particular to hackers. In this system, known as "eleet," "1337," and "leet-speak," "a" is commonly replaced with 4, "o" with 0, in an effect to render language codelike and opaque.[17] el8's 2002 manifesto calls for "Pr0j3kt M4yh3m," and channels *Fight Club* directly:

> we r h4rdkore h4krz who clean your toilets, the h4rdkore k0derz who forcefully w1pe y0ur wind0wz @ st0pl1ghtz and intersekti0nz, the h4rdk0re phre4krZ who mow your l4wn, the h4rdk0re cr4krz who ste4l cl0thez from the salvati0n army, we take yor order at burger k1ng, we steal yor hubk4pz, we even put k4meraz in port 'o pottiez. *_DO_* *_NOT_* *_FUCK_* *_WITH_* *_US_*.[18]

This is, of course, an adaptation of Tyler's warning to the police commissioner with which this chapter began. Though the warning appears verbatim in both Palahniuk's novel and Fincher's adaptation, Larholm (and, later, Olson) is correct in identifying the film, not the book, as el8's inspiration. Reflecting on the difference between the two mediums illuminates the film's special attraction to hacker culture. In the novel, Tyler's warning occurs *after* the narrator has begun to suspect that he and Tyler are the same person. Tyler's epistemic stability is on the wane, a point underscored by several novelistic devices: the scene is presented

---

puter and network security communities. The goal is not to ultimately discourage the publication of all security-related news and developments, but rather, to stop the disclosure of all unknown or non-public exploits and vulnerabilities" ("Antisecurity")

17. Thomas, writing of hacker orthography, describes acts of translation that attest to language's inherent infidelity, its vulnerability to technology, and technology's necessary reliance on language. In a move that recalls *Fight Club*'s ethos, he writes that hacker language games do violence to reveal violence: "The more earnestly technology is hidden within the dynamics of language, the more violence it does to technology itself. Hackers recover, and make explicit, the ways in which language has relied on technology. It is a mode that reveals what has continually been concealed in language itself—technology" (58).

18. Translation: "We are the hardcore hackers who clean your toilets, the hardcore coders who forcefully wipe your windows at stoplights and intersections, the hardcore phreakers who mow your lawn, the hardcore crackers who steal clothes from the salvation army, we take your orders at burger king, we steal your hubcaps, we even put cameras in port'o'potties. DO NOT FUCK WITH US!"

as a flashback, as reported speech, and its violence is mitigated by time, perspective, and *ressentiment*: "The people you depend on" speech is separated from "don't fuck with us" by the reflection "We are the middle children of history, raised by television to believe that someday we'll be millionaires and movie stars and rock stars, but we won't" (*FC* 1996, 166; the film sets this sentence in another context). The film, in contrast, infuses Tyler's warning with the menace of physical proximity and bodily threat. Tyler and his gang have physically overpowered the commissioner. He doesn't bother to cover his face. He speaks directly to the camera, with his head inverted—visually underscoring the reversal of power relations. His followers are holding a knife to the commissioner's testicles as he speaks (in the novel, the testicles were released *before* the warning is issued). "Do not fuck with us" is marked by a small jump cut that has Tyler speaking as if directly to the viewer (the effect of the jump cut is mimicked, by el8, with the last sentence appearing in all caps).

By defining themselves as black-hat hackers, or "crackers," el8 affirms the negative stereotypes that began to surface around images of hackers in the media at the time—*Fight Club* resonates with people aligned more with The Mentor's Manifesto than with Levy's Hacker Ethic.[19] But the paradigms of cyberspace, in which physical proximity must be simulated, require some revision to the original text. In the film, Tyler describes a service sector that cooks, hauls, connects, drives, and guards, and whose ability to cause mischief depends on their reliable access to physical infrastructure—the situation of hackers before the rise of the home computer and the personal modem. In el8's adoption, this class identity falls away: el8 claims to be an outlaw culture, one defined as a collection of nouns rather than verbs (hackers, coders, phreakers, crackers), deliberately underemployed, working at the margins, treating industry as a point of entry for access to infrastructure and opportunities for mayhem. Schooled not by the Hacker Ethic but by The Mentor's

---

19. Raymond elaborates on the hacker/cracker distinction: "There is [. . .] a group of people who loudly call themselves hackers, but aren't. These are people (mainly adolescent males) who get a kick out of breaking into computers and phreaking the phone system. Real hackers call these people 'crackers' and want nothing to do with them. Real hackers mostly think crackers are lazy, irresponsible, and not very bright, and object that being able to break security doesn't make you a hacker any more than being able to hotwire cars makes you an automotive engineer. Unfortunately, many journalists and writers have been fooled into using the word 'hacker' to describe crackers; this irritates real hackers to no end" (196). In Raymond's implication that crackers are less "real" than hackers we can see the stakes of this issue: the claiming of reality in cyberspace. I return to this point in my discussion of #OpIsrael 2.0, below.

X attitude, the mainstreaming of the internet, and the globalization of technology (el8's ezines claim to be "the definitive src for the Japan h/p scene," or the "Haiti h/p scene," or "the Afghan h/p scene" or "the Porno h/p scene"), and, again like The Mentor, who poetically claims and describes cyberspace ("This is our world now, the world of the electron and the switch"), el8 channels *Fight Club* as an assertion of ownership and immediacy in its call for "Pr0j3kt M4yh3m": "we k0me 2 t4ke b4ck wh4t iz r1ghtfully 0urz,—CYBERSPACE—. and eye'll b d4mned iph we k0ntinue t0 let the c0rper4ti0nz c0ntr0l *OUR* *WORLD*. G3T 0FF UR A$$, AND KAUZE S0ME MAAAAAAAYH3M."[20]

DO NOT TALK ABOUT /B/:
Fight Club and Anonymous

In an afterword to the reissue of the novel, Chuck Palahniuk describes the origin of *Fight Club* as a formal experiment in a short story. "Instead of walking a character from scene to scene in a story, there had to be some way to just—cut, cut, cut. To jump. From scene to scene. Without losing the reader. To show every aspect of a story, but only the kernel of each aspect. The core moment. Then another core moment. Then, another" (213). To produce this effect of movement without space ("cut, cut, cut. To jump. From scene to scene"), intensity without context ("The core moment. Then another core moment. Then, another"), Palahniuk developed a set of rules. These would work as "a kind of glue" that would "act to signal a jump to a new angle or aspect" (213). It is these rules, Palahniuk insists, and not the fantasy of violence, that gave birth to the book. "The whole idea of a fight club wasn't important. It was arbitrary. But the eight rules had to apply to something so *why not a club where you could ask someone to fight?* [. . .] The *fighting* wasn't the important part of the story. What I needed were the *rules*" (213).

Truth or myth, Palahniuk's reflection on the function of rules in the formation of *Fight Club* is telling, given the centrality of *Fight Club* to the rules of that most anarchic, intense, and mobile of nonspaces, the internet. The "Rules of the Internet" were developed in discussion on /b/, the "random" forum on the image board 4chan (4chan was created by

---

20. Translation: "We come to take back what is rightfully ours—CYBERSPACE—and I'll be damned if we continue to let the corporations control OUR WORLD. Get off your ass, and cause some mayhem!"

Christopher Poole in 2003). No registration was required for 4chan, and it was not necessary to create an account in order to post. If users did not post with a handle or name (and most did not), 4chan would assign the name Anonymous to the default empty name field. This structure of 4chan was important for two reasons: its mobility (4chan was not archived: discussions existed in real time, not unlike fight club, "which only exists between the hours when fight club starts and fight club ends" [*FC* 1996, 1999]) and the reimagining of identity that this made possible. "Unlike other sites, where being anonymous means not using your 'real' name or identity, most posts on /b/ are disconnected from *any* identity" (Bernstein et al. 3). The freedom offered by this anonymity seemed to fulfill *Fight Club*'s promise of a radical erasure of identity: "Who you were in fight club is not who you were in the rest of the world" (*FC* 1996, 1999). Ancillary sites and wikis like *Encyclopedia Dramatica* developed to document and parody (the distinction is not a stable one in the cyber community) the culture that developed on 4chan and /b/, "the obsessions of participants, the memes they created, and also the members unfortunate enough to gain some notoriety within the community" (Auerbach). Echoing the first and second rules of *Fight Club*, the first rule of the internet is, "do not talk about /b/," and the second rule of the internet is: "do NOT talk about /b/." Discussions on /b/ about the applicability of these rules indicate their origin in the need for secrecy in trolling and raids (so as not to indicate where a raid is originating from) and in retaining the quality of the forum (to keep noobs, or newbies, from crashing it), but, as *Encyclopedia Dramatica* puts it in its entry on the Rules, "/b/ *is* Fight Club, bitch" ("Rules 1 and 2").[21] *Encyclopedia Dramatica* also has an entry on the film, in which the rules for *Fight Club* are listed under this heading: "Rules of ~~the internet~~ Fight Club" ("Fight Club").

The third rule of the internet, "we are anonymous," was adopted by the collective that emerged from /b/ and came to prominence in 2008 with some high-profile DDoS attacks, defaces, leaks, raids, and street demonstrations in which people appeared in Guy Fawkes masks (I return to the masks at the end of this chapter). Project Chanology, instigated by the Church of Scientology's attempts to remove an interview

---

21. The origin of the rules of the internet is uncertain. They were probably developed around 2006, and certainly preceded Anonymous's highly publicized attacks on Scientology in 2008. According to knowyourmeme.com, "The idea of making a set of rules, similar to Netiquette for 4chan users, was initially talked about on Anonymous-related IRC channels before an entry was submitted to Encyclopedia Dramatica sometime in late 2006 and archived on January 10th, 2007" ("Rules of the Internet").

with Tom Cruise from YouTube, was launched in the name of freedom of the internet and brought Anonymous to the news; the 2010 Operation Payback was initialized in response to Aiplex's DDoS assault on the file-sharing site The Pirate Bay and, later, in support of WikiLeaks. Like Project Chanology, Operation Payback established Anonymous's reputation as a faceless crusader for freedom of information worldwide.

Anonymous, E. Gabriella Coleman writes, is "by nature and intent difficult to define: a name employed by various groups of hackers, technologists, activists, human rights advocates, and geeks; a cluster of ideas and ideals adopted by these people and centered around the concept of anonymity; a banner for collective actions online and in the real world that have ranged from fearsome but trivial pranks to technological support for Arab revolutionaries" ("Our Weirdness"). Like X, Anonymous's resistance to easy definition is part of its attraction; again like X, Anonymous refuses to be aligned with a coherent philosophy or platform. "Beyond a foundational commitment to anonymity and the free flow of information, Anonymous has no consistent philosophy or political program," writes Coleman. "It has no definite trajectory. Sometimes coy and playful, sometimes macabre and sinister, often all at once, Anonymous is still animated by a collective will toward mischief—toward 'lulz,' a plural bastardization of the portmanteau LOL" ("Our Weirdness"). Coleman traces the "spirit of lulz" to the Dadaists and Yippies, the Situationists, Up Against the Wall Motherfuckers, and The Yes Men. But the anarchic, intermedial, affectless, disaffected X ethos of *Fight Club* needs to join this group.

This is not to say that Anonymous is composed of members of Generation X. It is, rather, to use this X text to situate cultural aspects of this contemporary phenomenon, to have Palahniuk's anarchic myth join Michel de Certeau, Gilles Deleuze, Ernst Bloch, Eric Hobsbawm, and other revered theorists (all cited by Coleman) in understanding action, tactics, politics, the subject, and violence after X. Like Palahniuk's vision of anarchic disorder that emerged from rules, Tyler's lulz, and those of Project Mayhem, are predicated on transparency and opacity, cooperation and co-option, the uncanny ability to disappear here, to reclaim selfhood by erasing it. Much of Anonymous's attraction and mystique has to do with this menace of invisibility that, Thomas notes, has always been characteristic of the hacker underground. The Mentor's promise, "you can't stop us all, after all, we're all alike," is the menace of replication, the assembling of an anonymous army. Tyler does the same, promising to his acolytes: "You are not special. You are not a beautiful or unique snowflake. You're the same decaying organic matter as everything else" (*FC* 1996, 1999). This simultaneity of abjection and transcendence first attracts and then horrifies the narrator, but the final frames of the film, in which he and Marla are revealed to be mirror images, suggest that he has never been more than a replicant, "a copy of a copy of a copy" (*FC* 1996, 1999).

For Coleman, anonymity represents a unique kind of freedom from the enforced hypersociality of Web 2.0. "In a world where we post the majority of our personal data online, and states and corporations wield invasive tools to collect and market the rest, there is something profoundly hopeful in Anonymous's effacement of the self" ("Our Weirdness"). The attraction of this hope, its magnetic quality, a promise not unlike the satori state she identifies, in *Coding Freedom,* as one of the aesthetic attractions of hacking, is the state sought by *Fight Club*'s narrator: "look into the stars and you're gone" (*FC* 1996, 1999). Both Anonymous and *Fight Club* draw the public's attention by combining the philosophies of two seemingly incompatible traditions, existentialism and activism, lurking online and taking to the streets (the existentialist journal *Stirrings Still* devoted an entire issue to Palahniuk, who may have drawn inspiration for *Fight Club* from his experience in the anarchic activist group The Portland Cacophony Society). As Coleman, summing up the Anonymous phenomenon, puts it: "At the same time that Anonymous represents a shadowy lack—evasive, shifty, nomadic—they also represent at the same time an intense fullness. In contrast to criminal groups who go out of their way to remain hidden, Anonymous has managed to be a media sensation, to be spectacularly present, to become total spectacle. They sit at the cusp of visibility and invisibility" ("Anonymous from Lulz to Activists").[22] Even as X's tendency to cross out and mark the spot lines up well with Anonymous's intersection of plenitude and erasure, Anonymous's power, their attraction, and their menace reside in this X factor: the uncanny ability to disappear here.[23]

---

22. She continues: "Their visibility is channeled via pranks and interventions (the lulz securing some of their most audacious and irreverent interventions) and their invisibility broadcast via semiotic messages of anonymity which inculcates and elevates [. . .] a different version of what it might mean to be an individual" ("Anonymous from Lulz to Activists").

23. During Operation Payback, AnonOpsIRC was established—a more stable forum than /b/ for discussions of future activities. The high-profile hacks of HBGary Federal and the real-time defacing of the Westboro Baptist Church website were planned and executed from that forum. LulzSec (Lulz Security) emerged from AnonOps in 2011, claiming for its purpose a combination of "mayhem and lulz." Olson, who traces the

"WE ARE COMING TO RELEASE GAZA":
#OpIsrael 2.0

In the conclusion to his book about 1990s hacking, Thomas reflects on the media fascination with hacking and hackers, the association of hackers with shadowy, threatening presence, and their demonization by governments, corporations, and legal institutions. He concludes that much of this fascination and fear relies on the anxiety that traditionally accompanies technological developments. For many, Thomas writes, borrowing a term from Freud, technology represents an "expectant anxiety," one "aimed at the future" that "calls into question almost every aspect of daily human interaction" (217). "Expectant anxiety," he continues, is predicated on technology's ambivalence about the body.[24] "The fear attached to the body that begins with the discourse of television reaches its zenith with discussions of 'virtual reality' and the actual disappearance of the body," writes Thomas (218); the virtual makes the body disappear even as, by posing a threat to the body (disabling or altering it), technology underscores the body's presence. The body that can both vanish and appear is characterized by Thomas in terms of a ghost: "A virtual presence is a threat to the living precisely in terms of its incorporeal existence. The virtual 'haunts' the physical world. It is a dead presence, a 'spirit'" (218). It is in the context of this reciprocal haunting that I want to return to my opening point: AnonGhost's deface message and Anonymous's #OpIsrael.

In contrast to el8, AnonGhost quotes not the film *Fight Club* but the less well-known 1996 original. By doing so, AnonGhost resurrects the text's reference to a service class with physical access to infrastructure.

---

rise of LulzSec from Anonymous (she also notes the echoes of *Fight Club* in Anonymous culture [12]), notes the visual similarities between el8's e-zine and LulzSec's pastebin posts (285). Just as /b/'s interface appeared as a throwback to 1990s web design (Bernstein et al.), LulzSec's own public statements affirm their alliance with the GenX decade. In a taunt directed to the FBI, LulzSec writes: "The Anonymous bitchslap rings through your ears like hacktivism movements of the 90s. We're back—and we're not going anywhere. Expect us" ("Joint Statement"). In a farewell communication to its followers, LulzSec reaffirms its allegiance to early Antisec. "Behind the mask, behind the insanity and mayhem, we truly believe in the AntiSec movement. We believe in it so strongly that we brought it back, much to the dismay of those looking for more anarchic lulz. We hope, wish, even beg, that the movement manifests itself into a revolution that can continue on without us" ("50 Days").

24. For Thomas, schooled in Foucault's work on panopticism and discipline, much of the legal discourse surrounding hackers has to do with creating bodies that can be subjected to the law's regulatory power (217–18).

Also in contrast to el8, who channeled and adapted the 1999 *Fight Club* (or, more likely, the 2000 DVD, the means by which the film achieved its cult status), to elicit immediacy for the cyber realm, AnonGhost's warning precisely replicates page 166 of Palahniuk's book, with a single exception: the insertion of the sentence "We are everyone you come into contact with on a daily bases." By virtue of both its fidelity to the original *and* its departure from it, the deface warning resurrects *Fight Club*'s applicability to issues of class and labor in a globalized, corporatized economy; with "we are coming soon to release Gaza," it puts *Fight Club* in service not of antisecurity (a relatively abstract concept with an ethos of transparency) but of a concrete place with a gritty, bloody history. Thomas writes that the virtual quality of expectant anxiety has to do with the body's potential to disappear. AnonGhost's wielding of *Fight Club* seems to resurrect this body, grant it flesh and, crucially, a voice: the text, while precisely quoted, has also been marked with small infidelities so that it reads like an improperly recalled impression of the warning by a nonnative English speaker (none of the ESL markings in this warning appear on AnonGhost's Twitter feed).

AnonGhost (also known as The Mauritania Hacker Team) was a major player in #OpIsrael 2.0, Anonymous's cyberattack on Israel in April 2013. A revival of #OpIsrael, the cyberattack of November 2012 to protest Israeli actions in Gaza, #OpIsrael 2.0 was launched on April 7, 2013, the day Israel commemorates the Holocaust, and was accompanied by a threat from Anonymous to "erase Israel from cyberspace" ("OpIsrael"). Though Israel is no stranger to cyberwarfare or cyberattacks, the coincidence of symbolic and existential erasure has real reverberations for the population, and the threat was taken seriously in the media. Pro-Israeli hackers, responding to the threat, quickly defaced #OpIsrael's website, and a group of hackers calling themselves Israeli Elite Force (iEF) fought back against Anonymous with a number of initial leaks and doxes, designed to cull supporters and media attention in the days leading up to the scheduled attack. On April 7 proper, iEF tweeted: "We dedicate this BLITZ to all holocaust survivors! We are proud to be your modern Bielski partisans!" Though both AnonGhost and iEF tweet primarily in English, iEF's tweet included a link to a pastebin file with this message in Hebrew: "A personal message to all Israelis. In this attack we have chosen to act because we see that our folks are worried. We have come to prove that you have nothing to fear! Jewish hackers will always prevail. The 'attacks' from the Arabs are not serious, they are not professional. Therefore, till now, we have been silent. We see that the public is beginning to fear this nonsense so we have decided to respond."[25]

At work here is the claiming of reality, of the immediacy of real violence, and of the power to be a "real" threat; the Holocaust plays a crucial role for these purposes. The timing of #OpIsrael 2.0 to coincide with Israel's Holocaust Remembrance day, and the phrase "erase Israel from cyberspace," evoked historical genocide—the erasure of a people—to confer reality on an expectation of cyberviolence. Israel's media noted that Yad Vashem, the center for documenting the Holocaust, was one of Anonymous's targets, with one of the participants encouraging, "fire at the holocaust."[26] With the reference to "modern Bielski partisans," iEF publically (i.e., in English) takes up the Holocaust rhetoric (though in private, with a pastebin message directed to Hebrew speakers only, they reinscribe this threat in terms of Jews' and Arabs' competing claims for land). By adapting and wielding the Holocaust, iEF resurrects the rhetorical power of an existential threat. For both sides of the conflict, the Holocaust functions as Tyler's warning does: a model of immediate violence, available to be appropriated and utilized—in other words, hacked.

The effects of #OpIsrael 2.0 indicated that AnonGhost and the other participants in the project were no more able than traditional do-gooders to navigate the complexities of the facts on the ground. Ill equipped to distinguish between Israeli, Israeli Arab, West-Bank and Gaza-based Palestinian institutions, and acting on misinformation fed to them by iEF hackers working undercover in IRC channels, Anonymous DDoSed Sakhnin Teacher's College (an Arab institution in Northern Israel) and the Israeli Human Rights organization B'Tzelem.[27] The choice of the latter target—and iEF's subsequent public bragging about it on Twitter—underscores the detachment of #OpIsrael from the specificities of the conflict and, indeed, from any national context or nationalist agenda. For its part, Anonymous hacked a number of Facebook pages, including that of GazaYouthBreakOut who, on April 8, 2013, tweeted: "We love #Anonymous but we hate that they hacked

---

25. Translation mine. The message concludes with a reference to Proverbs 27:24, referring to the transience of power, and a quotation from Jeremiah 51:5 ("For Israel has not been forsaken, nor Judah of his God"), a verse that is generally interpreted as affirming the historical role of the Jews as God's chosen people.

26. The chat image appears in "The CyberAttack."

27. In private communication with the author iEF claimed responsibility for misdirecting Anonymous to Sakhnin Teacher's College as part of an undercover operation.

our FB page. Dudes, We're palestinians, you got the wrong address. . COME ON."

Perhaps no other context underscores so clearly the imbrications of faith and fact, image and experience, history and fiction, this book has attempted to describe. Israel/Palestine has been hypermediated since its inception. Each side of the conflict (and there are more than two!) proclaims itself to be the real victim of real violence. Each offers compelling evidence to underwrite these claims. All identify as misrepresented and misunderstood, document demonization by the Western media, and claim to be silenced. All know, with faultless certainty, that *violence is real*, and witness the range of forms that real violence can assume. Torn, open bodies do not call a halt to this work. They are its condition of possibility. In its very ineffectiveness, its epic fail, #OpIsrael 2.0 underscored how, after X, immediacy and immediate violence have become available to be claimed, disclaimed, appropriated, and mobilized, even—or especially— here: a site politically vexed, historically fraught, ideologically volatile, and literally visceral.

FIND SOME CAUSE:
Jack's Revolution

Fight Club's revolution is literally visceral, too. The narrator, squatting with Tyler in an abandoned house on Paper Street, discovers a series of articles in which human organs speak in the first person. Initially reporting information about functionality ("I am Jack's medulla oblongata. Without me, Jack could not regulate his heart rate, blood pressure, or breathing" [*FC* 1999]), these organs accrue volition and menace: "I am Jack's raging bile duct," "I am Jack's cold sweat" (*FC* 1999). As Marla interrupts the narrator's symbiotic coexistence with Tyler, the conceit, with repetition, abandons the physical and becomes psychological ("I am Jack's inflamed sense of rejection" [*FC* 1999]) and metaphorical: "I am Jack's broken heart" (*FC* 1999). The DVD perpetuates this conceit: it identifies itself as "Jack's movie," complete with "Jack's Chapter Selections" and "Jack's Audio Commentary" (*FC* 2000). In the novel, the body housing the organs is named not Jack but Joe, and the narrator's description of Project Mayhem resonates with an image of organs in revolt, a potential fifth column in the body politic: "The idea is to take some Joe on the street who's never been in a fight and recruit him. Let him experience winning for the first time in his life. Get him to explode" (*FC* 1996, 119–20). If the novel relied on a careful reader to make this connection, the film is more explicit. When the narrator recites "I am Jack's colon," Tyler replies immediately: "I get cancer. I kill Jack" (*FC* 1999).

Fight Club's vision of revolution is thus predicated on the expectation that the body will betray. It will unveil its unbridled multiplicity (imaged by cancer) and it will turn its own defense system against itself (imaged by AIDS). For Xer Palahniuk, writing in 1996, cancer and AIDS are explicitly linked (Palahniuk has been open about his homosexuality since 2003). In the novel, the narrator, who has witnessed friends and family die of cancer, recalls, while feeling a lump in Marla's breast, his own experience as the object of intense medical scrutiny when a birthmark was mistaken for Kaposi's sarcoma. The specter of acquired immune deficiency is imaged, in the novel, by syntactic reversal (the narrator was told about "a new kind of cancer that was getting young men") and ontic inversion: "the cancer that I don't have is everywhere now" (*FC* 1996, 105–6). Though this scene was not included in the film adaptation, Palahniuk has identified the AIDS epidemic as part of its generational appeal: "The 'Fight Club' generation is the first generation to whom sex and death seem synonymous" (qtd. in Lim). For Xers, schooled on the logic of AIDS, "That old saying, how you always kill the one you love, well, look, it works both ways" (*FC* 1996, 1999) reverberates with the general collapse of bodies that require fidelity in order to be sustained: family, corporation, religion, nation.

Xers notoriously have no cause to fight for, nothing to believe in, and if the very nature of hacking is, as Coleman puts it, turning a system against itself, the image of the body as a system that can be invaded and appropriated, turned against itself, is not only powerful but uniquely useful for thinking about violence's contemporary manifestations, after X. The hacked body reveals and conceals, articulating a coming into presence of a shadowy, unlocatable multiplicity. In *Fight Club*, this hacking is imaged by the figure of organs in revolt, by the metastasizing cells of cancer, capitalism, and terror, and by the subliminal images of Tyler on the DVD. All predicated on the body, they counter the somatic, tracing a movement away from perception. The subliminal images, not designed to be seen with a naked eye, explicitly reject the body's claims for certainty and are viewable only through instruments and devices— the remote, the slow-motion, the blood test, the microscope, the computer screen.

Hence my choice of *Fight Club,* with its invisible, silent programming function, over *V for Vendetta,* the far more visible face—or mask—of contemporary revolution. No anarchist geek could fail to note that in Moore's and Lloyd's classic graphic novel, V excels, in addition to all else, at hacking: he appropriates "Fate," the computer system adored by his nemesis, the fascist Adam Susan. Meditating on his love for Fate, Susan extolls this disembodied quality. "She has no eyes to flirt or promise, but she sees all. Sees and understands with a wisdom that is godlike in its scale. [. . .] Her soul is clean, untainted by the snares and ambiguities of emotion. She does not hate. She does not yearn. She is untouched by joy or sorrow" (*V* 1988, 38).²⁸ Like the narrator's and Tyler's relationship, in which "the gun, the anarchy, the explosion, is really about Marla Singer" (*FC* 1996, 1999), V's philosophy is the product of a love triangle, according to which Susan stole Justice, V's lover, driving V to the arms of Anarchy. V, apostrophizing Justice, scolds her for her infidelity with the fascist Susan ("Liar! Slut! Whore! Deny that you let him have his way with you, him and his armbands and jackboots!" [*V* 1988, 40]). Susan has forgotten Justice, and is inappropriately attached to Fate, whom he describes as his "bride," kissing and caressing the screen. Speaking of Susan to his protégé, Eve, V indicates his awareness of this misplaced affect: his hacking is a personal vendetta, as well as a metaphorical move.²⁹ "My rival, though inclined to roam, possessed at home a wife that he adored. He'll rue his promiscuity, the rogue who stole my only love, when he's informed how many years it is"—at this point the sequential oblong frames are replaced by a single rectangular frame, revealing V seated at an immense computer—"since first I bedded his" (*V* 1988, 201).

Hacking Fate enables V to acquire and disseminate information, access and deploy infrastructure, and represents the final step of V's plan, described admiringly by Eve as "purposeful," "benign, almost like surgery . . . Your foes assumed you sought revenge upon their flesh alone, but you did not stop there . . . you gored their ideology as well" (*V* 1988, 260). This characterization of V's violence as both visceral and philosophical is striking, because Eve's relation to V is characterized by her refusal of violence. She dissociates herself from V's killing even as she affirms his mission. "I'll not help them kill. The age of killers is no more.

---

28. Henceforth the graphic novel *V for Vendetta* is cited as *V* 1988, and the film adaptation as *V* 2005.

29. V's protégé, Evey Hammond, is rechristened "Eve" by V in part 3 of the graphic novel. In the film adaptation, she is "Evey" throughout.

FIGURE 7. *V For Vendetta* © DC Comics. Fascist leader Adam Susan covers his face in despair as V's defacement message appears on one of the terminals of his beloved computer system Fate, the first move in V's final plan—as indicated by the tipping of the domino in the preceding panel. V's hacking feat does not appear in the 2005 film adaptation. Note the Guy Fawkes mask in the lower right-hand corner of the panel. These appear periodically in the graphic novel, and serve a function similar to the subliminal images of Tyler in *Fight Club*.

They have no place within our better world" (*V* 1988, 260). Eve—aptly named, as she will bring this new world into being—hesitates over V's dead body, wondering whom she will see when she removes the mask. Various options appear and are discarded. Finally she recognizes her own face. "And at last I know. I know who V must be" (*V* 1988, 250). She then affirms his mask, takes his mission, and adopts her own protégé (a young man).

V's hacking feat vanishes from the 2005 adaptation, as does the computer system Fate, the love triangle imagery, and—most crucially—Eve's affirmation of V's mask and mission. The film opens with Evey—diminutized from Eve—proclaiming her fidelity to "the man" over and above the idea he represents. After reciting, "remember remember the fifth of November," she asks: "But what of the man?" (*V* 2005). Evey's attachment to the man lies in her attention to his physical vulnerability.[30] "We

---

30. Evey, unlike Eve, affirms an affiliation with the precariousness that, Judith Butler writes, defines political life. But Butler's ethical theory seems somewhat limited by her reliance on notions of individuality, classical subjectivity, a desire to "return to a sense

are told to remember the idea, not the man, because a man can fail. He can be caught, he can be killed and forgotten . . . but you cannot kiss an idea, cannot touch it, or hold it . . . ideas do not bleed, they do not feel pain, they do not love . . . And it is not an idea that I miss, it is a man" (*V* 2005). In the film's concluding scenes, Evey completes V's plan, and ignites the explosives V has set. Confirming imagery of multiplicity that had been building in the course of the film (raindrops; dominoes; computer screens), a vast crowd appears, all in full Guy Fawkes regalia, to witness the destruction of the Houses of Parliament. With the explosion, as Evey intones "He's Edmond Dantes, and he is my father, and my mother, my brother, my friend, he is you, and me, he is all of us" (*V* 2005), the crowd members remove their masks and the faceless horde is revealed as individuals: unique, diverse, hopeful.[31]

Anonymous, of course, retains the mask. By doing so, the hacker collective resurrects both the graphic novel original with its masked hacker hero (and heroine) *and* the multitudinous imagery of the Wachowski adaptation. But they do so with a uniquely X attitude, one that is accustomed to reverse or refuse temporal progression, construct causality and disavow it. Here, too, the *Fight Club* precedent is instructive. Tyler hacks and screens pornography. He seeds films with X-rated images and screens them to unsuspecting audiences. In other words: though the novel describes projectionists who assemble "epic" collections of pornographic images from single frames they clip and collect (Fincher recalls seeing such collections as a teenager [*FC* 2000]), Tyler reverses this process: rather than accumulating images, he disseminates them. In just such a manner Anonymous rewinds the final frames of the *V for Vendetta* film: not unmasking but masking, not refusing but assuming the Guy Fawkes symbol, a symbol that, as Lewis Call puts it, is mobile, nomadic, and "important precisely because it is never faithful to itself" (170). With the Anonymous phenomenon, hackers adopt the *V for Vendetta* program of revolution, adapt and export it, making it available to

---

of ethical outrage that is, distinctively, for an Other, in the name of an Other" and her demand to "hear the agonized cry or be compelled or commanded by the face" (150).

31. Call argues that the film is an improvement over the graphic novel original because of its radical employment of the mask: by multiplying it, rendering it mobile, the film affirms the anarchic history that the Guy Fawkes mask represents. "Moore's Bildungsroman may have been an inspirational story about one woman's journey to political engagement, but the film is something more than that: a post modern narrative about a subversive political symbolism which can spread through a culture like a virus or meme, rewriting that culture as it goes" (170). This would be true only if the crowd members retained their masks. But they do not.

an international market (Tunisia and, more recently, Istanbul), format-
ted in such a way as to enable its use by another application (Project
Chanology; Occupy Wall Street).

But just like Tyler, who spins out of control and drags the narrator
kicking and screaming in his wake, mastery of the image does not ensure
or safeguard intent. As the image migrates outward, from the page or the
screen and into the world, it assumes a life of its own, one unfettered by
affect, ideals, or even physical integrity. In both the film and novel version of *Fight Club,* the narrator vainly attempts to apprehend Tyler and
halt Project Mayhem. Eventually, he shoots himself in the head. The bullet does not kill him, but it leaves the narrator with a gaping wound in
his jaw.

In the novel, this wound is imaged as a scar that disfigures the narrator: like the Joker in Moore's classic Batman graphic novel, *The Killing
Joke* (1988), the scar manifests as a smile, underscoring the ground-
lessness of affect. The V mask smiles as well, and, describing a Project
Mayhem attack orchestrated by Tyler, *Fight Club*'s narrator evokes a
similarly affectless, smiling mask: strategically placed fires transform an
office building into "a grinning, five-story mask. [. . .] The face is an
angry pumpkin, Japanese demon, dragon of avarice hanging in the sky"
(*FC* 1996, 118). Slashed with Tyler's bullet, the narrator's face becomes
a similar mask, a mask the reader is expected to recognize: "a jagged
smile from ear to ear. Yeah, just like an angry Halloween pumpkin. Japanese demon. Dragon of avarice" (*FC* 1996, 207). With these sentences,
Project Mayhem manifests as written on the narrator's body, though
the body's assumption of physical integrity is crossed out. He has, the
concluding pages of *Fight Club* reveal, always been multiple, unreliable, hacked. He was always also Tyler, his rival, nemesis, lover, brother,
father, and friend.

In the film, the bullet leaves the narrator wounded, but he is still able
to speak, though his voice is altered. One of Tyler's acolytes approaches,
and the narrator croaks, "find some gauze" (*FC* 1999). Or perhaps he
says: "find some cause"—with a mouthful of blood and broken teeth,
the plosives *c* and *g* are indistinguishable.[32] This leaves open the question of whether the wound is to be covered up or the organized potential of Project Mayhem is to be rechanneled, redirected. The answer,
again, lies in the body: this time, not the narrator's or Tyler's but the
viewer's. She has witnessed how Tyler's insertion of images, in films he

---

32. I am grateful to my student Boynton Allen for this observation.

hacks, has direct effect. People shudder and weep when they see them, even though, as the images flicker too quickly to be registered, they do not know why they are acting. Tyler's hacks turn these spectators into zombies. Not merely an image for the posthuman that incites affect and thwarts it, eradicating and mobilizing the invaded, ruined body, the zombie—that corpselike, spectral figure wherein violence, in all its problematic potential, is revealed—is also a computer connected to the internet that has been hacked. Such a zombie or bot can be operated remotely without the owner's knowledge. It can be mobilized, its power claimed for some goal or cause or purpose. As the image of a penis flickers over the final scenes, *Fight Club* announces that it, too, has been hacked: Tyler, by splicing pornography into the film, informs its viewers of their own appropriated agency. He is you, and me. He is all of us.

Fight Club's claim to hack its viewers, to turn them into zombies, linked and formed in an organic, human botnet even as it enjoins them to "find some cause," affirms the force and efficacy of violence after X. Like the silent, masked, emptily smiling horde of *V for Vendetta*'s final scenes that inspired early Anonymous activists to don the mask, the mindless, apathetic consumers of popular culture, with no cause to fight for, nothing to believe in, represent the full power and potential of Jack's revolution. But where will this force will be directed? By whom it will be channeled? And in what name?

conclusion
. . . .

X Out

FIGURE 8. Expect Anonymous Fight Club Soap. Image by Mar Williams. This is one of several illustrations that accompany Joshua Corman's series on Anonymous. The soap's hot pink color and the angle of the letters recall the promotional materials that accompanied *Fight Club*'s film adaptation. Note the Guy Fawkes mask, visible in the bubbles and froth.

X: The generation without a name. That is, literally, anonymous.

EXPECT US: The slogan of Anonymous, the hacker collective that rose to prominence in 2008.

EXPECT ANONYMOUS: One of Mar Williams's illustrations for "Building a Better Anonymous," an online essay series by Joshua Corman and Brian Martin on the future of digital hacktivism, or "illegal hacking to achieve a political goal."

Hacking is commonly imaged as a malevolent act, the work of cruel youths or cynical criminals. But, Corman and Martin stress, hacking cannot be simply dismissed, demonized, or controlled. Reflecting on the Anonymous phenomenon they imagine a process by which the unruly anarchy of Anonymous is affirmed, and the phenomenon of digital hacktivism improved and mobilized. "It is an inevitable fact that Anonymous, or similar groups, will become bigger, stronger, and more effective," they write. "We seek to explore the ideas of making such a group truly better." But "better," the authors stress, does not conform to any traditional sense of virtue. It does not attest to an underlying or overarching morality or *ism*. "'Better' does not mean more criminal acts in the name of the greater good, it means a more efficient organization. [. . .] We envision a group with better defined goals, more accountability, a healthy dose of humor and the legendary resolve of the sabertooth squirrel." (The final image refers to Scrat, a character from the film *Ice Age*, who instigated the separation into continents of the landmass Pangaea and other global cataclysms.)

"We are Anonymous. We are legion. We do not forgive. We do not forget. Expect us," intones a faceless silhouette. Anonymous rose to prominence with a series of online and in-person activities in which the participants wore masks, as if recreating, on the streets of major cities worldwide, the final scenes of the film *V for Vendetta*. But behind or through or under these intertexts—the bar of soap itself, its off-putting color, and the font, shape, and angle of the letters on it—is *Fight Club*, the 1999 cult film where disaffected, disillusioned, middle-class men meet for bare-knuckle fistfights because the experience of violence (both beating and being beaten) offers them a sense of community and existential affirmation otherwise denied them. It is denied them because they are members of Generation X.

Disappear Here has probed Generation X's attitude toward violence to determine violence's forms and functions in the world that Xers grew up in. In this world, the line between fiction and fact is permeable, fungible; the relationship of violence to action is characterized by complicity, giving pause to ethics; "reality" is produced for television and marketed for consumption, and fiction—in the sense of fashioning and fabricating, as well as illusion and delusion—assumes an important role in the creation, construction, and preservation of "real violence." *After* Generation X, in the twenty-first century, the nature of "real violence" is an open question—a point that Millennials or members of Generation Y, who live online, via avatars, on social networking sites, have already begun to sense. Overt revolutionary attempts of the Millennial generation—such as the Occupy movement—emerge directly from X's dyad of presence and absence, the visceral and the metaphysical. Formed in the wake of the global 2008 recession, Occupy articulated the wreckage wrought by dividend traders and bankers, violence invisible to the naked eye.

The novels of Bret Easton Ellis, Jay McInerney, Douglas Coupland, and Colson Whitehead have helped me describe Generation X's unique attitude toward violence. As I recounted in "Why X Now? Crossing Out and Marking the Spot," this attitude was formed by developments in politics, culture, and technology in the 1980s and 1990s, the years that Xers were coming of age. "Nevermind: An X Critique of Violence" articulated the specific questions that Generation X poses to representation and critique, drawing on theories of media, the image, state power, and pain, as well as Richard Linklater's seminal film *Slacker*, to articulate the shifting grounds of representation after (that is, according to) Generation X. Turning to the work of Bret Easton Ellis (one of the authors most firmly associated with the "Nevermind" attitude and ethos), in "The Game That Moves: Bret Easton Ellis, 1985–2010," I showed how Ellis's novels trace the disappearance of the sign of the real and document a subtraction of reality from representation in the quarter century between 1985 (when his first novel, *Less Than Zero*, was published) and 2010 (when he published *Imperial Bedrooms*, which revisits the characters from *Less Than Zero*). "Disappear Here" is Ellis's phrase, and it returns and reappears in four of his six novels (as well as in music and film inspired by his work).[1]

---

1. *Disappear Here* is the title of a 2010 music album by the British electronica group Hybrid and a 2012 album by the U.S. punk band Callow. British indie rock group Bloc Party's 2007 album *A Weekend in the City* includes a track titled "Song for Clay (Disappear Here)," which quotes a number of lines from *Less Than Zero*. At the time of this writing, a Kickstarter campaign is underway to raise funds for a film to be directed by Matthew Mishory titled *Disappear Here* (expected release date was 2014).

"Something Empty in the Sky: 9/11 after X" studied the literary response to the spectacular terror attacks of September 11, 2001, by Xers Frédéric Beigbeder, Claire Messud, and Jess Walter, as well as by Ken Kalfus, McInerney, and Don DeLillo. These novels show how 9/11, still widely described as a "return of the real," attests repeatedly to the inextricability of the real from mass media; what "returns" takes the form of a familiar spectacle of disaster inscribed and televisually marked *as* real; not violence but its reality is re-cognized. With the help of Jonathan Safran Foer's fiction about cataclysmic historical events (the Holocaust, the firebombing of Dresden, and the terror attacks of September 11, 2001), "Not Yes or No: Fact, Fiction, Fidelity in Jonathan Safran Foer" described how, for Xers, the distinction between perpetrator and victim is fragile and contingent, the effect of an ever-shifting-object of fidelity rather than a brute manifestation of historical fact. Finally, tracing the online presence of the X phenomenon *Fight Club* (both Chuck Palahniuk's novel and David Fincher's film adaptation), "I Am Jack's Revolution: *Fight Club*, Hacking, Violence after X" reflected on the implications of Generation X's thinking on violence for our globalized, networked, new millennium, as information is mobile, contagious, and subject to leaks, and fiction—fashioning and fabricating, assembling and making, programming and hacking—creates, constructs, and preserves "real violence," and dictates action in its wake.

Now I want to reflect on some of the broader issues raised by this book, issues that revolve around *Disappear Here*'s situation on the cusp of the twenty-first century, and that emerge from my call for a new approach to violence and fiction today.

"Today," of course, changes daily. I wrote earlier that Generation X's association with movement, with acceleration, with time running out at the millennium's edge, is also the question of certainty's shifting terrain under the spell of velocity. X's avowed dislike of certainties, its association with youth, newness, and movement, concretizes the challenge that contemporaneity poses to study. As Timothy Bewes puts it in "Temporalizing the Present," "since understanding can only be achieved by turning one's head backward, any entity is frozen into stasis by the analytical gaze" (159). Or, as Crasher complains in *13thGen*, "it's like trying to read the song title on a record that's spinning" (Howe and Strauss 23).

A number of transient magazines and websites, too many to list, are also named "Disappear Here."

As presentation and representation increasingly, swiftly, interpenetrate, and the title or text is a moving target, how we read, what we read, and to what purpose is an open and urgent question.

The idea that texts simultaneously affirm and deny the power structures that dictated their production, reception, and resilience dominated literary criticism in the 1980s and 1990s. For scholars and teachers schooled in poststructuralism, deconstruction, and ideology critique, delving into the text, penetrating its surface, reveals hidden, ossified hegemonies, melts them into air, and soberly puts readers face to face with the real. This depth model was, of course, driven by dialectic, the thesis-antithesis-synthesis engine by which Hegel imaged history and Marx revolution; even after Francis Fukuyama, following Hegel, declared an end of history, dialectical thought continued to propel Marx's postmodernist, poststructuralist, and deconstructionist heirs who, despite having witnessed communism's horrific costs, shared Marx's distrust of fixed relations, his commitment to undoing ancient prejudices and opinions, and his intolerance of oppression. This depth model was also informed by psychoanalysis, a field driven by faith in the underlying, unexpressed, and inexpressible forces beneath the surface of things, and in the centrality of interpretation in co-creating truth: the critic, like the analyst, elicits from the opaque image an account of what the surface disavows. Hence the ambiguity, complexity, and the much-derided opacity associated with Judith Butler's and Jacques Derrida's early work: these are hard to read for a reason. A difficult text reveals and conceals, points to what it cannot confess, and affirms, again and again, that truth is not a simple fact. Acclaimed X authors like Mark Z. Danielewski and Ben Marcus rely on their readers' affinity with this important tradition, as well as their faith in its value.

The X authors discussed in this book, in contrast, are notoriously easy to read. Their work has been dismissed as cultlike and cartoonish (especially in its portrayal of violence), without intrinsic value or literary heft, their popularity nothing but a passing phase. Precisely because of their presumed superficiality, though, these texts offer insight into debates about the value and limits of the depth model. In recent years these debates have occupied literary scholars who are reflecting on the ethical and political potential of what they do. Stephen Best and Sharon Marcus describe a recent turn from the depth model (what they call "symptomatic reading") to "modes of reading that attend to the surfaces of texts rather than plumb their depths" (1–2). In advocating surface reading, Best and Marcus suggest that much is to be gained by "relinquishing the freedom dream that accompanies the work of demystification" (17) and attending to the text's "assembly"—what I have called, in *Disappear Here,* its fictive quality, its forming or fashioning. This tendency toward surface reading, Best and Marcus claim, emerged with images of violence that ushered in the new millennium: the Abu Ghraib torture photographs, the Hurricane Katrina coverage, and the orchestrated theatre of the Bush administration all "hammered home the point that not all situations require the subtle ingenuity" associated with late-twentieth-century deconstruction and ideology critique (2). Of course, as *Disappear Here* has demonstrated, this resolute superficiality is hardly new. "Surface surface surface was all that anyone found meaning in," wrote Ellis in *American Psycho* (375).

"Surface reading" does have its discontents. Carolyn Lesjak, for example, condemns it as politically quietist. The drive to surface reading, she argues, disavows history; it is reactionary, and proscribes revolution and progressive action. Lesjak advocates opacity, "reading surfaces as perverse rather than as obvious, as never identical to themselves in their 'thereness,' and always found within and constitutive of complex spatial relations, both seen and not seen, deep and lateral, material and figural" (251). Though she describes this approach as a lost cause, she nonetheless urges fidelity to it: "fidelity to the lost cause of reading dialectically [. . .] is the only way to keep faith with history" (264). Taking a middle ground in these debates, Timothy Bewes imagines an approach to fiction that consistently attends to that which "escapes ethical reflection [or] succeeds in abolishing perspective" ("Reading" 21). Bewes eschews reading for ethical or political purpose, preferring "the potentiality that inheres in those aspects of the text that are not exhausted by the referential function" (28). Seeking to set the reader in an immanent relation to the text, so that the act of reading illuminates reader and text simultaneously, underscoring their mutual complicity, Bewes imagines abolishing the oppositional relation between reader and text: "the object is no longer an object" (28).

Like the tattoo of a scar that looks like a gash, X reveals and obscures what's under erasure, marks a moving spot on the surface of things, and sets these debates in a broader perspective. Best and Marcus's affirmation of surface, their disavowal of grand ideals, and their willingness to relinquish the fantasy of the critic-as-hero (a willingness that Bewes shares) evince an X dislike and distrust of Boomer-centered *isms.* But so does Lesjak's affirmation of ambiguity, her attention to the uneasy quality of presence, and her stubborn fidelity to a lost cause. If Best and

Marcus's aesthetic credo was captured, decades earlier, by Ellis, both Lesjak and Bewes, for all their differences, seek what Xer Donna Tartt, in the final pages of her novel *The Goldfinch,* describes as the "middle zone" between the catastrophe of human existence and the work of art: "between 'reality' on the one hand, and the point where the mind strikes reality [. . .] where two very different surfaces mingle and blur to provide what life does not" (770).

That blurring, of course, is *Disappear Here*'s point of departure, and the wager of this book is that it extends to violence—itself commonly posed as a point of departure that both representation and interpretation reflect, traumatically repeat, neurotically obscure, or, in the name of Ethics, disavow. The underlying assumption of this project—its crux—is that violence, like any other aspect of reality, is subject to representation, and hence to misrepresentation, distortion, and denial—in short, to fiction. And yet, as I have maintained throughout this book: *violence is real,* though its reality is hard to find, and is ultimately indistinguishable from fiction. Consequently, after Generation X, we are called upon to navigate what is real, determine what is true, and act accordingly.

Or not; given Xers' notorious apathy and detachment, action does not come easily. For many Xers, "Resistance is Futile," the Borg's menacing mantra in *Star Trek: The Next Generation* (1987–94) rings true, and political engagement is most likely to be evinced by the ironic disavowal of ideological fervor that drove the "Rally to Restore Sanity and/ or Fear" led by Xers Jon Stewart and Stephen Colbert on the National Mall in Washington, DC (October 30, 2010). But Xers could never be scolded into caring. The rise of trauma theory in the 1980s and 1990s was affect-laden, ethically invested, urgent in its invocations of justice, and sometimes shrill in its warnings about the potential of damage that irresponsible representation can do to victims, to history, to truth, and to reality itself. Many Xers tuned these warnings out, and grew attuned to the limits of ethics, the exhaustion of critique, the evacuation of affect, the emptying out of revolutionary promise. *After* X, the complicity of all these *ism*s with faith-based structures comes to the fore, laying bare the fictive quality of faith—even, or especially, in secular, ideological, or political pursuits.

When fidelity—what you are compelled, by conviction, attitude, marketing, and imagery, to believe—dictates what presents as real, phenomena as diverse as the Arab Spring, the 2014 Israel–Hamas War, and the prevalence, in the United States, of "truther" movements (around President Barack Obama, 9/11, or Sandy Hook) begin to coalesce under a general revision of the value traditionally ascribed to epistemic validity, even—or especially—in the context of violence. Xer Stephen Colbert coined the term "truthiness" to capture this phenomenon. But this deep complicity with the image-driven discourse of commodity culture (a point that the Brat Pack authors of the early 1980s knew well, and which blank fiction practitioners in the 1990s demonstrated over and over) sutures X into contemporary aesthetic production, for which complicity, as Johanna Drucker has pointed out, needs to replace the paradigm of radical critique on which the ideological potential of art was premised by modernism.[2] *Disappear Here* has traced the implications of this complicity for reality, for violence, and for action today.

"Complicity" is a formidable term because of its association with a criminal charge. Charges elicit judgments of innocence or guilt. But in his meditations on complicity in ghettos and in Auschwitz, Primo Levi articulated a more nuanced approach. Complicity is different, Levi notes, from collaboration and culpability. Collaboration is a charge; culpability is a verdict. Both are well within judgment's sphere. But to be complicit, Levi stressed, is to stand in a relation to this sphere on which judgment *has yet* to fall. Levi's seminal articulation of this "gray zone" situates the subject in relation to violence without condemning or exonerating her. By distinguishing questions about complicity from the judgment that condemns, and clarifying that complicit actions within an evil system do not endorse or support the system and its evil, Levi poses complicity as a starting point for questions about ethics.[3] Precisely because it is not itself

---

2. Drucker's study of contemporary fine art suggests the term "complicit formalism" to articulate how artists in the 1990s and early 2000s articulated, within the formal properties of their works, "embedded conditions of meaning" (xvi). Drucker chooses "complicity" (a term she acknowledges is "deliberately provocative, since it implies a knowing compromise between motives of opportunism and circumstantial conditions—whether on the plane of production, or reference, or within institutional and social situations" [xvi]) in part to signal a departure from the oppositional model that defined the art of the avant-garde and that still (she writes in 2006) characterizes the theoretical bent of most academic work (xiv), and in part to exit the critical impasse of judgment that designates art objects "good" or "bad," and renders toothless art's potential for enacting change: "Criticism's prescriptive effect paralyzes the inventive impulse of making and locks artists into an impoverished 'poststudio' position in which art making is conceived largely as a conceptual or symbolic act. But this simply isn't true. For all the critical significance of conceptualism, art is never only an idea" (xv).

3. I am building, here, on the conclusion to my 2006 book *Against the Unspeakable*. That book discussed how, in the wake of events like the Holocaust, slavery, and the atomic bombings of Hiroshima and Nagasaki, complicity is generally posited as a problem, an irritant, or an ethical inconsistency that must be identified and abolished in the quest for moral clarity. Such a quest, I maintain, is a fool's errand. It misses the

a judgment (though it invites and expects it), complicity dwells in the tension between the particular and the paradigmatic, the demographic and as the point of view, a tension that has pervaded studies of Generation X from its inception.

This does not mean that complicity is, itself, ethical. In the seminal formulations of postmodernism by Baudrillard, Lyotard, and Jameson, complicity was an inevitable paradox with which postmodernism must wrestle and fail to resolve—fail, because a resolution will affirm a totality and certainty that is antithetical to the ethical and political projects with which postmodernism is aligned. For some scholars and theorists of postmodernism, complicity was a productive point from which difference can be investigated and embraced (Linda Hutcheon posits "complicitous critique" as a starting point for postmodern ethics). For others (like Christopher Norris), it was lamented: a sign of postmodernism's political inefficacy. But the simultaneity of affirmation and negation, of documentation and hypothesis, of refusal and co-option, of presence and representation that "X" captures has uniquely equipped Generation X to dwell in, or to occupy, complicity's domain. Studies of complicity by Mark Sanders and Christopher Kutz, like Levi's, conceive of complicity spatially, a temporary ground: complicity is a zone (Levi), a domain (Kutz), or a "footing" from which, as Sanders writes, "opposition takes its first steps" (9). Today, in our virtual, networked reality, "domain" names not just dwelling place but a system that offers access to the internet. Think of complicity as such a domain, governed, as web domains are, by protocols that offer network access, opening us to the being of other beings.[4] Complicity aligns and binds us to those whose suffering affects us even as "real violence" increasingly eludes our grasp, moving between the world and the screen, manifesting as an ever-shifting object of fidelity, migrating in and out of fiction.

This migration has informed my methodology, which draws on U.S. popular culture to articulate and address issues that reverberate in a global postcolonial contemporary. I know that the export of U.S. culture

---

fundamental value of complicity in a world where violence—on the page, screen, couch, or battlefield—leaves no one untouched.

4. Kutz proffers what he calls a "complicity principle," in which "I am accountable for what others do when I intentionally participate in the wrong they do or harm they cause" (122), suggesting that complicity is a logical precedent for accountability: first you are complicit, only then can you be accountable for evil, or to others. Sanders extends this logic by describing complicity as "the very basis for responsibly entering into, maintaining, or breaking off a given affiliation or attachment" (x).

was a crucial tool in the Cold War, a kind of cultural armament. But tools can be used to build and dismantle, and arms find their way into unexpected hands. As I arm and aim, I am driven by the conviction that much like French poststructuralism, with its inarguable and transformative contribution to feminism, Critical Race Theory, and cultural studies, U.S. popular culture is an enabling paradigm; it cannot be discarded merely because of its complicity with global hegemony.[5] Indeed, as Mark LeVine notes, the development, in the 1980s, of satellite TV that exposed Xers to "everything from MTV's 'Headbangers Ball' and *Dallas* to Spanish-language telenovelas and German pornography" (301), makes such a paradigm absolutely necessary. Like Henseler (a Hispanicist), Tara Brabazon (Australia), LeVine (who specializes in the Middle East), and Lisa Parks and Shanti Kumar, the editors of *Planet TV* (who write from a South Asian perspective), I see in U.S. popular culture useful tools for critical work in a global context. The idea is *not* to assert

---

5. In my insistence on X's global bent, I am guided by Christine Henseler, perhaps the most prolific scholar of Generation X today. Her edited volume and digital project, *Generation X Goes Global,* instantiates her earlier observation in *Spanish Fiction in the Digital Age: Generation X Remixed*: Generation X, writes Henseler, "unsettled critics' traditional, nationalist, and purely word-oriented critical perspectives; its 'X' factor simultaneously allowed them to acknowledge and discredit the moniker's North American and popular cultural alliances" (*Spanish Fiction* 5). *The X Factor*—a global television music competition franchise that originated from *Pop Idol* in the United Kingdom and spawned *American Idol* in the United States—marks the spot from which Generation X, heirs to unprecedented technological and telecommunications developments, may offer a timely critique of power and agency in contemporary media studies, one that creatively, even playfully, engages U.S. popular culture from a variety of national and post-national sites. Writing of global television studies, Parks and Kumar assert that blanket assumptions of cultural imperialism fatally discount the significance of audience agency: "One of the ways that television scholars have approached the debates over globalization is through cultural imperialism, which forcefully foregrounds the inequities of media resources and flows in international communication. However, in recent years, cultural imperialism has come under heavy criticism for its inability to adequately theorize the power of audiences to creatively subvert the power of global television. As a result, it has become a less fashionable academic position in the 1990s than it was during the 1970s and 1980s" (11). For Generation X, as Henseler writes in *Spanish Fiction,* "globalization both universalizes and individualizes culture" (16); hence her conviction of the need to shift focus from "traditionally 'passive' or 'victimized' notions centered on the influence of North American corporate culture to more dynamic, active exchanges and innovations" (*Spanish Fiction* 121). But even as Henseler's subsequent edited volume and digital project, *Generation X Goes Global,* claimed for this cohort the mantle of "the first fully *global generation*" (*Global* 15), its contributors (with characteristic ambivalence and suspicion) questioned the very basis for the project. "Generation X does not necessarily go global for everybody," admits Henseler; "[the project's] central premise may quake as it crosses tectonic plates" (*Global* 17).

the value of U.S. culture over and above that of others. Indeed, most of the GenX novels and authors discussed in this book have widely been derided for their *lack* of value and values, or for an (unearned) excess of value placed on them at certain moments in their careers.

My previous work on large-scale global violence (slavery, the Holocaust, and Hiroshima, all commonly imaged, especially in the 1980s and 1990s, as unspeakable) examined the implications of representation's limits for those who define themselves by and through them. That work was attuned to what is at risk when the reality of violence is questioned or denied; it also propelled me toward *Disappear Here* by giving me a clear sense of how the absolute empirical validity of these events legislates their interpretation and dictates the political configurations of identities that define themselves by a history of suffering. *Disappear Here* has pursued that argument, taking as its object not the representation of events that historically occurred but works of fiction that explore the assumption of validity that commonly attach to them. It is this investment with validity that unites the many different types of violence (physical, psychological, empirical, epistemic) that I bring together in this book. Rather than adjudicating among these types (labeling some as dangerous, others as benign; identifying some as causes, others as effects) and rather than discriminating between contexts in which violence occurs (the family, the state, the institution, the environment), I have argued that the underlying stakes of such work have to do with claims on the real. Precisely because of the association of violence with reality, identifying the presence or traces of violence works to claim empirical validity in an increasingly virtual world—one in which "reality" is as urgent as it is elusive.

For the generation that witnessed a receding of the real, its assumption into the image, and its subsequent retrieval from the image and concretization in experience—experience often described as mediated by television, or "just like a movie"—fiction is crucial. Since his seminal 1994 film *Pulp Fiction,* Xer Quentin Tarantino's work has underscored the role that fiction plays in forming our relation to violence. In striking contrast to Boomer Steven Spielberg's *Schindler's List* (1993) and *Amistad* (1997), which were purported to be based on precise historical facts (though scholars do quibble) about the Holocaust and the American slave trade, Tarantino's *Inglourious Basterds* (2009) and *Django Unchained* (2012) revisit the history of Nazi Germany and U.S. slavery, respectively, but embrace an antihistoricist bent, pursuing the logic of revenge and genre over and above fidelity to historical fact. Unlikely to heed the atavistic call to fidelity, to enlist in the name of a nation, a people, a history, a god, Xers are uniquely poised to create, rather than destroy. *After* Generation X, these creations (think of Amazon.com and Google, both a brainchild of Xers) are, like Shelley's poets, the unacknowledged legislators of our world.

Violence in this world moves in and out of fiction, from the content of the text to the context of its reception, from image to disaster and back. This movement is evident in fiction and film by Xers from many nations. Victor Pelevin's *Homo Zapiens* (Russia, 1999) echoes the conceit of the Wachowskis' global hit *The Matrix* (1999), positing local politics and the Chechen war as the products of simulation by advertising agencies; the protagonist himself is finally scanned, replicated, and disseminated digitally. Tom McCarthy's *Remainder* (UK and France, 2005) traces this process in reverse: the protagonist, a survivor of a crippling disaster, generates a concrete reality from a sense of déjà vu. Sayed Kashua, a Palestinian Israeli who writes in Hebrew, traces permutations of fidelity in each of his books: his *Second Person Singular* (2010) combines the trope of passing (a Palestinian assumes an Israeli man's identity) with the specter of marital infidelity to articulate the vicissitudes of identity against a background of occupation, terror, and war. Park Chan-wook's popular 2003 South Korean revenge flick *Oldboy* is rife with images of torture, mutilation, and murder (inflicted mostly with a hammer); the image of a hammer-wielding figure in the video diary of mentally disturbed Virginia Tech student Cho Seung-Hui (released after the murders of spring 2007) further testifies to violence's potential to burst the bounds of fiction, and to its terrible cost.

Like *Oldboy*, Koushun Takami's novel *Battle Royale* (Japan, 1999), a controversial hit when it was published, pushed the envelope with extreme and graphic violence. Takami's account of young people battling to the death developed from his experience growing up in a Japan haunted by memories of U.S. air raids during World War II. Suzanne Collins's young adult series *The Hunger Games* (U.S., 2008; the 2012 film adaptation was a worldwide hit) bears striking similarities to *Battle Royale*. But Collins claims not to know of Takami's novel; her dystopian vision was defined by the prevalence of media she observed in the lives of young people (she added a live TV element, an echo of the 1987 film *Running Man*). Unlike Takami's novel, in which characters' allegiances prove sincere and reliable, Collins's protagonist, Katniss Everdeen, never ascertains the extent to which her affections are genuine, simulated, or performed for the necessity of survival. Katniss's inability to determine or pin down her own affect, her attempt to locate herself in the stylized images produced around her, locates her within a tradition of X authors for whom the stakes are, as for Katniss, life and death. Such an author is Québécoise Nelly Arcan. In her *Whore* (2001), violence, in the form of the deep systemic dictates of gender, functions as a source of attraction and fascination and, ultimately, destruction. Arcan is the pen name of Isabelle Fortier, whose background is remarkably similar to that of her unnamed narrator: a student of literature who prostitutes herself out of a dependency on male desire. *Whore* elicited much speculation as to whether the book was autobiographical, encouraged by Arcan herself in essays and interviews and, especially, in her second novel, *Folle*, narrated by an ex-prostitute turned writer named Nelly Arcan. As if heeding her protagonist's repeated assertions about the inevitability of suicide, the author hanged herself in 2009.

Despite its life-or-death stakes (or, more likely, because of them), violence in fiction has been treated as an exception from reality, rather than a sadly inevitable part of it. But to dismiss violence as a fiction is often to perform a violence of a different order, though such epistemic or discursive violence is itself often countered (and even dismissed) by gestures back to "the real." The outrage generated by phenomena like Xer James Frey's *A Million Little Pieces* and JT LeRoy's unmasking as Xer Laura Albert focuses on the fictionalization of the violence supposedly inflicted on the authors, and evidence the truism that violence demands accuracy, though the object of that accuracy continually eludes.[6] In the second half of the twentieth century, this wedding of violence to its reality extended from fiction and its limits to the fact- and truth-making work of history, philosophy, and aesthetics. For philosopher Jean-François Lyotard, who frames his extensive meditation on *The Differend* as a response to Holocaust denier Robert Faurisson, the reality of violence poses special demands on the historian and the

---

6. Frey's *A Million Little Pieces* was marketed as a memoir and lauded by Oprah Winfrey. Subsequent to investigative reporting in *The Smoking Gun* and a public apology by Frey, the book has been recategorized and its reader instructed, on the copyright page, to consider it a work of fiction. LeRoy was a cult figure whose searing novel *Sarah* and short-story collection *The Heart Is Deceitful Above All Things* encouraged readers to believe his persona's backstory of child prostitution, drug abuse, abandonment, and addiction. Writing of the rash of *faux memoirs* published in 1990 and the early twenty-first century, Mihaela P. Harper wonders whether the phenomenon "is due to a need for reassurance that the external reality of the past, solid and immutable, is still 'out there,' in spite of or maybe because of its terrifying brutality; or, on the contrary, this interest is incited by a desire to question the need for such a reality, and is symptomatic of a contemporary confusion about what is real and what is not" (228).

philosopher: Auschwitz is "the most real of realities" (58). This tradition has proved resilient: after 9/11, Jean Baudrillard's and Slavoj Žižek's treatments of the terror attacks as an opportunity to rethink the nature of the real were countered by vehement assertions of these events' unquestionable facticity: "most real of all real" (as Versluys puts it), "a bedrock of fact" (Frow).

These assumptions and premises were precisely what the opening chapters of this book attempted to X out, and my own work, in this process, was always guided by this axiom: *violence is real*. It is real, or it is not "really" violent. Violence is also everywhere: from the brutal positive manifestations of violent actions on bodies, buildings, and ecosystems, to hidden, structural, systemic relations between institutions, ideas, and discourses. In the 1970s and the 1980s, scholarship in feminism and Critical Race Theory underscored this invisible, pervasive, insidious quality. These fields were definitive in demonstrating how, even if the fact of violence is subjected to skepticism and doubt (by silencing or disqualifying the victim or the witness), or if the nature of its effects are disputed or dismissed (the conspiracy, the cover-up), violence *has* occurred, but on another register. The effect of this work (which was informed by poststructuralism and deconstruction) was a simultaneous acknowledgment and disavowal of violence's availability to knowledge. Coming, as I do, at the end of these traditions, distinguishing violence from fiction seems like a pointless exercise. Like Saussure's sign, memorably imaged by two sides of a sheet of paper, violence and fiction are inextricable. In the face of this deep complicity of art and life, I offer an X critique of violence, suggesting that we tarry in the noncommittal, withhold judgment, pause, and abide in the flickering light of the unmoored image, the image that orients without reference. I foresee a new economy of representation, one with no room for the time-honored labor of determining the presence or absence of a causal link between violent images and violent behavior, or the critical work of condemning some representations of violence and exonerating others.

To X out these distinctions is perilous, of course. But risk is intrinsic to creative thought. I have, in this book, attempted to outline the possibilities and perils that X-ing out opens up. X out means, also, to have the final word: one last call-out before dropping the mic. As I X out here, I offer a reckoning of my own X origins, the intersection from which *Disappear Here* emerges or erupts.

I hail from multiple countries and continents, none or all of which I can claim as my own. My grandparents, robbed of their homes in

Austria and Transylvania, built lives in Puerto Rico and the United States; my parents abandoned those lives to create yet another new life in Israel. To build a life in a new country and a foreign language is not easy. It takes a toll on bodies, minds, and bank accounts. My childhood was defined by movement: departures: disruptions: all in the bleak light of the Holocaust. For my parents, Zionism promised a refuge in a world in which homes and lives can be stolen or abandoned, nothing can be trusted, and no one is ever truly safe. But the Israel I came of age in saw that promise disappear. Palestine emerged from silence and denial, threat and fear, to political position and partisan pursuit, manifesting in our lives as inexorable fact. Israeli Xers who, like me, were schooled in the heroic narratives of our young country's history and drafted into the army at the age of eighteen lived a very different story than our parents': not the just war, the struggle to survive, the phoenix emerging from Auschwitz, ours was the story of invasion, occupation, terror, Intifada (the 1987 Intifada coincided with my own army service), and the self-directed violence, a kind of national psychic suicide, of the assassination of Prime Minister Yitzhak Rabin. Coming of age in Israel in those decades attuned me to the fragility of all ideals, the cultural reverberations of trauma, the solace of silence, and its deadly price; generations of migration schooled me in the contingencies of life without a safety net. I am not unfamiliar with war and terror. I have seen what violence can do. I have witnessed its capacity to turn bodies and buildings and minds and lives inside out, as well as the reverberations of this inversion that extend beyond the physical to the ways we make sense of the world. But the deadly debris of discrimination, occupation, and infrastructure, like the collateral damage of construction and critique, are inextricable from the stories we tell, the images we make, the maps we draw, the dreams we dream. Traditional and comfortable distinctions between victim and perpetrator, oppressor and oppressed, past and present, presence and absence are no refuge as past violence stalks us, as faraway atrocities reverberate at home, and even homes are haunted by the stolen land on which they rest.

I have described *Disappear Here* as a form of theft: one that acknowledges and erases origin, affirms and disavows or denies it. X captures the existential ambivalence of "disappear here," prompting me to affirm and disavow the historical specificity of my own perspective. Personal experience, like the historical events, political issues, technological developments, and cultural concerns that this book documents, and the images from 1980s and 1990s U.S. fiction, film, and popular culture that ground this work and define its scope, are the contested ground (because all ground is contested) from which I arm and aim at this: my target: violence, the real, and "real violence" today. To that end I export X from its generational source, its specific temporal, cultural, and experiential context. I hack it, pwn it (to pwn is a hacker term meaning to own or control), and wield it to execute *Disappear Here*'s program of opposition, multiplicity, intersection, variability, precision, erasure, and, maybe, revolution.

And I am not alone. The changes that X has witnessed and wrought have now become mainstream. As Xers negotiate local and global crises, and battle disasters the self-evidence of which are, increasingly, a matter of interpretation, conflicting evidence, image analysis, and faith, what violence is, where and how it occurs, and what kind of action, if any, can be brought to bear on this complex phenomenon is not only an open question but a moving target. For this challenge X is uniquely equipped. Born of change, formed from disaffection, the generation with no cause or credo crosses out *and* marks the spot. It's where it's at when "it" is on the move. Xers are artists, critics, teachers, scholars, and leaders; they are the arbiters of culture and society. Their affectless, apathetic ethos is no longer a problem to be corrected (if it ever was) but a beacon, a guide to be followed as, turning to the future, after X, we consider our children, our students, our victims, our executors, who will inherit the world that X has made.

works cited

. . . .

"126 More Websites Hacked by AnonGhost." *Hackread.com.* 27 Jan. 2013. Web. 21 June 2013.

Aaron, Michele. "(Fill-in-the) Blank Fiction: Dennis Cooper's Cinematics and the Complicitous Reader." *Journal of Modern Literature* 27.3 (2004): 115–27. Print.

Abel, Marco. "Don DeLillo's 'In the Ruins of the Future': Literature, Images, and the Rhetoric of Seeing 9/11." *PMLA* 118.5 (2003): 1236–50. Print.

———. "Judgment Is Not an Exit: Toward an Affective Criticism of Violence with *American Psycho.*" *Angelaki* 6.3 (2001): 137–54. Print.

———. *Violent Affect: Literature, Cinema, and Critique after Representation.* Lincoln: U of Nebraska P, 2007. Print.

Acker, Kathy. *Bodies of Work: Essays.* London: Serpent's Tail, 1997. Print.

Adler, Jerry. "The Year of the Yuppie." *Newsweek* 31 Dec. 1984: 14. Print.

Agamben, Giorgio. *State of Exception.* 2003. Trans. Kevin Attell. Chicago: U of Chicago P, 2005. Print.

Ahmed, Sara. *The Cultural Politics of Emotion.* New York: Routledge, 2004. Print.

Anderson, Benedict. *Imagined Communities: Reflections on the Origin and Spread of Nationalism.* 1983. Rev. ed. New York: Verso, 1991. Print.

Annesley, James. *Blank Fictions: Consumerism, Culture and the Contemporary American Novel.* London: Pluto, 1998. Print.

———. "Brand Ellis: Celebrity Authorship in *Lunar Park.*" Mandel, *Bret Easton Ellis* 143–47.

"Antisecurity." *Internet Archive Wayback Machine.* Internet Archive, 1 Mar. 2001. Web. 7 June 2013. <http://web.archive.org/web/20010301215117/http://anti.security.is/>

Antonowicz, Anton. "My Verdict: She Didn't Show Any Remorse: Anton Antonowicz Comments on Louise Woodward's Interview with the BBC." *Daily Mirror* 23 June 1998: 7. Print.

Arcan, Nelly. *Folle.* Paris: Éditions du Seuil, 2004. Print.

———. *Whore.* 2001. Trans. Bruce Benderson. New York: Grove, 2004. Print.

Ardoin, Paul. "A Very Unrigid Cosmopolitanism: Shame, Laughter, and Flexibility in Jonathan Safran Foer's *Everything Is Illuminated.*" *Lit: Literature Interpretation Theory* 24.3 (2013): 185–201. Web.

Arendt, Hannah. *On Violence.* New York: Harcourt Brace Jovanovich, 1969. Print.

Armstrong, Nancy, and Leonard Tennenhouse, eds. *The Violence of Representation: Literature and the History of Violence.* New York: Routledge, 1989. Print.

Ashraf, Nauman. "187 websites hacked by AnonGhost." *Thehackerspost.com.* 24 Feb. 2013. Web. 24 Jan. 2014.

Atchison, S. T. "'Why I Am Writing from Where You Are Not': Absence and Presence in Jonathan Safran Foer's *Extremely Loud & Incredibly Close.*" *Journal of Postcolonial Writing* 46.3–4 (2010): 359–68. Print.

Auerbach, David. "Anonymity as Culture: Case Studies." Coleman and Auerbach n. pag.

Augé, Marc. *The War of Dreams: Studies in Ethno Fiction.* 1997. Trans. Liz Heron. London: Pluto, 1999. Print.

Ayers, Sheli. "*Glamorama* Vanitas: Bret Easton Ellis's Postmodern Allegory." *Postmodern Culture* 11.1 (2000): n. pag. Web. 26 July 2009.

Badiou, Alain. *Being and Event.* 1988. Trans. Oliver Feltham. London: Continuum, 2005. Print.

———. *The Century.* 2005. Trans. Alberto Toscano. Cambridge: Polity, 2007.

———. *Ethics: An Essay on the Understanding of Evil.* 1998. Trans. Peter Hallward. London: Verso, 2001. Print.

———. *Handbook of Inaesthetics.* 1998. Trans. Alberto Toscano. Stanford: Stanford UP, 2005. Print.

———. *Polemics.* Trans. Steve Corcoran. New York: Verso, 2006. Print.

Baelo-Allué, Sonia. *Bret Easton Ellis's Controversial Fiction: Writing Between High and Low Culture.* London: Continuum, 2011. Print.

Baker, Timothy C. "The (Neuro)-Aesthetics of Caricature: Representations of Reality in Bret Easton Ellis's *Lunar Park.*" *Poetics Today* 30.3 (2009): 471–515. Print.

Bataille, Georges. *Erotism: Death and Sensuality.* 1962. Trans. Mary Dalwood. San Francisco: City Lights, 1986. Print. Trans. of *L'Erotisme.* Paris: Les Editions de Minuit, 1957.

Baudrillard, Jean. *The Spirit of Terrorism and Other Essays.* Trans. Chris Turner. New York: Verso, 2003. Print.

Baxter, Tara, and Nickki Craft. "There Are Better Ways of Taking Care of Bret Easton Ellis Than Just Censoring Him . . . ." Russell 245–53.

Beaudoin, Tom. *Virtual Faith: The Irreverent Spiritual Quest of Generation X.* San Francisco: Jossey-Bass, 1998. Print.

Beck, Stefan. "Kinderkampf." *New Criterion* 23.10 (2005): 92. Print.

Beigbeder, Frédéric. *Windows on the World.* Paris: Grasset, 2003. Print.

———. *Windows on the World.* 2002. Trans. Franck Wynne. New York: Hyperion, 2004. Print.

Benjamin, Walter. "Critique of Violence." 1921. Trans. Edmund Jephcott. *Reflections: Essays, Aphorisms, Autobiographical Writings.* Ed. Peter Demetz. New York: Harcourt Brace Jovanovich, 1978. 277–300. Print.

———. "The Work of Art in the Age of Its Technical Reproducibility." 1936. Trans. Harry Zohn and Edmund Jephcott. Leitch 1051–71.

Benzon, Kiki. "Revolution 2: An Interview with Mark Z. Danielewski." *electronic book review.* "writing under constraint." Ed. Joseph Tabbi. 20 Mar. 2007. Web. 10 Aug. 2014.

Bernstein, Michael S., Andres Monroy-Hernandez, Drew Harry, Paul Andre, Katrina Panovich, and Greg Vargas. "4chan and /b/: An Analysis of Anonymity and Ephemerality in a Large Online Community." *Follow the Crowd.* 15 Aug. 2011. Web. 5 June 2013. <http://crowdresearch.org/blog/?p=1528>

Best, Stephen, and Sharon Marcus. "Surface Reading: An Introduction." *Representations* 108.1 (2009): 1–21. Print.

Bewes, Timothy. "Introduction: Temporalizing the Present." *Novel: A Forum on Fiction* 45.2 (2012): 159–74. Print.

———. "Reading with the Grain: A New World in Literary Criticism." *d i f f e r e n c e s: A Journal of Feminist Cultural Studies* 21.3 (2010): 1–33. Print.

Bird, Benjamin. "History, Emotion, and the Body: Mourning in Post-9/11 Fiction." *Literature Compass* 4.3 (2007): 561–75. Print.

Black, Joel. *The Aesthetics of Murder: A Study in Romantic Literature and Contemporary Culture.* Baltimore: Johns Hopkins UP, 1991. Print.

Bloom, Allan. *The Closing of the American Mind.* New York: Simon and Schuster, 1987. Print.

Bolter, Jay David, and Richard Grusin. *Remediation: Understanding New Media.* Cambridge: MIT P, 1999. Print.

Borradori, Giovanna. *Philosophy in a Time of Terror: Dialogues with Jürgen Habermas and Jacques Derrida.* Chicago: U of Chicago P, 2004. Print.

Boswell, James. *Life of Johnson.* Ed. G. B. Hill. Rev. ed. L. F. Powell. 6 vols. Oxford: Oxford UP, 1935. Print.

Brabazon, Tara. *From Revolution to Revelation: Generation X, Popular Memory and Cultural Studies.* Burlington, VT: Ashgate, 2005. Print.

Brand Nubian. "Down for the Real." *Everything Is Everything.* Elektra Entertainment, 1994. CD.

Bredekamp, Horst. "From Walter Benjamin to Carl Schmitt, via Thomas Hobbes." *Critical Inquiry* 25 (1999): 247–66. Print.

Brooks, Peter. "Repetition, Repression, and Return: *Great Expectations* and the Study of Plot." *New Literary History* 54.4 (1987): 494–526. Print.

Brownrigg, Sylvia. "Frenchman's Take on Doomed Towers." *San Francisco Chronicle* 20 Mar. 2005: E3. Print.

Butler, Judith. *Precarious Life: The Powers of Mourning and Violence.* New York: Verso, 2004. Print.

Caldwell, John Thornton. *Televisuality: Style, Crisis, and Authority in American Television*. New Brunswick: Rutgers UP, 1995. Print.

Call, Lewis. "A is for Anarchy, V is for Vendetta: Images of Guy Fawkes and the Creation of Postmodern Anarchism." *Anarchist Studies* 16.2 (2008): 154–72. Web. 1 Aug. 2014.

"Carl Schmitt." *Stanford Encyclopedia of Philosophy*. Stanford University, 7 Aug. 2010. Web. 29 May 2014.

Carlson, Elwood. "20th-Century U.S. Generations." *Population Bulletin* 64.1 (2009): 1–17. www.prb.org. Web. 30 June 2014.

Carroll, Hamilton. "'Like Nothing in This Life': September 11 and the Limits of Representation in Don DeLillo's *Falling Man*." *Studies in American Fiction* 40.1 (2013): 107–30. Print.

Carter, Kevin. *Vulture Watching Starving Child*. Sudan, Mar. 1993. Photograph.

Caruth, Cathy. *Unclaimed Experience: Trauma, Narrative, and History*. Baltimore: Johns Hopkins UP, 1996. Print.

Chaplinsky, Joshua. "Bret Easton Ellis: 1985–2010." Interview with Bret Easton Ellis. *The Cult: The Official Chuck Palahniuk Site*. A Writer's Cult LLC, 28 June 2010. Web. 21 June 2013.

Charney, Leo. "The Violence of a Perfect Moment." Slocum, *Violence and American Cinema* 47–62.

Chesnutt, Vic. "Free of Hope." *Is the Actor Happy?* 1995. New West Records, 2004. CD.

Clark, Michael P. "Violence, Ethics, and the Rhetoric of Decorum in *American Psycho*." Mandel, *Bret Easton Ellis* 19–35.

Codde, Philippe. "Keeping History at Bay: Absent Presences in Three Recent Jewish American Novels." *MFS: Modern Fiction Studies* 57.4 (2011): 673–93. Print.

———. "Philomela Revisited: Traumatic Iconicity in Jonathan Safran Foer's *Extremely Loud and Incredibly Close*." *Studies in American Fiction* 35.2 (2007): 241–54. Print.

Colby, Georgina. *Bret Easton Ellis: Underwriting the Contemporary*. New York: Palgrave Macmillan, 2011. Print.

Coleman, E. Gabriella. *Coding Freedom: The Ethics and Aesthetics of Hacking*. Princeton: Princeton UP, 2012. Print.

———. "Gabriella Coleman Anonymous from Lulz to Activists Dec 1 2011." Online video clip. *YouTube*. YouTube, 4 Dec. 2011. Web. 10 Aug. 2014.

———. "Our Weirdness Is Free: The Logic of Anonymous—Online Army, Agent of Chaos, and Seeker of Justice." Coleman and Auerbach n. pag.

Coleman, E. Gabriella, and David Auerbach. *Here Comes Nobody: Essays on Anonymous, 4chan and the Other Internet Culture*. New York: Triple Canopy, 2012. Ebook.

Collado-Rodriguez, Francisco. "Ethics in the Second Degree: Trauma and Dual Narratives in Jonathan Safran Foer's *Everything Is Illuminated*." *Journal of Modern Literature* 32.1 (2008): 54–68. Print.

Collins, Suzanne. *The Hunger Games*. New York: Scholastic, 2008. Print.

Conte, Joseph M. "Don DeLillo's *Falling Man* and the Age of Terror." *MFS: Modern Fiction Studies* 57.3 (2011): 559–83. Print.

Cooper, Cynthia A. *Violence on Television: Congressional Inquiry, Public Criticism, and Industry Response*. London: UP of America, 1996. Print.

Cooper, Dennis. *Frisk*. New York: Grove Weidenfeld, 1991. Print.

Corman, Josh, and Brian Martin. "'Building a Better Anonymous' Series: Part 0." *Cognitive Dissidents*. Joshua Corman, 20 Dec. 2011. Web. 1 June 2014.

Cornell, Drucilla, Michael Rosenfeld, and David Gray Carlson, eds. *Deconstruction and the Possibility of Justice*. New York: Routledge, 1992. Print.

Coupland, Douglas. *Generation X: Tales for an Accelerated Culture*. New York: St. Martin's, 1991. Print.

———. "Generation X'ed." *Details* June 1995: 72. Print.

Crash. Dir. David Cronenberg. Fineline Features, 1996. DVD.

Crowdus, Gary. "Getting Exercised Over *Fight Club*." *Cinéaste* 25.4 (2000): 46–48. Print.

"The CyberAttack." *The Marker*. Haaretz, 7 Apr. 2013. Hebrew. Web. 23 June 2013. <http://www.themarker.com/technation/1.1986489>

Danielewski, Mark Z. *House of Leaves*. 2nd ed. New York: Pantheon, 2001.

Dawes, Birgit. "On Contested Ground (Zero): Literature and the Transnational Challenge of Remembering 9/11." *Amerikastudien* 52.4 (2007): 517–43. Print.

Dawson, Alene. "Study Says Generation X Is Balanced and Happy." *CNN.com*. CNN, 27 Oct. 2011. Web. 21 June 2013.

Dean, Jodi. "Uncertainty, Conspiracy, Abduction." Friedman 293–312.

Delgado, Richard, and Jean Stefancic, eds. *Critical Race Theory: The Cutting Edge*. 2nd ed. Philadelphia: Temple UP, 2000. Print.

DeLillo, Don. *Falling Man*. New York: Scribner, 2007. Print.

———. "In the Ruins of the Future: Reflections on Terror and Loss in the Shadow of September." *Harper's Magazine* Dec. 2001: 33–40. Print.

Delvaux, Martine. "The Exit of a Generation: The 'Whatever' Philosophy." *The Midwest Quarterly* 40.2 (1999): 171–86. Print.

DeRosa, Aaron. "Alterity and the Radical Other in Post-9/11 Fiction: DeLillo's *Falling Man* and Walter's *The Zero*." *Arizona Quarterly: A Journal of American Literature, Culture, and Theory* 69.3 (2013): 157–83. Print.

Derrida, Jacques. "Autoimmunity: Real and Symbolic Suicides." Borradori 85–136.

———. "Force of Law: The 'Mystical Foundation of Authority.'" Trans. Mary Quaintance. Cornell, Rosenfeld, and Carlson 3–67.

Derrida, Jacques, and Maurice Blanchot. *The Instant of My Death / Demeure: Fiction and Testimony*. Trans. Elizabeth Rottenberg. Stanford: Meridian, 2000. Print.

Douthat, Ross G. "After Tragedy." *National Review* 20 June 2005: 48–50. Print.

Drucker, Johanna. *Sweet Dreams: Contemporary Art and Complicity*. Chicago: U of Chicago P, 2006. Print.

Durand, Alain-Philippe. "Beyond the Extreme: Frédéric Beigbeder's *Windows on the World*." Durand and Mandel 109–20.

Durand, Alain-Philippe, and Naomi Mandel, eds. *Novels of the Contemporary Extreme*. London: Continuum, 2006. Print.

Duvall, John N. "Homeland Security and the State of (American) Exception(alism): Jess Walter's *The Zero* and the Ethical Possibilities of Postmodern Irony." *Studies in the Novel* 45.2 (2013): 279–97. Print.

Duvall, John N., and Robert P. Marzec. "Narrating 9/11." *MFS: Modern Fiction Studies* 57.3 (2011): 381–400. Print.

Eaglestone, Robert. "'The Age of Reason Is Over . . . an Age of Fury was Dawning': Contemporary Anglo-American Fiction and Terror." *Wasafiri* 22.2 (2007): 19–22. Print.

Elias, Amy J. *Sublime Desire: History and Post-1960s Fiction.* Baltimore: Johns Hopkins UP, 2001. Print.

Ellis, Bret Easton. *American Psycho.* New York: Vintage, 1991. Print.

———. *Glamorama.* New York: Random House, 1998. Print.

———. *Imperial Bedrooms.* New York: Knopf, 2010. Print.

———. *Less Than Zero.* 1985. New York: Random House, 1998. Print.

———. *Lunar Park.* New York: Knopf, 2005. Print.

———. *The Rules of Attraction.* New York: Penguin, 1988. Print.

———. "Unfollow. Unfollow. Unfollow. Please God unfollow." 20 Nov. 2012, 1:28 AM. Tweet.

Enzensberger, Hans Magnus. *Civil Wars: From L.A. to Bosnia.* 1993. New York: New Press, 1994. Print.

Eugenides, Jeffrey. *The Marriage Plot.* New York: Picador, 2011. Print.

Eve 6. "Inside Out." *Eve 6.* RCA Records, 1998. CD.

Ferguson, Niall, ed. *Virtual History: Alternatives and Counterfactuals.* New York: Basic Books, 1999. Print.

Fetveit, Arild. "Reality TV in the Digital Era: A Paradox in Visual Culture?" Friedman 119–37.

Feuer, Menachem. "Almost Friends: Post-Holocaust Comedy, Tragedy, and Friendship in Jonathan Safran Foer's *Everything Is Illuminated.*" *Shofar: An Interdisciplinary Journal of Jewish Studies* 25.2 (2007): 24–48. Print.

Fight Club. Dir. David Fincher. Twentieth-Century Fox, 1999. DVD 2000.

"Fight Club." Review. *Entertainment Weekly.* 19 Jan. 2001: 24. Print.

"Fight Club." *Encyclopedia Dramatica.* Encyclopedia Dramatica, 22 May 2013. Web. 5 June 2013.

Flory, Richard W., and Donald E. Miller. *Finding Faith: The Spiritual Quest of the Post-Boomer Generation.* New Brunswick: Rutgers UP, 2008. Print.

Flynn, Gillian. *Gone Girl.* New York: Crown, 2012.

Foer, Jonathan Safran. *Everything Is Illuminated.* Boston: Houghton Mifflin, 2002. Print.

———. *Extremely Loud and Incredibly Close.* Boston: Houghton Mifflin, 2005. Print.

Foucault, Michel. *Discipline and Punish.* 1975. Trans. Alan Sheridan. New York: Vintage, 1979. Print.

Fox, James Alan, and Jack Levin. *Extreme Killing: Understanding Serial and Mass Murder.* London: Sage, 2005. Print.

Fradinger, Moira. *Binding Violence: Literary Visions of Political Origins.* Stanford: Stanford UP, 2010. Print.

Freccero, Carla. "Historical Violence, Censorship, and the Serial Killer: The Case of *American Psycho.*" *Diacritics* 27.2 (1997): 44–58. Print.

Friedländer, Saul, ed. *Probing the Limits of Representation: Nazism and the "Final Solution."* Cambridge: Harvard UP, 1992. Print.

Friedman, James. "Introduction." Friedman 1–22.

———, ed. *Reality Squared: Televisual Discourse on the Real.* New Brunswick: Rutgers UP, 2002. Print.

Friend, David. *Watching the World Change: Stories Behind the Images of 9/11.* New York: Farrar, Straus and Giroux, 2006.

Frow, John. "The Uses of Terror and the Limits of Cultural Studies." *symplokē* 11.1–2 (2003): 69–76. Print.

Fukuyama, Francis. *The End of History and the Last Man.* New York: Free Press, 1992. Print.

———. "The New World Disorder." Rev. of *Civil Wars: From L.A. to Bosnia* by Enzensberger. *New York Times.* New York Times, 9 Oct. 1994. Web. 11 Apr. 2014.

Gander, Forrest. Liner Notes. *Is the Actor Happy?* New West Records, 2004. CD.

Gardner, Sue. "The New Youth Culture Turns Into the New Youth Market." *Toronto Star* 15 May 1993: J13. Print.

Gates, Henry Louis Jr., ed. *Black Literature and Literary Theory.* New York: Routledge, 1990.

Gessen, Keith. "Horror Tour." *New York Review of Books* 52.14 (2005): 68–72. Print.

Gewirtz, Paul. "On 'I Know It When I See It.'" *The Yale Law Journal* 105.4 (1996): 1023–47. Print.

Giles, James R. *The Spaces of Violence.* Tuscaloosa: U of Alabama P, 2006. Print.

———. *Violence in the Contemporary American Novel: An End to Innocence.* Columbia: U of South Carolina P, 2000. Print.

Godden, Richard. "Bret Easton Ellis, *Lunar Park,* and the Exquisite Corpse of Deficit Finance." *American Literary History* 25.3 (2013): 588–606. Print.

———. "Fictions of Fictitious Capital: *American Psycho* and the Poetics of Deregulation." *Textual Practice* 25.5 (2011): 853–66. Print.

Gomel, Elana. *Bloodscripts: Writing the Violent Subject.* Columbus: The Ohio State UP, 2003. Print.

Gordinier, Jeff. *X Saves the World: How Generation X Got the Shaft but Can Still Keep Everything from Sucking.* New York: Viking, 2008. Print.

Gornick, Vivian. "About a Boy." *The Nation* 25 Apr. 2005: 29–32. Print.

Grassian, Daniel. *Hybrid Fictions: American Literature and Generation X.* Jefferson, NC: McFarland, 2003. Print.

Gray, Richard. *After the Fall: American Literature Since 9/11.* Malden, MA: Wiley Blackwell, 2011. Print.

Greenberg, Judith, ed. *Trauma at Home: After 9/11.* Lincoln: U of Nebraska P, 2003. Print.

Gubar, Susan. *Poetry after Auschwitz: Remembering What One Never Knew.* Bloomington: Indiana UP, 2003. Print.

Guillory, John. *Cultural Capital: The Problem of Literary Canon Formation.* Chicago: U of Chicago P, 1993. Print.

Hallward, Peter. *Badiou: A Subject to Truth.* Minneapolis: U of Minnesota P, 2003. Print.

Hamblett, Charles, and Jane Deverson. *Generation X*. London: Tandem, 1964. Print.

Hanson, Peter. *The Cinema of Generation X*. Jefferson, NC: McFarland, 2002. Ebook.

Hanssen, Beatrice. *Critique of Violence: Between Poststructuralism and Critical Theory*. New York: Routledge, 2000. Print.

Hardt, Michael, and Antonio Negri. *Empire*. Cambridge: Harvard UP, 2000. Print.

Harper, Mihaela P. "Turning to Debris: Ethics of Violence in Wilkomirski's *Fragments* and Beigbeder's *Windows on the World*." *symplokē* 20.1–2 (2012): 227–40. Print.

Harris, Andrea L. "Generation X X: The Identity Politics of Generation X." Ulrich and Harris 268–94.

Hayles, N. Katherine. *How We Became Posthuman: Virtual Bodies in Cybernetics, Literature, and Informatics*. Chicago: U of Chicago P, 1999. Print.

Hebdige, Dick. *Hiding in the Light: On Images and Things*. London: Routledge, 1988. Print.

Heffernan, Julián Jiménez, and Paula Martin Salván. "'The stricken community': Recidivism and Restoration in American 9/11 Fiction." *Arizona Quarterly* 69.2 (2013): 145–69. Print.

Heise, Thomas. "*American Psycho:* Neoliberal Fantasies and the Death of Downtown." *Arizona Quarterly: A Journal of American Literature, Culture, and Theory* 67.1 (2011): 135–60. Print.

Hell, Richard, and the Voidoids. "Blank Generation." *Blank Generation*. Sire Records, 1977. Music recording.

Henseler, Christine, ed. *Generation X Goes Global: Mapping a Youth Culture in Motion*. New York: Routledge, 2013. Print.

———. "Generation X: What's in the Label?" *Huff Post: The Blog*. The Huffington Post, 27 May 2014. Web. 7 July 2014.

———. "*Short-Changed:* In Defense of Generation X." *ChristineHenseler.com*. Christine Henseler, n.d. Web. 11 July 2013.

———. *Spanish Fiction in the Digital Age: Generation X Remixed*. New York: Palgrave Macmillan, 2011. Print.

Henseler, Christine, and Randolph D. Pope, eds. *Generation X Rocks: Contemporary Peninsular Fiction, Film, and Rock Culture*. Nashville: Vanderbilt UP, 2007. Print.

Herrnstein Smith, Barbara. *Scandalous Knowledge: Science, Truth and the Human*. Durham: Duke UP, 2005. Print.

Hirsch, E. D. Jr. *Cultural Literacy: What Every American Needs to Know*. New York: Houghton Mifflin, 1987. Print.

Holohan, Siobhan. *The Search for Justice in a Media Age: Reading Stephen Lawrence and Louise Woodward*. Burlington, VT: Ashgate, 2005. Print.

Holtz, Geoffrey T. *Welcome to the Jungle: The Why Behind "Generation X."* New York: St. Martin's Griffin, 1995. Print.

Homes, A. M. *The End of Alice*. New York: Scribner, 1996. Print.

Hornblower, Margot. "Great Xpectations." *Time International (Canada Edition)*. Time, 7 July 1997: 26. Web. 10 Aug. 2014.

Howe, Neil, and Bill Strauss. *13thGen: Abort, Retry, Ignore, Fail?* New York: Vintage, 1993. Print.

Hume, Kathryn. *Aggressive Fictions: Reading the Contemporary American Novel*. Ithaca: Cornell UP, 2012. Print.

———. *American Dream, American Nightmare: Fiction since 1960*. Chicago: U of Illinois P, 2000. Print.

Hungerford, Amy. *The Holocaust of Texts: Genocide, Literature, and Personification*. Chicago: U of Chicago P, 2003. Print.

———. "How Jonathan Safran Foer Made Love." *American Literary History* 25.3 (2013): 607–24. Print.

Hutcheon, Linda. *The Politics of Postmodernism*. New York: Routledge, 1989. Print.

Ingersoll, Earl. "One Boy's Passage, and His Nation's: Jonathan Safran Foer's *Extremely Loud and Incredibly Close*." *CEA Critic* 71.3 (2009): 54–69. Print.

Irom, Bimbisar. "Alterities in a Time of Terror: Notes on the Subgenre of the American 9/11 Novel." *Contemporary Literature* 53.3 (2012): 517–47. Print.

Israeli Elite Force (IsraeliElite). "We dedicate this BLITZ to all holocaust survivors! We are proud to be your modern Bielski partisans! A msg from us http://pastebin.com/UfVS-3fcW." 7 Apr. 2013, 3:27 p.m. Tweet.

Jameson, Fredric. *The Political Unconscious: Narrative as a Socially Symbolic Act*. New York: Cornell UP, 1981. Print.

Jay, Martin. *Refractions of Violence*. New York: Routledge, 2003. Print.

Jenkins, Keith. "Ethical Responsibility and the Historian: On the Possible End of a History 'Of a Certain Kind.'" *History and Theory* 43.4 (2004): 43–60.

Jenkins, Philip. *Decade of Nightmares: The End of the Sixties and the Making of Eighties America*. Oxford: Oxford UP, 2006. Print.

Kakutani, Michiko. "Like Humbert Humbert, Full of Lust and Lies." Rev. of *The End of Alice*. *New York Times*. New York Times, 23 Feb. 1996. Web. 10 Aug. 2014.

Kalfus, Ken. *A Disorder Peculiar to the Country*. New York: HarperPerennial, 2006. Print.

Kaplan, E. Ann, ed. *Regarding Television: Critical Approaches—An Anthology*. Los Angeles: University Publications of America, 1983. Print.

Karnicky, Jeffrey. "'An Awfully Good Impression': Truth and Testimony in *Lunar Park*." Mandel, *Bret Easton Ellis* 117–29.

Kashua, Sayed. *Second Person Singular*. 2010. Trans. Mitch Ginsburg. New York: Grove, 2012. Print.

Kauffman, Linda S. "The Wake of Terror: Don DeLillo's 'In The Ruins of the Future,' 'Baader-Meinhof,' and *Falling Man*." *MFS: Modern Fiction Studies* 52.2 (2008): 353–77. Print.

Kavaldo, Jesse. "The Fiction of Self-Destruction." Schuchardt 13–34.

———. "With Us or Against Us: Chuck Palahniuk's 9/11." Kuhn and Rubin 103–15.

Keeble, Arin. "Marriage, Relationships, and 9/11: The Seismographic Narratives of *Falling Man, The Good Life,* and *The Emperor's Children*." *Modern Language Review* 106.2 (2011): 355–73. Print.

Kirn, Walter. "Everything Is Included." *New York Times Book Review*. New York Times, 3 Apr. 2005: 1. Web. 10 Aug. 2014.

Kleinman, Geoffrey. "Chuck Palahniuk, Author of *Fight Club*." Interview. *DVD Talk*. DVD-Talk.com, n.d. Web. 18 Jun. 2013.

Kuhn, Cynthia, and Lance Rubin, eds. *Reading Chuck Palahniuk: American Monsters and Literary Mayhem*. New York: Routledge, 2009. Print.

Kushner, David. *Masters of Doom: How Two Guys Created an Empire and Transformed Pop Culture*. New York: Random House, 2003. Print.

Kutz, Christopher. *Complicity: Ethics and Law for a Collective Age*. New York: Cambridge UP, 2000.

La Berge, Leigh Claire. "The Men Who Make the Killings: *American Psycho*, Financial Masculinity, and 1980s Financial Print Culture." *Studies in American Fiction* 37.2 (2010): 273–96. Print.

LaCapra, Dominick. *History and Its Limits: Human, Animal, Violence*. Ithaca: Cornell UP, 2009. Print.

———. *Representing the Holocaust: History, Theory, Trauma*. Ithaca: Cornell UP, 1994. Print.

———. *Writing History, Writing Trauma*. Baltimore: Johns Hopkins UP, 2001. Print.

Lacey, Josh. "Minute by Minute." *The Guardian*. Guardian News, 11 Sep. 2004. Web. 10 Aug. 2014.

Lainsbury, G. P. "Generation X and the End of History." Ulrich and Harris 184–95.

Lang, Berel. *Holocaust Representation: Art within the Limits of History and Ethics*. Baltimore: Johns Hopkins UP, 2000. Print.

———. *Post-Holocaust: Interpretation, Misinterpretation, and the Claims of History*. Bloomington: Indiana UP, 2005. Print.

Lee, J. "35+ Israeli & 115 Other Sites hacked by @AnonGhost_" *Cyberwar News*. EHN, 18 Jan. 2013. Web. 21 June 2013.

Lehmann-Haupt, Christopher. "'Psycho': Whither Death Without Life?" *New York Times* 11 Mar. 1991. *ProQuest Historical Newspapers*. Web. 29 June 2009.

Leitch, Vincent B., ed. *The Norton Anthology of Theory and Criticism*. 2nd ed. New York: W.W. Norton & Company, 2010. Print.

Lesjak, Carolyn. "Reading Dialectically." *Criticism* 55.2 (2013): 233–77. Print.

Less Than Zero. Dir. Marek Kavievska. Twentieth-Century Fox, 1987. DVD.

Levi, Primo. *The Drowned and the Saved*. Trans. Raymond Rosenthal. New York: Vintage, 1989. Trans. of *I sommeri e I salvati*. Turin: Einaudi, 1986.

Levin, Aaron. "Experts Refute Myths Linking Mental Illness, Violence." *Psychiatry Online*. American Psychiatric Publishing, 28 Mar. 2014. Web. 30 June 2014.

LeVine, Mark. "Generation G Comes of Age: Youth and Revolution in the Middle East and North Africa." Henseler, *Generation X Goes Global* 293–314.

Levy, Steven. *Hackers: Heroes of the Computer Revolution*. New York: Doubleday, 1984.

———. "Loitering on the Dark Side." *Newsweek Online*. Newsweek, 2 Mar. 1999. Web. 10 Aug. 2014.

Leys, Ruth. *Trauma: A Genealogy*. Chicago: U of Chicago P, 2000. Print.

Lim, Dennis. "'Fight Club' Fight Goes On." *New York Times*. New York Times, 6 Nov. 2009. Web. 19 June 2013.

Linklater, Richard. *Slacker*. Detour Film Production, 1991. DVD.

Loshitzky, Yosefa. "Introduction." *Spielberg's Holocaust: Critical Perspectives on Schindler's List*. Ed. Yosefa Loshitzky. Bloomington: Indiana UP, 1997. 1–17. Print.

The Lulz Boat (lulzsec). "50 Days of Lulz statement: http://pastebin.com/1znEGmHa." 25 June 2011, 7:03 p.m. Tweet.

———. "This is a joint statement from #Anonymous (@AnonymousIRC) and Lulz Security (@LulzSec) to the FBI (@FBIPressOffice)—http://pastebin.com/RA15ix7S." 21 July 2011, 9:05 a.m. Tweet.

Lyotard, Jean-François. *The Inhuman: Reflections on Time*. 1988. Trans. Geoffrey Bennington and Rachel Bowlby. Stanford: Stanford UP, 1991. Print.

Mailer, Norman. "Children of the Pied Piper." *Vanity Fair* 54.4 (Mar. 1991): 154–59, 220–21. Print.

Malewitz, Raymond. "Regeneration through Misuse: Rugged Consumerism in Contemporary American Culture." *PMLA* 127.3 (2012): 526–41. Print.

Mandel, Naomi. *Against the Unspeakable: Complicity, the Holocaust, and Slavery in America*. Charlottesville: U of Virginia P, 2006. Print.

———. "Fiction et fidélité: *Windows on the World*." French Trans. Matthieu Dalle. *Frédéric Beigbeder et ses Doubles*. Ed. Alain-Philippe Durand. Amsterdam: Rodopi, 2008. Print.

———. "The Value and Values of Bret Easton Ellis." Mandel, *Bret Easton Ellis* 1–14.

———, ed. *Bret Easton Ellis: American Psycho, Glamorama, Lunar Park*. London: Continuum, 2011. Print.

Markovits, Benjamin. "The Horrors of History. A Novel of Post-9/11 Trauma Is Let Down by Its Obsessive Whimsy." *NewStatesman.com*. The New Statesman, 6 June 2005. Web. 11 Nov. 2008.

The Matrix. Dir. Andy and Lana Wachovski. Warner Bros., 1999. DVD.

Mauro, Aaron. "The Languishing of the Falling Man: Don DeLillo and Jonathan Safran Foer's Photographic History of 9/11." *MFS: Modern Fiction Studies* 57.3 (2001): 584–606. Print.

McHale, Brian. *Postmodernist Fiction*. New York: Methuen, 1987. Print.

McCarthy, Tom. *Remainder*. 2005. New York: Vintage, 2007. Print.

McInerney, Jay. Biography. Jaymcinerney.com. n.d. Web. 12 Aug. 2013.

———. *Bright Lights, Big City*. New York: Vintage, 1984. Print.

———. *Brightness Falls*. New York: Knopf, 1992. Print.

———. *The Good Life*. New York: Knopf, 2006. Print.

McVeigh, Timothy. "Letter to Fox News." *The Outpost of Freedom*. Gary Hunt, 10 June 2001. Web. 2 July 2014.

McWilliams, Brian. "White-Hat Hate Crimes on the Rise." *Wired*. Condé Nast, 13 Aug. 2002. Web. 7 June 2013.

The Mentor. "The Conscience of a Hacker." *Phrack* 1.7 (1986): n. pag. Web. 10 Aug. 2010.

Messud, Claire. *The Emperor's Children*. New York: Vintage, 2006. Print.

Michaels, Walter Benn. "Empires of the Senseless: (The Response to) Terror and (the End of) History." *Radical History Review* 85 (2003): 105–13. Print.

Miller, Kristine. "Reading and Writing the Post-9/11 Cop: Trauma, Personal Testimony, and Jess Walter's *The Zero.*" *Arizona Quarterly: A Journal of American Literature, Culture, and Theory* 70.1 (2014): 29–52. Print.

Miller, Laura. "*Windows on the World* by Frédéric Beigbeder." *Salon.com.* Salon Media Group, 20 Mar. 2005. Web. 10 Aug. 2014.

Mitchell, W. J. T. *Picture Theory: Essays on Verbal and Visual Representation.* Chicago: U of Chicago P, 1994. Print.

Moore, Alan, and David Lloyd. *V for Vendetta.* New York: DC Comics, 1990. Print.

Morrison, Toni. "Unspeakable Things Unspoken: The Afro-American Presence in American Literature." Tanner Lecture. *Michigan Quarterly Review* 28.1 (1989): 1–34.

Munson, Sam. "In the Aftermath." *Commentary* 119.5 (2005): 80–85. Print.

Musil, Robert. *The Man Without Qualities.* Vol. 1. 1930. Trans. Sophie Wilkins and Burton Pike. New York: Vintage, 1996. Print.

Myers, B. R. "A Bag of Tired Tricks." *The Atlantic Monthly* May 2005: 115–19. Print.

Natoli, Joseph. *This Is a Picture and Not the World: Movies and a Post-9/11 America.* Albany: State U of New York P, 2007. Print.

Navajas, Gonzalo. "A Distopian Culture: The Minimalist Paradigm in the Generation X." Henseler and Pope 3–14.

Nielsen, Henrik Skov. "Telling Doubles and Literal-Minded Reading in Bret Easton Ellis's *Glamorama.*" Durand and Mandel 20–30.

———. "What's in a Name? Double Exposures in *Lunar Park.*" Mandel, *Bret Easton Ellis* 129–42.

Nirvana. "Smells Like Teen Spirit." *Nevermind.* Geffen, 1991. CD.

Norris, Christopher. *What's Wrong with Postmodernism: Critical Theory and the Ends of Philosophy.* Baltimore: Johns Hopkins UP, 1990. Print.

Norris, Margot. *Writing War in the Twentieth Century.* Charlottesville: U of Virginia P, 2000. Print.

Oldboy. Dir. Park Chan-wook. Show East, 2003. Film.

Olson, Parmy. *We Are Anonymous: Inside the Hacker World of LulzSec, Anonymous, and the Global Cyber Insurgency.* New York: Little, Brown, 2012. Print.

"OpIsrael V. 2.0." *AnonNews: Everything Anonymous.* N.d. Web. 5 July 2013.

Palahniuk, Chuck. *Fight Club.* New York: Henry Holt, 1996. Print.

Pan, David. "Wishing for More." *Telos* 76 (1988): 143–54. Print.

Parker, Deborah, and Mark Parker. "Directors and DVD Commentary: The Specifics of Intention." *The Journal of Aesthetics and Art Criticism* 62.1 (2004): 13–22. Print.

Parks, Lisa, and Shanti Kumar, eds. *Planet TV: A Global Television Reader.* New York: NYU P, 2003. Print.

Patay, Douglas Lane. "Johnson's Refutation of Berkeley: Kicking the Stone Again." *Journal of the History of Ideas* 41.1 (1986): 139–45. Print.

Pelevin, Victor. *Homo Zapiens.* 1999. Trans. Andrew Bromfield. New York: Penguin, 2000. Print.

Perniola, Mario. *Art and Its Shadow.* Trans. Massimo Verdicchio. London: Continuum, 2004. Print.

Petersen, Per Serritslev. "9/11 and the 'Problem of Imagination': *Fight Club* and *Glamorama* as Terrorist Pretexts." *Orbis Litterarum: International Review of Literary Studies* 60.2 (2005): 133–44. Print.

Pew Charitable Trusts. "Economic Mobility and the American Dream: Examining Generational Differences." *PewTrusts.org*. Economic Mobility Project, Mar. 2012. Web. 23 Jan. 2013.

Porter, Stephen, John C. Yuille, and Darrin R. Lehman. "The Nature of Real, Implanted, and Fabricated Memories for Emotional Childhood Events: Implications for the Recovered Memory Debate." *Law and Human Behavior* 23. 5 (1999): 517–37. Print.

"projekt MAYHeM."*~el8 (2)*. El8, n.d. Web. 7 June 2013. <http://web.textfiles.com/ezines/EL8/el8.2.txt>

Punter, David. "e-texuality: Authenticity after the Postmodern." *Critical Quarterly* 43. 2 (2001): 68–91. Print.

Quiney, Ruth. "'Mr. Xerox,' the Domestic Terrorist, and the Victim-Citizen: Masculine and National Anxiety in *Fight Club* and Anti-Terror Law." *Law and Literature* 19.2 (2007): 327–54. Print.

Radwin, Jon. "Generation X and Postmodern Cinema: *Slacker.*" *Post/Script* 19.2 (2001): 34–48. Print.

Randall, Martin. *9/11 and the Literature of Terror*. Edinburgh: Edinburgh UP, 2011. Print.

Raymond, Eric S. *The Cathedral and the Bazaar: Musings on Linux and Open Source by an Accidental Revolutionary*. Rev. ed. Sebastopol, CA: O'Reilly, 2001. Print.

Rebein, Robert. *Hicks, Tribes, and Dirty Realists: American Fiction after Postmodernism*. Lexington: UP of Kentucky, 2001. Print.

Redding, Arthur. "'Merely Political': Glam Terrorism and Celebrity Politics in Bret Easton Ellis's *Glamorama*." Mandel, *Bret Easton Ellis* 98–112.

———. *Raids on Human Consciousness: Writing, Anarchism, and Violence*. Columbia: U of South Carolina P, 1998. Print.

Reel, Guy, Marc Perrusquia, and Bartholomew Sullivan. *The Blood of Innocents: The True Story of Multiple Murder in West Memphis, Arkansas*. New York: Pinnacle, 1995. Print.

Rehling, Nicola. "*Fight Club* Takes a Beating: Masculinity, Masochism and the Politics of Disavowal." *Gramma: Journal of Theory and Criticism* 9 (2001): 187–205. Print.

Ribbat, Christoph. "Nomadic with the Truth: Holocaust Representations in Michael Chabon, James McBride, and Jonathan Safran Foer." *Anglistik und Englischunterricht* 66 (2005): 199–218. Print.

Richardson, Brian. *Unnatural Voices: Extreme Narration in Modern and Contemporary Fiction*. Columbus: The Ohio State UP, 2006. Print.

Rosenblatt, Roger. "Snuff This Book! Will Bret Easton Ellis Get Away With Murder?" *New York Times Book Review* 16 Dec. 1990: 3, 16. Print.

———. "The Year Emotions Ruled. (Cover Story)." *Time* 22 Dec. 1997: 64. Print.

Rovner, Adam. "Alternate History: The Case of Nava Semel's *IsraIsland* and Michael Chabon's *The Yiddish Policemen's Union*." *Partial Answers* 9.1 (2011): 131–52. Print.

"Rules." Def. 3d. *Oxford English Dictionary Online*. Web. 6 Aug. 2014.

"Rules 1 and 2." *Encyclopedia Dramatica*. Encyclopedia Dramatica, 28 May 2012. Web. 5 June 2013.

"Rules of the Internet." *KnowYourMeme.com*. Cheezburger Inc., Web. 5 June 2013.

Rushkoff, Douglas, ed. *The GenX Reader*. New York: Ballantine, 1994. Print.

Russell, Diana E. H., ed. *Making Violence Sexy: Feminist Views on Pornography*. New York: Teacher's College P, 1993. Print.

Saal, Ilka. "Regarding the Pain of Self and Other: Trauma Transfer and Narrative Framing in Jonathan Safran Foer's *Extremely Loud & Incredibly Close*." *MFS: Modern Fiction Studies* 57.3 (2011): 451–76. Print.

Sanders, Mark. *Complicities: The Intellectual and Apartheid*. Durham: Duke UP, 2002.

Scarry, Elaine. *The Body in Pain: The Making and Unmaking of the World*. New York: Oxford UP, 1985. Print.

Schehr, Lawrence R. "Effondrements: Frédéric Beigbeder's *Windows on the World*." *French Cultural Studies* 21.2 (2010): 131–41. Print.

Schmid, David. "The Unusual Suspects: Conspiracy, Celebrity, and Objective Violence in *Glamorama*." Mandel, *Bret Easton Ellis* 69–83.

Schuchardt, Read Mercer, ed. *You Do Not Talk About Fight Club: I Am Jack's Completely Unauthorized Essay Collection*. Dallas: Benbrella, 2008. Print.

Sebald, W. G. *On the Natural History of Destruction*. New York: Random House, 2003.

Seltzer, Mark. *Serial Killers: Life and Death in America's Wound Culture*. New York: Routledge, 1998. Print.

———. *True Crime: Observations on Violence and Modernity*. New York: Routledge, 2007. Print.

Serpell, C. N. "Repetition and the Ethics of Suspended Reading in *American Psycho*." *Critique: Studies in Contemporary Fiction* 51.1 (2010): 47–73. Print.

Shaviro, Steven. *Connected, or What It Means to Live in the Network Society*. Minneapolis: U of Minnesota P, 2003. Print.

———. "*Lunar Park*." *The Pinocchio Theory*. Steven Shaviro, 29 Aug. 2005. Web. 29 June 2009.

Sicher, Efraim. *The Holocaust Novel*. New York: Routledge, 2005. Print.

Siegle, Robert. *Suburban Ambush: Downtown Writing and the Fiction of Insurgency*. Baltimore: Johns Hopkins UP, 1989. Print.

Silver, Bruce. "Boswell on Johnson's Refutation of Berkeley: Revisiting the Stone." *Journal of the History of Ideas* 54.3 (1993): 437–48. Print.

Simpson, David. *9/11: The Culture of Commemoration*. Chicago: U of Chicago P, 2006. Print.

Slocum, J. David. "Violence and American Cinema: Notes for an Investigation." Slocum 1–34.

———, ed. *Violence and American Cinema*. New York: Routledge, 2001. Print.

Slotkin, Richard. *Gunfighter Nation: The Myth of the Frontier in Twentieth-Century America*. New York: Atheneum, 1992. Print.

Smith, Rachel Greenwald. "Organic Shrapnel: Affect and Aesthetics in September 11 Fiction." *American Literature: A Journal of Literary History, Criticism, and Bibliography* 83.1 (2011): 153–74. Print.

Solomon, Deborah. "The Rescue Artist." *New York Times Magazine* 25 Feb. 2005: 40–45. Print.

Sontag, Susan. *On Photography*. New York: Farrar, Straus and Giroux, 1973.

———. *Regarding the Pain of Others*. New York: Picador, 2003. Print.

Sorel, Georges. *Reflections on Violence*. Trans. T. E. Hulme. London: George Allen & Unwin, 1915. Print.

Stam, Robert. "Television News and Its Spectator." Kaplan 23–43.

Stephenson, Neal. *In the Beginning . . . Was the Command Line*. New York: HarperCollins Perennial, 1999. Print.

Swanson, Jeffrey W. "Explaining Rare Acts of Violence: The Limits of Evidence from Population Research." *Psychiatric Services* 62.11 (2011): n. pag. Web. 30 June 2014.

Ta, Lynn M. "Hurt So Good: *Fight Club*, Masculine Violence, and the Crisis of Capitalism." *Journal of American Culture* 29.3 (2006): 265–77. Print.

Tabbi, Joseph. *Postmodern Sublime: Technology and American Writing from Mailer to Cyberpunk*. Ithaca: Cornell UP, 1995. Print.

Takami, Koushun. *Battle Royale*. 1999. Trans. Yuji Oniki. San Francisco: Haikasoru, 2009. Print.

Talking Heads. "Crosseyed and Painless." *Remain in Light*. Rec. 1980. Sire, 1990. CD.

Tanner, Laura E. "Holding On to 9/11: The Shifting Grounds of Materiality." *PMLA* 127.1 (2012): 58–76. Print.

Tartt, Donna. *The Goldfinch*. New York: Little, Brown, 2013. Print.

Taylor, Paul A. *Hackers: Crime in the Digital Sublime*. New York: Routledge, 1999. Print.

Terada, Rei. *Feeling in Theory: Emotion after the "Death of the Subject."* Cambridge: Harvard UP, 2001. Print.

Thomas, Douglas. *Hacker Culture*. Minneapolis: U of Minnesota P, 2002. Print.

Thompson, Stacy. "Punk Cinema." *Cinema Journal* 43.2 (2004): 47–66. Print.

Touré. *I Would Die 4 U: Why Prince Became an Icon*. New York: Atria, 2013. Print.

Turkle, Sherry. *The Second Self: Computers and the Human Spirit*. 1984. 2nd ed. Cambridge: MIT P, 2005. Print.

Ulrich, John M. "Generation X: A (Sub)Cultural Genealogy." Ulrich and Harris 3–37.

Ulrich, John M., and Andrea L. Harris, eds. *GenXegesis: Essays on Alternative Youth (Sub) Culture*. London: U of Wisconsin P / Popular, 2003. Print.

Updike, John. "Mixed Messages." *The New Yorker* 81.4 (2005): 138. Web. 10 Aug. 2014.

"U.S. Literature: Blank Fiction." *Contemporary Narrative in English Research Group*. Contemporary Narrative in English Research Group, n.d. Web. 28 Dec. 2011.

Uytterschout, Sien, and Kristiaan Versluys. "Melancholy and Mourning in Jonathan Safran Foer's *Extremely Loud and Incredibly Close*." *Orbis Litterarum* 63.3. (2008): 216–36. Print.

V for Vendetta. Dir. Andy and Lana Wachovski. Warner Bros., 2005. DVD.

Versluys, Kristiaan. *Out of the Blue: September 11 and the Novel*. New York: Columbia UP, 2009. Print.

Videodrome. Dir. David Cronenberg. Universal Pictures, 1983. DVD.

Walker, Joseph S. "A Kink in the System: Terrorism and the Comic Mystery Novel." *Studies in the Novel* 36.3 (2004): 336–51. Print.

Wallace, David Foster. "E Unibus Pluram: Television and U.S. Fiction." 1993. *A Supposedly Fun Thing I'll Never Do Again: Essays and Arguments*. Boston: Little, Brown, 1997. 21–82. Print.

Walter, Jess. *The Zero*. New York: Harper, 2006. Print.

———. "Zero PS." Interview. *JessWalter.com*, n.d. Web. 29 Apr. 2014.

Walter, Patrick F. "Cyberkill: Melancholia, Globalization and Media Terrorism in *American Psycho* and *Glamorama*." *Arizona Quarterly: A Journal of American Literature, Culture, and Theory* 68.4 (2012): 131–54. Print.

Wark, McKenzie. *A Hacker Manifesto*. Cambridge: Harvard UP, 2004. Print.

Watt, Ian. *The Rise of the Novel: Studies in Defoe, Richardson, and Fielding*. Berkeley: U of California P, 1957. Print.

Whitehead, Colson. *The Intuitionist*. New York: Random House, 1999. Print.

Williams, Mar. *Expect Anonymous Fight Club Soap*. Jpg. "'Building a Better Anonymous' Series: Part 1." *Cognitive Dissidents*. Joshua Corman, 20 Dec. 2011. Web. 10 Aug. 2014.

"Words of the Year." *AmericanDialect.com*. The American Dialect Society, n.d. Web. 30 June 2014.

Wurtzel, Elizabeth. *Prozac Nation: Young and Depressed in America*. Boston: Houghton Mifflin, 1994. Print.

Worthington, Marjorie. "The Fleeting '9/11 Effect' in *The Good Life* and *Lunar Park*." *Journal of the Midwest Modern Language Association* 44.2 (2011): 111–25. Print.

Wyatt, Edward. "After a Long Wait, Literary Novelists Address 9/11." *The New York Times* 7 Mar. 2005: E1. Print.

Young, Elizabeth, and Graham Caveney. *Shopping in Space: Essays on America's Blank Generation Fiction*. London: Serpent's Tail, 1992. Print.

Zelizer, Barbie. "Photography, Journalism, and Trauma." Zelizer and Allan 48–68.

Zelizer, Barbie, and Stuart Allan, eds. *Journalism after September 11*. New York: Routledge, 2002. Print.

Žižek, Slavoj. "The Ambiguity of the Masochist Social Link." *Perversion and the Social Relation*. Eds. Molly Anne Rothenberg and Dennis Foster. Durham: Duke UP, 2003. 112–25. Print.

———. *Violence: Six Sideways Reflections*. London: Profile, 2008. Print.

———. *Welcome to the Desert of the Real*. New York: Verso, 2002. Print.

index
· · · · · ·

absence: as fragmenting narrative, 112; resonance of, 14; simultaneity of presence and, 116, 129–30, 149, 175, 212, 224; trauma as, 119; vs. presence, 15, 30, 40

Abu Ghraib, 61, 143–44, 146, 215

abuse, 68; repressed memories of, 45

acceleration, 26, 28, 57, 213

accuracy, 21; factual, 159; impetus to, 176; and inaccuracy, 115; and violence, 222

Acker, Kathy, 35, 95, 96

action, 19, 25, 42, 59, 66, 91, 213, 217; challenges to, 27, 67; and image, 51; and violence, 211

activism, 199; antisecurity, 180; online, 11; solidarity with, 2; youthful, 20

aesthetics, 55–56, 83; of fragmented texts, 154; of trauma, 127; violence and, 34, 59

affect, 39, 57, 65–66, 77, 127, 222; detachment from, 81; divorce of critique from, 50; evacuation of, 28, 216; knowledge as, 90; moralization of, 72; violence of, 41

affectlessness, 32, 39, 52, 77, 132, 198

Agamben, Giorgio: *State of Exception,* 62–63, 73–75

agency, 10, 53; appropriated, 209; attribution of, 154; limits of, 16; zones of, 76

AIDS, 2, 19, 70, 204

Albert, Laura (aka JT LeRoy), 31, 222. *See also* LeRoy

alienation, 13, 20, 187

Allison, Dorothy, 95

alterity, 13n3: erasure of, 126; terroristic, 114n2

Al Qaeda, 143–44, 171

Althusser, Louis, 43n2, 72, 87, 95

ambiguity, 70, 214–15; moral, 155, 181

ambivalence, 4, 22, 57; ethical investment in, 21; toward presence, perception, and parrhesia, 10

Amis, Martin: *Time's Arrow,* 133

analogy, 143–46, 154, 174

anarchy, 52n14, 179, 181, 184, 198, 211

anomie, 73–74, 77; law and, 74